Race and the Brazilian Body

Race and the Brazilian Body

Blackness, Whiteness, and Everyday Language in Rio de Janeiro

JENNIFER ROTH-GORDON

University of California Press

University of California Press, one of the most distinguished university presses in the United States, enriches lives around the world by advancing scholarship in the humanities, social sciences, and natural sciences. Its activities are supported by the UC Press Foundation and by philanthropic contributions from individuals and institutions. For more information, visit www.ucpress.edu.

University of California Press
Oakland, California

Library of Congress Cataloging-in-Publication Data

Names: Roth-Gordon, Jennifer, author.
Title: Race and the Brazilian Body : blackness, whiteness, and everyday language in Rio de Janeiro / Jennifer Roth-Gordon.
Description: Oakland, California : University of California Press, [2017] | Includes bibliographical references and index.
Identifiers: LCCN 2016031605| ISBN 9780520293793 (cloth : alk. paper) | ISBN 9780520293809 (pbk. : alk. paper)
Subjects: LCSH: Blacks—Race identity—Brazil—Rio de Janeiro. | Brazil—Ethnic relations. | Human skin color—Social aspects—Brazil—Rio de Janeiro. | Blacks—Language—Social aspects—Brazil.
Classification: LCC F2659.N4 R68 2017 | DDC 305.800981—dc23
LC record available at https://lccn.loc.gov/2016031605

Manufactured in the United States of America

24 23 22 21 20 19 18 17 16
10 9 8 7 6 5 4 3 2 1

For Derek
Thank you for taking this journey with me

Contents

Acknowledgments   ix

1. BRAZIL'S "COMFORTABLE RACIAL CONTRADICTION"   1

2. "GOOD" APPEARANCES: RACE, LANGUAGE, AND
   CITIZENSHIP   42

3. INVESTING IN WHITENESS: MIDDLE-CLASS
   PRACTICES OF LINGUISTIC DISCIPLINE   69

4. FEARS OF RACIAL CONTACT: CRIME, VIOLENCE, AND
   THE STRUGGLE OVER URBAN SPACE   95

5. AVOIDING BLACKNESS: THE FLIP SIDE OF
   BOA APARÊNCIA   128

6. MAKING THE *MANO*: THE UNCOMFORTABLE
   VISIBILITY OF BLACKNESS IN POLITICALLY
   CONSCIOUS BRAZILIAN HIP-HOP   161

   CONCLUSION: "SEEING" RACE   185

   Notes   195

   References   203

   Index   223

Acknowledgments

Once upon a time, I set out to study slang in Rio. I am eternally grateful to my academic mentors at Brown University and Stanford University who set me on the course of linguistic anthropology and nurtured my passion for studying language in sociopolitical context: Bill Beeman, Penny Eckert, Jim Fox, Miyako Inoue, and John Rickford. Penny Eckert consistently set a high bar, and I wouldn't be where I am now without her. I have been fortunate to have received guidance and support from senior colleagues and peers, and I would like to acknowledge, in particular, H. Samy Alim, Sarah Benor, Mary Bucholtz, Rudi Gaudio, Perry Gilmore, Lanita Jacobs, Shari Jacobson, Shoshanna Lurie, Bonnie McElhinny, Janet McIntosh, Jacqui Messing, Deborah Tannen, Kit Woolard, and Leisy Wyman. My academic interests evolved to include the study of race, and I thank Matt Guterl for welcoming me into the world of ethnic studies. I hope our research paths will continue to converge. I have been honored to have been a part of the Linguistic Anthropology program at the University of Arizona since 2004, where Jane Hill, Norma Mendoza-Denton, Susan Philips, and Qing Zhang have all been incredibly supportive and fun to work with. I also gratefully acknowledge the support of colleagues Bert Barickman, Ana Maria Carvalho, Mark and Mimi Nichter, John Olsen, Ivy Pike, and Dani Triadan.

My graduate students have offered semester after semester of inspiration, and I look forward to many years as their colleague and friend. I am especially grateful to those I worked most closely with: Julie Armin, Micah Boyer, Joon-Beom Chu, Ufuk Coşkun, Mary Good, Lauren Hayes, Parvaneh Hosseini, Ben McMahan, Melanie Medeiros, Keri Miller, Jessica Nelson, Dana Osborne, Lucero Radonic, Antonio Bacelar da Silva, Ashley Stinnett, Angela Storey, and Maisa Taha. My "failed whiteness" reading-writing group, including Lori Labotka, Sarah Raskin, and Megan Sheehan, helped pave the way for me to successfully think through and complete this book. Joon-Beom Chu, Jessica Nelson, and Tom-Zé da Silva provided excellent assistance in the final editing stages of this book. Abby Mogollón, Erika Robb Larkins, and Rich Rothblatt all offered assistance and support during a key phase of the publication process. Fellow anthropologist Victor Braitberg has contributed valuable feedback on my work over the years, in addition to sharing his family for weekends of camaraderie and relaxation. Abby Mogollón, Ellen Ruble, and Lisa Soltani provided critical sources of friendship and moral support, as did a whole host of friends from Providence, to Tucson, to Rio de Janeiro. I treasure you all.

I am happily indebted to Susan Shaw and Terry Woronov, who helped me navigate life as an assistant professor through tenure to the publication of this book. I am so grateful for their years of support and detailed feedback on my work. Brazilian anthropologist Leticia Veloso has been an unbelievably generous and insightful colleague to think with, and she provided invaluable comments on this manuscript. I look forward to our ongoing collaboration. Tom-Zé da Silva was always more of a colleague than a mentee, and he has contributed to this book in countless ways, from his friendship, to writing sessions in coffee shops, to his Portuguese transcription assistance. My research assistant, "CW," is all over the pages of this book, from the cover to the many recorded conversations in Cruzada that uphold and make possible my analysis. His heart, his desire for a better world for his community, and his energy to make it happen have all been the inspiration for this book since we met. I gratefully acknowledge his friends, my middle-class research assistants and their families, and DJTR and MV Bill for their participation in my research. I am profoundly honored that Marcelo Santos Braga and Tatiana Medeiros Veloso generously contributed their amazing artistic talent for the photos and maps in this book. I also wish to thank Charles Frank, Breanne Hoke, and Brandon Butler of the Glushko-Samuelson Intellectual Property Clinic at American University's Washington College of Law. For permission to use lyrics and images, I gratefully acknowledge Angeli, Hugo Nicolau Barbosa de Gusmão, MV Bill (CQ Rights), Racionais MC's, André Mello, AGÊNCIA O GLOBO, and Ultraje: Nós Vamos Invadir Sua Praia by Roger Rocha Moreira © 2008 WARNER/CHAPPELL EDICOES MUSICAIS LTDA. (ABRAMUS).

I would also like to gratefully acknowledge funding for various stages of my research that was provided by the National Science Foundation, Stanford University, the University of Arizona, the Ruth Landes Memorial Foundation, and the Wenner-Gren Foundation. The book has benefited from the insightful feedback provided by Jan Hoffman French, Kristina

Wirtz, and an anonymous reviewer though all remaining errors are my own. I am profoundly grateful to Kate Marshall, Bradley Depew, Cindy Fulton, Steven Baker, and Sandra Kimball for their efforts shepherding this book into the world.

I owe much love and thanks to my parents, Robert and Sharon; my siblings, Jill, Rachel, and Richard; and my extended family, which now includes Rothblatts, Seigels, Carps, Sowells, Gaspars, Wintners, and Gordons. During my twenty years researching in Brazil, I have been lucky enough to acquire *família de coração* (family of the heart): Marta, André, Bruna, Nana, Arnaldo, Lourenço, Daniel, Bruno, Alexandre, Eliane, Guilherme, Gustavo, Gabriela, Lica, Sammy, Márcia, Evandro, Leo, Wagner, Adriene, Bujica, and my "BFF group": Alessandra, Aline, Bernadete, Cris, Mayra, Mónica, Rocy, Simone, Tatiana, and Valéria. My husband, Derek Roth Gordon, has tolerated my penchant for planning, made fuzzy ideas become reality, and kept us all sane in the process. If you dream it, he can make it happen. My children have traveled the world with me, and I am grateful for their courage and their spirit of adventure. I thank fourteen-year-old Sam for joining me in late-night writing sessions that went way past his bedtime, eleven-year-old Henry for statistical assistance calculating the racial makeup of Rio's population, and eight-year-old Sophie for letting me write about her in the conclusion. Without the time and energy spent on their many extracurricular activities, carpools, bake sales, field trips, birthday parties, Halloween parties, homework projects, and bedtime Harry Potter reading sessions, a book would have been completed sooner. But it wouldn't be this book, and I wouldn't be its author.

1. Brazil's "Comfortable Racial Contradiction"

In 2013, Brazilian journalist Paulo Henrique Amorim was sentenced to one year and eight months in prison, a sentence later upheld by Brazil's Superior Tribunal de Justiça (Superior Court of Justice).[1] His crime? He had publicly criticized the powerful Brazilian media network Rede Globo for denying that racism exists in Brazil, and he had called out one particular journalist, Heraldo Pereira, for going along with this denial, describing him as a *"negro de alma branca"* (black with a white soul). Amorim was later accused of *racismo* (racism) and *injúria racial* (racial insult, or an "injury to one's honor"; see Racusen 2004:789) by both the network and Heraldo Pereira, and was found guilty of the latter. Amorim, who is politically liberal and often at the center of controversy, used as part of his defense the fact that he has long publicly supported antiracist efforts. He argued that he was merely exercising his freedom of speech in order to disagree with Pereira's implicit suggestion that any black person could work hard and become rich and famous in Brazil. Despite Amorim's desire to make Brazil's structural racism more visible, the expression that he chose to describe Pereira allowed the powerful (and conservative) media network and the courts to find him personally guilty of racism toward another individual. As the prosecutor explained, his use of this "highly racist" expression:

> sugere que as pessoas de cor branca possuem atributos positivos e bons, ao passo que os negros são associados a valores negativos, ruins, inferiores. É o mesmo que afirmar que os brancos são superiores aos negros e, nesse contexto, um negro de alma branca seria aquele que, embora seja preto, tem a dignidade ou a distinção que seriam próprias das pessoas de cor clara.[2]

> suggests that white people possess positive and good attributes, while black people are associated with negative, bad, and inferior values. It is

1

the same as saying that white people are superior to black people, and, in this context, a black person with a white soul would be a person who, despite being black, has the dignity or the distinction that belongs to light-skinned people.

Only a few decades ago, this widely used expression could have been considered a compliment by some in Brazil (Turra and Venturi 1995),[3] a saying that noted with approval Pereira's acquisition of "white" traits, including his higher level of education (he is trained as a lawyer), his use of standard Portuguese, and his behavioral refinement, all of which would help override the negative characteristics thought to accompany his dark skin and phenotypically black features. Another Brazilian expression, more commonly used in Bahia than Rio, describes those who demonstrate refinement and the right class status but aren't fair-skinned as *socialmente branco* or "socially white" (Azevedo 1975; Figueiredo 2002). These types of racial descriptions have long suggested a mismatch between phenotype and behavior. And yet this radically new reading of the expression *negro de alma branca*, as an example of a racial insult now subject to legal prosecution (Guimarães 2003; Racusen 2004), serves as an excellent introduction to current debates about Brazilian racism. If you criticize a dark-skinned person for not being antiracist, does that make you a racist? Is noticing race always racist? Does racism explain Brazilian inequality? Do the recent affirmative action policies (such as racial quotas for university admissions) create racism in Brazil? These questions, and controversies like the Paulo Henrique Amorim case, can be dizzying, and they illustrate how public discourse in Brazil over race and racism has changed considerably over the past few decades.

It's not just the public debate that feels new. Brazil has had laws against racial discrimination on the books since the Afonso Arinos Law of 1951, passed after an African American dancer, Katherine Dunham, was denied a room at a posh hotel in São Paulo. Brazil's 1988 constitution went even further, defining racial discrimination as a crime without bail or statute of limitations and punishable by imprisonment. Despite this "enlightened jurisprudence" (J. Dávila 2012:2), when I moved to Brazil to conduct dissertation research in 1997, no one had ever been convicted of either crime (Rosa-Ribeiro 2000:226; see also Racusen 2004). After I returned to Brazil in 2014 to begin a new research project, I met several people who had personally filed charges of racism against others. This included one woman who filed a legal complaint against the owner of the nail salon where she worked and another woman who filed charges against the principal at the public school that her daughter attended.[4] Very public racial incidents had garnered not just media attention but also legal, financial, and social repercussions. When a dark-skinned girl from the racially mixed state of Minas Gerais posted a picture of herself wrapped in the arms of her light-skinned boyfriend on Facebook, she was flooded with racist comments. The Brazilian Civil Police began to investigate those who had posted offensive comments, including those who alluded to plantation life and asked where the boy had purchased his "slave."[5] When losing soccer fans screamed "*macaco*" (monkey) at the dark-skinned goalkeeper of a rival team, one twenty-two-year old female fan from the southern state of Porto Alegre was caught on camera. She was banned from the stadium, and the team she was rooting for was given a R$50,000 fine (equivalent to over US$20,000 at the time).[6]

In a similar incident involving fan racism (this time while playing in Europe), Brazilian soccer player Daniel Alves spurred an online antiracist social media movement back in Brazil when he peeled and ate the banana that had been thrown onto the field by a (presumably European) fan. Brazilian celebrities, politicians, and supporters all posted selfies with peeled bananas, and his teammate, Brazilian fan favorite Neymar, used the opportunity to launch a hashtag campaign, #somostodosmacacos (we are all monkeys). Barely twenty years ago, academics described what felt like a "cultural censorship" around the topics of race and racism (Sheriff 2001; see also Twine 1998; Vargas 2004), yet public discussion of racism seems commonplace in twenty-first-century Brazil.

In one of my very first job interviews, a professor from Princeton University who had not worked in Brazil asked me a question I have not forgotten: "A few decades ago, anthropologists were studying Brazil because of its excellent race relations. Now all people seem to study is Brazilian racism. Did we just get it wrong back then, or have things changed?" The safest answer, of course, is both. Things have changed in Brazil, by a lot, not only since I began researching there in the mid-1990s but also since the United Nations commissioned scholars to study the country as a "racial democracy" that could serve as a role model to a world reeling from the horrors of state-sanctioned anti-Semitism after World War II. But even as the current sociopolitical context allowed for the complicated racial positionings that occurred as a "white," left-leaning journalist accused a "black," right-leaning colleague of being a "black with a white soul," and then was convicted for his racist insult, there are some strong currents of continuity.[7] While a conviction and a jail sentence for the crime of racial injury are definitely new, Amorim was ultimately punished for violating a very old Brazilian preference for "*racismo cordial*" (cordial racism), according to which individuals downplay racial differences that might lead to conflict or disagreement (Fry 1995–96; Sansone 2003; Turra and Venturi 1995).[8] His comment, which the general public has only recently understood as a racial insult, also willfully mocks the long-held belief that racism is not just personally abhorrent, but an insult to the nation. The better answer to the senior scholar's question, then, would have been this: Brazil, as a nation, has long lived with what I call a *comfortable racial contradiction.*

Historian Micol Seigel offers examples of how the Brazilian elite simultaneously "clung to racial hierarchies even as they loudly repudiated racism" (2009:210). In his book *Brazil: Five Centuries of Change* (1999), Thomas Skidmore, another Brazilianist historian, has declared that Brazil's "ultimate contradiction is between [its] justifiable reputation for personal generosity ('cordiality') and the fact of having to live in one of the world's most unequal societies" (xiii). Perhaps nothing sums up this contradiction better than the assertions of Brazil's own abolitionists who in the late 1800s widely proclaimed that Brazil had been fortunate to escape the racial hatred and division that characterized their neighbor to the north—at the same time that Brazilian slavery continued. Brazil retains the notorious reputation of being the last country in the Western Hemisphere to abolish slavery, which it did, at least in part, because of concerns over its international racial reputation. One abolitionist, Perdigão Malheiro described in 1871 a Brazilian context that increasingly included free people of African descent (such as manumitted slaves): "Since Negroes came to Brazil from the African coast there has never been that contempt for the African race to be found in other countries, especially the United States. . . . Gentlemen, I know many individuals of dark skin who are worth more than many of white skin. That is the truth. In the schools, higher faculties, and churches do we not see good colored students alongside our distinguished men?" (quoted in Skidmore 1974:23).

The idea that an individual of African descent could succeed in Brazil because of the country's lack of prejudice, while more than a million black people continued to be forcibly enslaved, was echoed by the more widely known Joaquim Nabuco: "Color in Brazil is not, as in the United States, a social prejudice against whose persistence no character, talent, or merit can prevail" (quoted in Skidmore 1974:24). Both abolitionists, their own century's equivalent of the antiracist, seem to lay the foundations for the *negro de alma branca.* They would have seen no contradiction in the belief in white superiority that this term implies existing alongside the pride they took in Brazil affording free people of African descent the opportunity of social mobility despite the unfortunate and obvious circumstance of their blackness (E. Costa 1985). Their focus on the possibilities of individual accomplishment as "exceptions to the rule" brings into sharp relief their dismissal of the significance of the widespread and structurally embedded racism amid which they lived. Drawing on what is now considered sensational and offensive language, this is essentially the same situation that Paulo Henrique Amorim felt compelled to critique nearly 150 years later.

I will describe this as Brazil's comfortable racial contradiction, but my choice of this term requires a few disclaimers. I do not mean to imply that this racial situation is "comfortable" for all of Brazil's residents, as it certainly is not (A. Costa 2016; Sheriff 2001), nor do I wish to ignore the contributions of activists or academics, past and present, who have long sought to expose and ameliorate this contradiction (see, for example, Carneiro 2011; Dzidzienyo 1971; A. Nascimento 1978). More important, however, I do not intend to examine Brazil or Brazilians as somehow unusual, or even extreme, in their ability to juggle competing racial ideologies. Instead, my choice of the term highlights the fact that Brazil handles these larger contradictions quite well, making them seem "comfortable" and commonsensical to many people, who adapt them to new situations and political climates. North Americans, in particular, have been drawn to Brazilian race relations because a lack of overt racial conflict, an absence of clear racial identities, and a situation of ambiguous racial boundaries seem so unusual and even (to some) "unnatural." Rather than asking how Brazil developed an "exceptional" set of racial beliefs (cf. Hanchard 1998), I examine day-to-day life as completely normal. I describe how Rio residents, in particular, live among these comfortable racial contradictions and how these contradictions structure what they see, what they say, and how they interact with others across race and class lines. I seek to explain what it means to live in a city of sharp racial disparities and obvious racial hierarchy, but in a country where one is not supposed to be influenced by or believe in racial difference.

This contradiction has been studied by both Brazilian and Brazilianist scholars across a range of academic disciplines including history, sociology, political science, and anthropology. Florestan Fernandes famously claimed that Brazilians have "the prejudice of having no prejudice" (1969:xv). Anthropologist Robin Sheriff described Brazil's racial democracy as simultaneously "a nationalist ideology, a cultural myth, and . . . a dream of how things ought to be" (2001:4). Michael Hanchard examines "the simultaneous production and denial of racial inequality" in Brazil (1998:155). For my part, I am less concerned with making sense of this contradiction than with understanding its effects. After all, Brazilians are not the only ones to smoothly juggle opposing ideals and realities. The United States remains a nation deeply wed to the notion of the American Dream and the seeming opportunity for any individual to succeed, even as income inequality has reached its highest levels since before the Great Depression. Shamus Khan refers to this as "democratic inequality" (2011:196). Nor does Brazil hold a monopoly on racial ironies. U.S. historian David R. Roediger reminds us of the question posed in the late 1980s by novelist Ralph Ellison: "What, by the way, is one to make of a white youngster who, with a transistor radio, screaming a Stevie Wonder tune, glued to his ear, shouts racial epithets at black youngsters trying to swim at a public beach?" (1998:359). At the end of the day, I am also not interested in assessing whether Brazil is more racist, less racist, or as racist as the United States, and, aside from offering a brief history of how the two nations have long been in dialogue and competed on racial matters (Seigel 2009), I attempt to avoid making what are often far more complicated comparisons. My goal instead is to understand how ubiquitous racial inequality, notions of white superiority, and a national disdain for racial prejudice play out in the mundane experiences of everyday life.

This book is based on twenty years of research in Rio de Janeiro, a city where 52 percent of the population identifies as *preto* (black) or *pardo* (brown), numbers that closely resemble the racial makeup of Brazil.[9] I draw on my training as a linguistic and cultural anthropologist to analyze what may be described as everyday racial strategizing that Rio residents employ as they present themselves to others and as they interpret the people they meet. I focus on daily interactions to shed light on how racial inequality, and the racial hierarchy on which it is based, is not just something people live in but also something that people actively negotiate and produce. As I present snapshots of everyday life across race and class lines, I argue that Rio residents "read" bodies for racial cues, examining not only phenotypical attributes—including skin color, hair texture, and facial features such as the shape of the nose or lips—but also paying careful attention to cultural and linguistic practices such as how one is dressed and how one speaks. My attention to daily practice is inspired by the work of sociologist Pierre Bourdieu (1984, 1994), and, as in his work, differences of socioeconomic class pervade the encounters that I describe. When I analyze the attention paid to levels of education, "proper" ways of speaking, and displays of cultural refinement (or the lack thereof), both North American and Brazilian readers may be drawn to read these as obvious signs of class status. The explicit intent of this book is to show how these embodied practices also convey racial meaning.

In what follows, I introduce the three main premises of Brazil's comfortable racial contradiction. They include the following racial "facts," which I will set up in further detail: (1) structural racism has always existed in Brazil; (2) Brazil continues to draw on and perpetuate notions of the superiority of whiteness and the inferiority of blackness, ideas that are globally shared; and (3) Brazil has long been proud of its racial mixture and its racial tolerance, ideas that have been both promoted—and enforced—by the Brazilian nation-state. Given this cultural contradiction, I do not restrict my analysis to situations in which people explicitly talk about race, because those are clearly not the only times that Brazilians are influenced by racial ideas, nor are racial terms (including *negro de alma branca*) the only way that race impacts ideas about language and actual linguistic practice.[10] In short, I invite the reader to dive into a study of the ways Rio residents make sense of ubiquitous signs of blackness and whiteness within a context that discourages them from describing what they see in racial terms.

POBREZA TEM COR (POVERTY HAS A COLOR)

In 1808, the Portuguese regent prince deceived Napoleon and fled Lisbon just as the French army invaded the city, sailing away with more than 15,000 members of the Portuguese court and arriving in their colony of Brazil as the first royals to ever step foot in the Americas. This tale is widely recognized as a defining moment in Brazilian history, when Europe literally came to Brazil, setting off a chain of events that would turn Brazil into the independent nation that it is today. As described in vivid detail in a best-selling book by Brazilian journalist Laurentino Gomes (2007), it was a serious adjustment for members of the Portuguese nobility to learn to live in the tropics. In the process, they remade Brazil and the city of Rio de Janeiro as they attempted to bring it up to European standards that included sidewalks, botanical gardens, a national library, a school of medicine, and the country's first bank. The contrast between the newcomers and the majority of the uneducated and "uncivilized" residents was extreme. At the time of the Portuguese court's arrival, only one in one hundred people was literate. One in three inhabitants of Brazil was a slave. Slaves were relatively affordable, and "anyone with a whiff of nobility could reap income from more humble labor without degrading themselves or callusing their hands" (Sérgio Buarque de Holanda, quoted in Gomes 2007:176). For those coming from Portugal, racial differences in Brazil were equally extreme: "For every white there were ten blacks, three *mulattos* [individuals of black and white ancestry], and three *caboclos* [individuals of mixed white and indigenous ancestry]" (D. Davis 1999:14).

Scholars of Brazilian race relations do not necessarily focus on this particular moment of Brazilian history, yet the image of the Portuguese royal court descending upon Rio de Janeiro, a city of only 60,000 inhabitants at the time, and the race, class, and cultural contrasts that ensued strike me as incredibly important for understanding the current situation of race and class inequality in Brazil. The gap between relatively small middle and upper classes and the "masses," who continue to lack access to decent education, health care, housing, and employment, is not just a statistical fact. It exists as a psychological reality of how the making of Brazil began and of how Brazil (unfortunately) continues to be. One of this book's central goals is to explain how beliefs in the superiority of whiteness and the inferiority of blackness allow Rio residents to justify or make sense of this continued divide. Indeed, according to basic definitions of structural racism, it does not matter whether people of color are intentionally placed at the bottom rungs of the social hierarchy, whether they occupy the bottom strata due to racial conflict, segregationist laws, or a legacy of slavery, or even if they find themselves among equally poor but lighter-skinned people while there. When people who are understood to be "black" are disproportionately concentrated at the bottom of society, and people who are viewed as "white" disproportionately enjoy the privileges and resources offered to those at the top, we may safely and productively describe the situation as one of structural racism.

One illustration helps demonstrate the continuities of patterns of structural racism found in colonial Brazil. In a brilliant political cartoon "Feriado: Dia da Consciência Negra" (Holiday: Black Consciousness Day), published in the newspaper *Folha de São Paulo* in 2006 and reposted several years in a row by fans on at least one blog,[11] cartoonist Angeli juxtaposes Brazil's current sociopolitical context with a legacy of racial inequality. He draws one of Rio's iconic South Zone beaches with their long stretches of sand packed with row upon row of pale, white sunbathers. Their dramatically consistent peachy skin is intentional, if not accurate: A long history of miscegenation and the fact that Brazilians, and Rio residents in particular, strongly prefer a good *bronzeado* (or "tan"; see Barickman 2009; Farias 2006) mean that many more Brazilians identify as *moreno* (brown) than white (Norvell 2002). In the foreground of the image, at the shoreline, four dark-skinned beach vendors carrying heavy loads hawk the drinks and other amenities that they sell for a living. Black Consciousness Day became an official national holiday in 2011, passed along with several other laws intended to increase awareness of the national contributions of Brazilians of African descent and to offer limited reparations to black Brazilians for previous racial "injuries" (including slavery). A law passed in 2003, for example, requires the teaching of Afro-Brazilian history and culture in all schools (see A. Costa 2014).

Black Awareness Day had long been celebrated on May 13, the day that Princesa Isabel signed the law that officially ended slavery in Brazil.

However, black activists did not want to continue to honor the princess for "freeing" the slaves. Many current-day black NGOs (nongovernmental organizations) emphasize this point: black people should not be referred to as *escravos*, or slaves, as the term would suggest that this was somehow their natural condition. Instead, they should always be described as *os escravizados* (the enslaved), a term that foregrounds unequal race and power relations and oppression by European colonizers (see Roth-Gordon and da Silva 2013). Along similar lines, black activists rediscovered and re-created Zumbi as a modern-day symbol of black resistance and freedom. Zumbi is now well known as the last leader of Brazil's largest escaped slave colony, the Quilombo dos Palmares, which was located in the Northeast of Brazil in the modern-day state of Alagoas. Zumbi led the maroon colony for many years, evading capture by the Portuguese. When Zumbi was killed on November 20, 1695 (the date chosen in accordance with recent estimates), his head was put on display to dispute the rumors of his immortality and to prevent further slave rebellion.

Although black NGOs and some *favelas* (shantytowns, where many people of African descent live) organize activities to celebrate black awareness and black pride on this day, temperatures in Rio can reach their summer highs, making it a crowded beach holiday. Angeli's tongue-in-cheek illustration thus makes the uncomfortable observation that whiter and wealthier Brazilians, including descendants of the Portuguese court and subsequent generations of European immigrants, can "honor" black history and the contributions Afro-Brazilians have made to Brazil by sitting on historically "white" beaches and being served by subsistence-wage workers who are the descendants of slaves.

Some who are familiar with Brazil could argue that Angeli's image, while originally printed in color, is too black and white. Not all of the beachgoers on Rio's most famous beaches are white; many would not racially describe themselves as such (Norvell 2002), and a good number of the low-income beach vendors are light-skinned. These observations form the basis of a critique that admits to widespread disparity in Brazil, and in Rio, but suggests that the phenotypical variation found within the middle class and especially among the poor points to socioeconomic class as the source of inequality. Race is not commonly thought to be the primary source of stigma, nor is it considered the "real" barrier to social mobility. Like Angeli, I have made the choice in this book to highlight the important role that race plays in upholding Brazilian inequality. Indeed, it is not because of, but rather in spite of, the intentional exaggeration that Angeli's point becomes readily understandable, even to those who prefer to emphasize class over race.

FIGURE 1.   "Feriado: Dia da Consciência Negra" (Holiday: Black Consciousness Day). Political cartoon originally published in *Folha de São Paulo,* November 20, 2006. Used with permission granted by Angeli.

FIGURE 2.   Worker taking chairs away from the beach at the end of the day. Photo by Marcelo Santos Braga.

As I detail in chapter 4, which takes up the topic of racial contact on the beach, not just some, but the vast majority of Copacabana, Ipanema, and Leblon residents and primary beachgoers are light-skinned. And not just some, but most, of the beach vendors are dark-skinned. More important, the nature of structural racism is at its clearest in this example. If one were to look for the darkest-skinned people on the beach, they would almost all, with rare exception, be on the move as workers, setting up beach chairs or carrying drinks, ice cream, and other beach amenities to well-heeled but currently barefoot patrons, so the latter may shop and refresh themselves without leaving their chosen place to lounge on the sand. The connections to colonial Brazil, where some lived in comfort off the toil of others, are most palpable when one watches the darkest-skinned bodies sweat and strain under heavy loads in the hot sun. Even if one wanted to criticize Angeli for simplifying matters, few who live in or have visited Brazil could fail to recognize the phenomenon he describes.

This fact of racial disparity is at the heart of the common expression *pobreza tem cor* (poverty has a color; see Carneiro 2011:57). While not all people who live in the shantytowns and suburbs of Rio are black, the vast majority of black people live in these impoverished areas. A fellow anthropologist once took a long walk through various neighborhoods. As he headed south through the city, he watched the overall mix of people turn from a medium shade of brown to lighter brown to nearly all white (Sean Mitchell, personal communication), a reminder of the racial geography of Rio or what anthropologist Keisha-Khan Perry has called the "racial politics of spatial exclusion" (2013:51). For this book, I draw on research that I conducted in 1997–98 in Cruzada, a South Zone *comunidade* (or "community," a new euphemism for a shantytown) where the majority of residents identified as *preto* (black) and my whiteness made me an obvious outsider. As I explain in chapter 2, Cruzada is technically a *conjunto habitacional* (akin to a housing project), a series of ten buildings built to house displaced residents after an unexplained fire destroyed a sprawling shantytown, Praia do Pinto, that took up some of Rio's most expensive real estate.[12] The contrast between the one long city block of Cruzada and the neighboring blocks and streets is visually startling, not only because of the juxtaposition of poorly maintained housing project buildings and luxurious and modern condominiums, but also because the racial makeup of the population is so clearly divergent from the surrounding area.[13]

I visited Brazil nearly every year after I left in 1998, and in 2014 I moved back to Rio de Janeiro to live in the wealthy neighborhood of Ipanema with my family, which by then included my white husband, one white biological

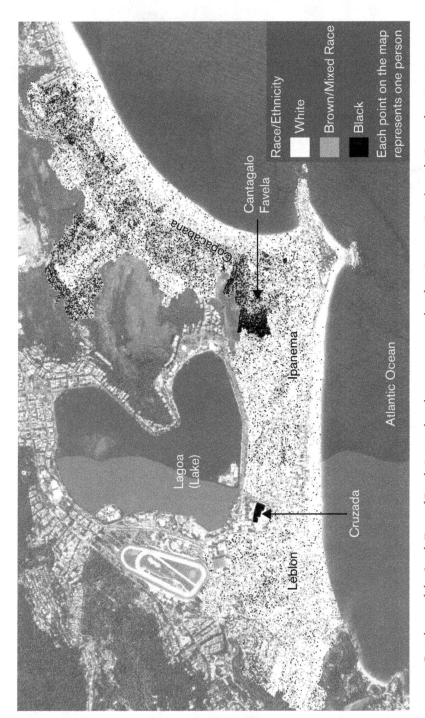

MAP 1. Racial map of the South Zone of Rio de Janeiro based on 2010 census data from Instituto Brasileiro de Geografia e Estatística (IBGE). Adapted from maps created by Hugo Nicolau Barbosa de Gusmão.

son, and two other children, one son and one daughter, both African American and adopted. We spent one year in Rio while I researched the daily lives of middle- and upper-middle-class families, and it was only then that the difference between brownness and blackness became crystal clear to me. (Both of my African American children are dark enough to be considered *negro/a* in Brazil.) The physical and social spaces that we frequented in Copacabana, Ipanema, and Leblon included expensive apartment buildings, members-only social clubs, private schools and extracurricular activities, shopping malls, vacation spots, and *casas de festas* (spaces rented to host children's birthday parties). These spaces almost always had dark-skinned workers who occupied service positions as cleaners, maids, nannies, waiters, doormen, and security guards. Visibly "black" Brazilians who actively participated as members and invited guests were few and far between (see Cicalo 2012a, 2012b; McCallum 2005).

During this research in middle-class spaces, I was never in a place where there were too many black people to count (generally on one hand), and my children got used to being the only dark-skinned people who were not minimum-wage workers. The experience of bringing a black and white (and thus highly visible) family to live in Rio offered me an unusual vantage point. Unlike most Brazilian families, ours had no smooth range from light brown to dark brown, nor did we "match" as an entirely dark-skinned or entirely light-skinned family. Brazilians seemed to quickly understand our situation, especially since my dark-skinned children were still young. One physically disabled man without legs who gets around on a skateboard and has lived for years on the streets around the public square near our apartment once called out to us, "Me adota também!" (Adopt me too!).

Throughout our many visits to Rio, my family and I experienced few instances of direct racism—I can also count these on one hand. One time when we stopped to speak to the waiter on the outside patio of a fancy Leblon restaurant (where we went for my husband's birthday), a security guard came over to ask if my two younger children were "with us." When we stayed to dine at the restaurant, and I spoke with the waiter and the manager to discuss what had happened and how my son (who was eight at the time) had noticed his symbolic exclusion from our family because of his skin color, both were very apologetic and sincere in their disapproval of the situation. Middle-class friends to whom I told of this incident afterward all readily agreed that it was a clear, and disturbing, example of Brazilian racism. Their willingness to discuss individual and more obvious situations of racism in which insult or exclusion was directed toward dark-skinned individuals, as in the Paulo Henrique Amorim case, did not mean that they

shared my interest in discussing the structural racism that we were all living in.[14]

When I asked friends why our shared private school, with more than fifteen hundred students ages two to eighteen, did not seem to have more than
a few dozen students of color, despite the fact that plenty of dark-skinned
youth lived in the poorer neighboring communities, they did not recognize
this as racism. My ever-aware son had also noticed the glaring absence of
dark-skinned students. But, illustrating the preference to think in terms of
class rather than race, my middle-class friends chalked this up to both class
discrimination and the financial inability of poorer people to enroll their children in a private school. "Don't you think it would cause an uproar if three
hundred black kids entered the school tomorrow?" I would ask. "Not if they
were middle-class kids," I routinely heard. "The uproar would only occur if
three hundred kids from the shantytowns or three hundred children of doormen came into the school." Our short-lived debate was hyper-hypothetical:
there were not three hundred middle-class or wealthy dark-skinned children
to be found, even if we had combed multiple South Zone neighborhoods.

Along similar lines, when I asked why there were no black teachers at
the school, friends said that they doubted that the school was turning away
qualified black candidates because of their race. One well-liked dark-skinned
library assistant named Rose whom I interviewed (and talked to parents
about) was considered poorly suited for classroom teaching because of her
"ungrammatical" speech. This meant that she acted as the full-time teaching librarian for the lower school, working twice as many hours as regular
teachers for half the pay. This, too, was seen as class discrimination, unrelated to her race. She may have reached the best position that she could
obtain, I was told, due to her class background. Rose had previously worked
as a nanny. My friends were likely right that there were few qualified black
teaching candidates prior to the recent implementation of college quotas.
Qualified applicants might also have been more likely to seek positions
through *concursos* (literally "contests") that offered jobs based on test
scores on publicly offered exams, reducing the chances that racism would
affect the outcome. They could therefore "earn" these positions and not
subject themselves to interviews and positions in primarily white spaces
that they may have found intimidating. By comparison, though Rose had
begun seeking out *concursos* that she could sit for, she was reluctant to
leave her position in such a prestigious space, one she had never dreamed
that she could occupy. Middle-class interpretations of the lack of racial mixture in these spaces were telling. The absence of black students and black
teachers was unfortunate but not surprising to them given the fact that

most black people in the area were poor and had access only to public (and thus substandard) schools. It was not understood to be related to racism.

Throughout this book, I emphasize how racial ideas shape the construction of social inequality, not because I wish to deny the importance of class (which is always relevant), but because the divide between rich and poor is so readily acknowledged in Brazil. One could also describe the arrival of the Portuguese court in 1808 as introducing a clash of dramatically different socioeconomic levels and lifestyles, from noble to slave. Slaves were also mostly uneducated (deliberately so) and thus "justifiably" ineligible for social mobility. And yet such a reading would obviously ignore the structural racism that was fed not only by differences in wealth, opportunity, and the situation of one's birth, but also by notions of the superiority of whiteness and the inferiority of blackness. Black people were not seen as equals; they were not generally understood to have the same intellectual capacities as people of European descent; and in this way their location at the bottom of the social hierarchy was made understandable. The historical continuation of these ideas from the nineteenth century to the present day offers the second guiding premise of this book.

"CIVILIZATION AND BARBARISM"

Brazil began to contemplate the end of slavery decades before it fully emancipated all slaves in 1888, and scholars and politicians at the time worried aloud about the country's lack of whiteness. It was the dawn of the era of scientific racism, during which whiteness was scientifically "proven" to be superior and miscegenation was widely understood to lead to degeneration and demise. Across Latin America, leading thinkers constantly monitored their global standing and strategized on how to racially improve their national population (Stepan 1991). Argentina's Domingo Sarmiento, in one of his nineteenth-century essays, "Civilization and Barbarism," described the difficulty a mixed-race Latin America would have promoting European values as the whiter United States successfully had done. As historian Darien Davis explains, "Barbarism was all that was South American; its indigenous roots, its African slavery, its miscegenation, and its cultural mixing" (1999:20). Blackness, in particular, was associated with slavery and held up as the opposite of modern civilization. Compared to the United States (as it perpetually was), Brazil suffered from a racially inferior climate (the tropics) as well as a severe racial imbalance. Because its black population had been over 50 percent for so long, racial separation was thought to be a near impossibility (Skidmore 1974:29).

The proposed solution of *embranquecimento*, or whitening, through facilitating and financially subsidizing European immigration, seemed to offer "an ingenious compromise between racist theory and the facts of Brazilian social life" (Skidmore 1974:136).[15] European immigrants would bring to the tropics "a flow of lively, energetic, and healthy Caucasian blood" (Joaquim Nabuco, quoted in Skidmore 1974:24) and would allow Brazilians to "cleanse themselves of the backward population" (D. Davis 1999:19). They could then be encouraged to *melhorar a raça* (improve, or "save," the race; see D. Davis 1999:18) through marriage and miscegenation with whiter stock. Even as they embraced whitening to solve their "problems" with blackness, Brazilian racial thinkers remained proud of their racial tolerance. As one proponent of whitening noted with relief: "We have been able to fuse all races into a single native population, because Portuguese colonization assimilated the savage races instead of trying to destroy them, thus preparing us to resist the devastating invasion of race prejudice" (quoted in Skidmore 1974:24). Both "savage races" and racial prejudice were to be carefully avoided in order to ensure the overall health, well-being, and future of the nation.

It is thus a source of continued pride that Brazil avoided explicitly segregationist laws, in sharp contrast to the United States—a country that spent nearly one hundred years after emancipation legally enforcing separation of the black and white races and legalizing explicit racial discrimination. And yet this comparison ignores the sometimes extralegal Brazilian policies that accomplished race-based restrictions and successfully limited the presence of undesirable blackness. For example, Brazil never passed a bill, proposed in the 1920s, that was intended to prohibit the immigration of people of African descent. Fears of tarnishing Brazil's reputation as a country with no racism, an image helpful to the nation both abroad and at home, ensured that the law did not pass. However, the Ministry of Foreign Affairs told representatives to put the law into effect anyway, as intercepted telegrams to U.S. consuls made clear, and African Americans were repeatedly denied even tourist visas (Seigel 2003:70). As Seigel notes, "Brazil may never have legislated racism, as comparers are so avid to note, but it often worked no less hard to enforce it" (2003:68).

Eugenic principles were written into Brazilian law in the 1934 Constitution, and beliefs in the racial superiority of whiteness explain immigration laws passed in 1945, as Brazil emphasized "the need to preserve and develop in the ethnic composition of the population the more desirable characteristics of its European ancestry" (E. Nascimento 2001:514). Concern over its international racial reputation had led Brazil to abolish slavery in the late nineteenth century and would later lead it to enact state-based affirmative action policies in the early twenty-first century (Telles 2004:237–38). Brazilian racial insecurities were voiced aloud in at least one public speech made by representatives of Hitler's Germany at an international conference: "It is unbelievable that I, a representative of Germany, only has [sic] the same vote that competes with those semi-savage countries of blacks from America like Brazil" (quoted in D. Davis 1999:182). Even as Brazil began to embrace the idea of its "mulatto" reputation, especially in soccer, there were still concerns, as late as 1958, about sending a predominantly nonwhite selection to represent Brazil in the World Cup (Owensby 2005:334).

The takeaway message from this era of Brazilian history, as Thomas Skidmore describes it in *Black into White* (1974), his detailed account of racial thought from 1870 to 1930, is that Brazil, along with Latin America in general, spent many a sleepless night worrying about its lack of whiteness and its extensive blackness.[16] To illustrate this perceived racial dilemma and Brazilians' beliefs in the possibilities and promise of whitening, I recount a Brazilian fairy tale, written in the early 1900s and later translated into an English version for a British audience (Young 1916). In the tale "A Princesa Negrina" (The Black Princess), which Brazilian anthropologist Lilia Moritz Schwarcz (1998) notes is a blend of Snow White, Cinderella, Beauty and the Beast, and (I would add) Rapunzel, a king and queen are granted a wish by a fairy godmother. As they have no children, the queen exclaims, "Como eu gostaria de ter uma filha, mesmo que fosse escura como a noite que reina lá fora!" (How I would love to have a daughter, even if she were as dark as the night that reigns outside!) The fairy godmother interprets this wish literally, and a daughter "preta como o carvão" (black as coal) is born, causing much commotion. Witnessing the despair of the royal couple, the fairy godmother offers to eventually turn the child white, if she is kept in the castle until her sixteenth birthday. At the age of fifteen, the princess (named Rosa Negra, or Black Rose) loses both of her parents and is tempted out of the castle by a snake. After she learns of the disobedience of the princess, the fairy godmother gives Black Rose one last chance and commands her to marry a monster that is half man and half beast. The princess agrees, but that night she cries desperately to the beast, explaining that she is sad not because of him, but because she has now lost her only chance to become white. They embrace, and at that moment, the beast turns into o Príncipe Diamante (the Diamond Prince), a handsome white nobleman, and she turns into a lovely white princess. And the couple lives happily ever after.[17]

My Brazilian friends were horrified when I told them the story of *A Princesa Negrina*, an outdated fairy tale that they had never heard of, and they were just as horrified that I would include such a story in my book on Brazilian race relations. I share this old-fashioned and obviously racist tale because it helpfully demonstrates how racial thought is both historically and culturally specific, at the same time that it retains a central coherence. This is a distinctly Brazilian fairy tale that makes little sense to North Americans who consider race fixed and largely determined by one's ancestry.[18] And yet more than one hundred years after it was written, the tale of "The Black Princess" confuses neither Brazilians nor North Americans with the main idea that whiteness is considered more valuable and more beautiful than blackness (even as we may vehemently disagree with this racial hierarchy). It is thus important to recognize that racial ideas seamlessly combine both the old and the new, as they span both time and space. As anthropologist Kristina Wirtz notes: "Blackness is neither a straightforward natural category nor a straightforward historical category. It is, rather, a complex series of cultural constructions whose various, overlapping histories encompass several continents and oceans over half a millennium" (2014:5).

Figuring out what to hold constant in these "overlapping" racial ideas is an obvious challenge. It is here that I must begin to explain why I do not limit my understanding of race to the actual visual marker of skin color. As I discuss further in what follows, it is quite common for Brazilians to believe that discrimination against people with lighter skin cannot possibly be related to race. In the absence of recognizable phenotypical markers associated with blackness (the trio of skin color, hair texture, and specific facial features), how could people come to be interpreted as black? And if they are treated poorly, isn't this a sign of discrimination due to socioeconomic class or place of residence (the stigma of living in a *favela* or a distant suburb)? One of the central arguments of this book is that racial ideas must be separated from the phenotypical cues we have learned to look for on bodies. As in the fairy tale, whiteness is granted to the princess (and, allegorically, to Brazil) because of her character; it is not guaranteed by or directly related to her skin color (or her ancestry). Indeed, in Portuguese, there are two possible words for whiteness (within academic studies): *brancura* and *branquitude*. Social psychologist Lia Vainer Schucman clarifies that *brancura* refers to a "white" phenotype, which includes light skin, narrow facial features, and straight hair, while *branquitude* refers to a position of privilege that one occupies in a racially hierarchical society (2014:169; see also Sovik 2009:50). Despite the happy ending in the fairy tale, in which everyone finally matches, these types of whiteness do not always overlap in "real" life.

There is no better example of this than the case of *nordestinos* who have migrated from the Northeast of Brazil and who live, along with their descendants, in poverty side-by-side with descendants of African slaves in the stigmatized *favelas* of the large cities of Brazil's South. Because the majority of *nordestinos* are lighter-skinned, and because they suffer from discrimination, poverty, and restricted social mobility, they are the clearest example of how social inequality is boiled down to class in Brazil. In *The Color of Modernity*, historian Barbara Weinstein (2015) makes the argument I have long wanted to make, though this is not the topic of my research: *nordestinos* aren't considered (racially) white.[19] Weinstein's careful and convincing study traces the development of regional identity in Brazil, describing the different trajectories of Brazil's "booming" industrial South versus the poverty-stricken and rural Northeast. As São Paulo became whiter with the importation of European immigrants, primarily from Italy, Spain, and Portugal, and as the region's economy grew, "tangible material differences between locales such as São Paulo and the Nordeste could be mobilized to legitimate narratives of modernity and backwardness" (Weinstein 2015:6). Here the nation appealed to ideas of innate and natural characteristics to explain how a white, hardworking, and prosperous South contrasted with the lazy, backward, and blacker Northeast. Weinstein explains: "Given that these 'racial' categories were themselves unstable, the labeling of a region as 'black' or 'white' has to be understood as a process that is not reducible to local inhabitants' skin color or origins. Central to my own work is the contention that *paulistas* [residents of São Paulo] have routinely represented themselves as 'white' and *nordestinos* as 'nonwhite' regardless of genetics or physical appearance" (2015:10).

Thus while many northeasterners can be described as lighter-skinned, though not generally as light as those of direct European ancestry, they are not understood to be racially white. They are commonly assumed to lack refinement, intellectual capacity, and civility. Indeed, Weinstein finds that people from São Paulo often call *nordestinos* "*baianos*" (people from Bahia), even though most northeasterners do not come from the state of Bahia. Bahia is, however, the most African of all Brazilian states, and thus this inaccurate generalization attempts to racialize northeasterners through symbolic connections made to blackness (Weinstein 2015:226; see also O'Dougherty 2002). Although I focus in this book on the more overbearing racial contrast made between blackness and whiteness, particularly in Rio, the process of racially reading bodies that I describe here also impacts Brazilians of indigenous ancestry (see, for example, Conklin 1997) and immigrants (mostly in São Paulo) from Asia and the Middle East (Lesser

2013). Brazil's "comfortable racial contradiction" thus employs ideas of racial superiority versus inferiority and presumed differential capacities for "*Ordem e Progresso*" (Order and Progress; the national motto emblazoned on the Brazilian flag) to explain and justify the reality of structural racism. The contradictory part of Brazilian race relations is introduced when we factor in equally commonsensical and deeply held beliefs in the nation's capacity for racial tolerance.

"WE ARE NOT RACIST"

Consider the following explanation of Brazilian race relations:

> Brazilians who are aware of social realities in their country [will not] deny that race prejudice is entirely lacking, or that a mild form of racial discrimination exists and is growing in certain areas. There are well-known stereotypes and attitudes, traditional in Brazil, which indicate dispraisal of the Negro and of the mulatto. There are also well-known barriers to the social ascension of "people of colour" who are the descendants of slaves. Increasing discrimination in such centres as São Paulo and Rio de Janeiro caused the National Congress to pass a law making racial discrimination a criminal offence. Yet most Brazilians are proud of their tradition of racial equality and of the racial heterogeneity of their people. They feel that Brazil has a great advantage over most Western nations in the essentially peaceful relations which exist between the people of various racial groups in their country. Industrial, technological and even educational backwardness may be overcome more easily than in areas of the world where racial cleavages divide the population. Brazilians have an important tradition to cherish in their patterns of interracial relations. . . . The world has much to learn from a study of race relations in Brazil. (Wagley 1952:8)

While anthropologist Charles Wagley made these observations in the 1950s in the midst of the UNESCO studies funded by the United Nations to help the world understand how Brazil had successfully achieved the status of a "racial democracy," I would argue that his comments hold true for Brazil today. In this section of the chapter, I seek to explain the historical foundation of how Brazil came to think about itself as an example of racial tolerance and cordiality. I prefer both of these descriptors to the term "racial democracy," as both of them allow for the "comfortable racial contradiction" that I have been describing. Historian Darien Davis describes racial tolerance, in Brazil and throughout Latin America, as relying on the definition of *to tolerate*, along the lines of "the acceptance of a necessary evil" (1999:17). The idea of cordiality similarly implies politeness and possibly even camaraderie, but it does not invoke notions of equality as the word *democracy* does. The description of Brazil as a "racial democracy" has led to a series of academic studies refuting the veracity of this claim (see, for example, Bailey 2009; Hasenbalg and Silva 1988; Telles 2004). Few would argue, however, with the fact that Brazil has long thought of itself as a racially tolerant nation, despite its structural racism. In what follows, I seek to provide the reader with a quick summary of how these ideas were first propagated, both at home and abroad, and how they were later enforced by a repressive and occasionally brutal military regime. These state policies, ranging from propaganda to censorship, continue to influence how Brazilians, foreigners, and academics think about race in Brazil.

It is perhaps interesting to note that both of Brazil's twentieth-century dictatorships were heavily invested in promoting the idea of Brazil's racial tolerance. It was President Getúlio Vargas (dictator from 1930 to 1945, democratically elected from 1951 to 1954) who sought to consolidate Brazil's federal system and actively promoted feelings of Brazilian nationalism. For Vargas, unity rested on notions of the "racially harmonious Brazilian national family" (D. Davis 1999:2). The idea of a Brazilian family that included African, European, and indigenous peoples was broadcast to the world even as recently as 2014 as three children (one white, one black, and one indigenous) were chosen to release white doves during the World Cup opening ceremonies.[20] Brazilian anthropologist Roberto DaMatta (1981) has famously described this national origin story as the "fábula das três raças" (the fable of the three races), which is supposed to represent the heritage of all Brazilians. Vargas's banner of *brasilidade* (Brazilianness) forced Brazilians to subsume ethnic, racial, and regional identities and profess a shared nationalism (Ferraz 2013; Lesser 2013).

Under the Vargas dictatorship, any attention to racial conflict or racial discrimination was considered an affront to national pride and an impediment to national progress (Daniel 2006:68). The trope of *mestiçagem* (racial mixture), made popular during the same era through the well-known work of Gilberto Freyre (1978 [1933]), also downplayed discussion of racial difference. According to Freyre, racial mixture and racial tolerance would lead to the creation of a Brazilian "meta-race." This pride in a racially mixed Brazilian identity and in a country that had achieved racial harmony and even "fraternity" was constantly evoked (and only made sense) in relation to North America's reputation as a land of racial hatred and violent conflict (Seigel 2009:217), a characterization supported by widely publicized incidents of racial lynching. Indeed, the propaganda around Brazil's racial tolerance was not intended merely for a Brazilian audience.[21] In 1951, Brazil's

Ministry of Foreign Relations distributed a pamphlet printed in English extolling the benefits of Brazil's race relations in comparison to those of the United States (Daniel 2006:177).

Despite the internationally publicized results of the UNESCO studies that found both subtle and statistical evidence of racial inequality throughout the country (as in the previous quote from Charles Wagley; see also Harris 1952), the idea that Brazil was a racially tolerant nation gained an even stronger foothold when it was legally enforced during Brazil's military dictatorship from 1964 to 1985. Racial inequality had not improved; racial hierarchy continued; and beliefs that connected blackness to inferiority were still widespread. But racism was not to be discussed and critiques of racial democracy (considered "acts of subversion") would not be tolerated (Nobles 2000:111). To make sure that quantitative studies that could measure racial inequality were not conducted, questions about race and racial identification were omitted from the 1970 census. Leading scholars who had participated in the earlier UNESCO studies and were active in what would later be called the São Paulo School of Race Relations were forced out of their university positions. These included sociologists Florestan Fernandes, Octávio Ianni, and Fernando Henrique Cardoso, who went into exile but later returned to become president of Brazil from 1995 to 2003. Black activist Abdias do Nascimento also went into "voluntary" exile in the United States, and black organizations, such as Nascimento's TEN, Teatro Experimental do Negro (Black Experimental Theater), were disbanded. The Commission of Military Inquiry confiscated books from Brazilian universities that addressed the theme of racial inequality (J. Dávila 2013:34).

Political scientist David Covin points to the deep racial contradictions that Brazil supported at the time: "Brazil [was] a racial democracy—under a *dictatorship*—one composed entirely of white men, in a mostly black country" (2006:36; see also J. Dávila 2012). The dictatorship fiercely protected national ideals of *mestiçagem* (race mixture) and racial tolerance through acts of censorship: "At the level of propaganda and communication, a disseminated image of national unity was paramount, and any mention of racial discord, either within or outside of Brazil, was prohibited. Film censors were instructed to assess whether a film depicted racial problems in Brazil, dealt with the Black Power movement in the United States, or referred to racial problems in any way that could impact upon Brazil" (Hanchard 1998:113). Historian Paulina Alberto (2009) documents a case in which a senior military official altered a report to explain that individuals were barred from entering private social clubs based on their social class and not, as the junior officer had written, because of their race (see also Azevedo 1975). Political scientist Michael Hanchard offers another example that indicates the severity and, at times, absurdity of racial censorship: the line "The whites have great material advantage while the blacks have almost no legal opening" was removed from a reprinted article from Britain's *Manchester Guardian,* even though it described a game of chess (1998:113).

Brazil began its political *abertura* (opening) in the early 1980s, and the country spent decades in a process of "redemocratization" (Holston 2008; Holston and Caldeira 1998; see also chapter 2). But during the second half of the twentieth century another important (and fairly recent) layer had been added to the story of Brazilian race relations. Extreme racial inequality, deep anxiety over a lack of whiteness and a strong fear of blackness were now entwined with a national pride in racial mixture and a rejection of racism that had been strictly enforced by the military government. The social imperative to ignore racial difference, despite the stigma of blackness/nonwhiteness and the existence of structural racism, has impacted decades of policy making and reactions to the country's *favelas.* Historian Brodwyn Fischer notes that discussions about race and racism in *favelas* were increasingly "muffled" or silenced even before the military dictatorship, and in the mid-1950s, Brazil's national congress managed to spend a full year debating a national law about *favelas* without once mentioning that the majority of residents were of African descent (2014:24). This despite the fact that an influential *favela* study produced around the same time "lament[ed] the supposed inability of 'Neolithic' rural migrants and ex-slaves to overcome their backwardness and join a productive proletariat" (quoted in Fischer 2008:77).

The ability to juggle the *favela's* negative associations of blackness with a silence on racism is fully developed in the internationally acclaimed film *Cidade de Deus* (City of God), which portrays "daily life" in the *favela* to millions of non-Brazilian viewers. The film vividly depicts scenes of crime, violence, and social marginalization, but never mentions race or racism, despite its largely black cast and the fact that the most dangerous and "evil" of characters has the darkest skin (Vargas 2004:443–44). Along similar lines, at least a half-dozen book-length treatments published in the past five years focus on the drug trade, violence, and disenfranchisement in Rio's *favelas,* but they rarely mention race as a significant factor of the residents' exclusion or daily experiences.

Despite these frequent omissions, it has been well documented that *favelas* in Rio are commonly thought of as *o lugar dos negros* (the place of black people; see Sheriff 2001:18), meaning that all who live there, regardless of skin color, bear the stigma of racial association through their contact with darker-skinned people (the descendants of slaves) and their inescapable contact with black spaces. "Even those who were not physically black were black in the minds of the social elites because they lived like black people among black people" (Covin 2006:39). As anthropologist João Costa Vargas notes, the *favela* became readily associated with "the very concepts that have been usually associated with black people, not only in Brazil, but throughout the Americas/Africa/Europe complex: dirt, promiscuity, aversion to work, violence, irrationality, lawlessness, danger, and subhumanity. . . . Urban space became a metaphor, a code concept for blackness, in the same way that the *favela* was rendered a code word for blacks" (2004:455). Thus even though racism is clearly not the only explanation for the growth and continued exclusion of *favelas* and their residents, it should be stated often and with no small amount of fanfare that the perceived nonwhiteness of *favela* and suburban residents (including northeastern migrants) is one of the reasons that middle-class city residents allow their neighbors to live in situations of such precariousness and insecurity (Penglase 2014). Continuing the long legacy of slavery to which the *favelas* are directly linked, *favela* residents are not understood to be the same as people from *o asfalto* (the asphalt, or the developed part of the city), which makes their suffering unfortunate but more tolerable. Deeply ingrained notions that accord only white people full humanity help structure a widespread societal resignation and denial of full citizenship rights (Alves 2014; Alves and Vargas 2015; C. Smith 2015, 2016; Vargas 2011; Vargas and Alves 2010).

Noticing racial difference in Brazil is thus invested with a host of meanings. It is personally damning, taken as a sign of one's lack of civility and refinement; it is unpatriotic and an insult to the nation; and it is politically risky, monitored by the state and now subject to legal action. Even asking about one's own personal racial identification can be taken as offensive and unnecessarily divisive (as in the Vargas era), as I found when I conducted surveys on slang in the late 1990s. One public high school student refused to respond to my request for racial classification in the section asking for personal information (including age, gender, socioeconomic class, and residential neighborhood). The light-skinned female youth bypassed the printed options that offered official racial census categories and wrote that she was, "Brasileira (o que importa a cor)" (Brazilian [what does color matter]).

Here this teenager articulates the still-widespread idea that to be Brazilian is to take pride in racial mixture and to demonstrate a lack of interest in racial difference. "*Democracia racial* [racial democracy] is as much a system of etiquette as it is an ideology, and as such it stipulates that Brazilians of all colors and classes eschew discourses that figure their nation as divided along a rigid color line" (Sheriff 2001:46). During her research on understandings of race in a Rio *favela* in the mid-1990s, Robin Sheriff encountered a strong preference to ignore or dismiss situations of racism and obvious racial disparity (as Twine [1998] also found). Sheriff described this as a "cultural censorship," a racial silence maintained even as coercion by the state had eased. Anthropologist João Costa Vargas has described the attention paid to race along with the audible silence as "the hyperconsciousness/negation of race dialectic . . . [which] allows us to understand how a system that is on the surface devoid of racial awareness is in reality deeply immersed in racialized understandings of the social world" (2004:443).

I have updated these terms in order to describe Brazil in terms of its "comfortable racial contradiction," because there is now loud discussion of acts of individual racism, as well as debates over public policy, even as the avoidance of noticing racial difference and a denial of structural racism persist. This new sociopolitical context has aggravated many Brazilians who argue, often passionately, that Brazil continues to be a land of racial tolerance and unity. Here again, we find continuities. In 2006 Ali Kamel, a journalist for the powerful and politically conservative newspaper *O Globo*, published the book *Não Somos Racistas: Uma Reação aos que Querem nos Transformar numa Nação Bicolor* (We Are Not Racist: A Reaction to Those Who Want to Turn Us into a Black-White Nation). This book, voted one of the ten most important of the year by the Brazilian news magazine *Veja*, sharply criticized the affirmative action quotas based on race that were being implemented in various prestigious public universities. An observation made by Emílio Willems in the *American Journal of Sociology* in 1949 puts an old spin on Kamel's "new" provocative title: "Assiduous readers of Brazilian newspapers may have noted that the question of whether or not race prejudice exists in Brazil is put with an insistence that certainly would be unnecessary if there were actually no doubt about it. Usually the answer is given by those who raise the question: They reaffirm that race prejudice does not exist in Brazil" (1949:403).

A deeply felt identification with racial tolerance clearly persists in Brazil, alongside the mounting evidence of racial disparity. But how to address this disparity and how to even talk about it remain highly controversial. In early 2016, the journalist Paulo Henrique Amorim was given another jail sentence, this time for five months and ten days (pending appeal), for the crimes of *injúria* (insult) and *difamação* (defamation) for accusing Ali Kamel of being a racist because of the publication of his 2006 book. Amorim described Kamel as "*trevoso*" (evil) and claimed that he "engrossa as fileiras racistas dos que bloqueiam a integração e a ascensão dos negros" (joins the already-large ranks of racists who block the integration and ascension of black people).[22] The court decided that Amorim is free to critique Kamel, but not to choose words "with the special intent to offend." Brazil's military dictatorship, with its active censoring of the mention of racial inequality, ended more than thirty years ago, but the Brazilian courts have just decided that accusing someone of racism can land you in jail. This latest Amorim conviction suggests that the bold assertion that someone else has paid attention to racial difference is the gravest of insults and dangerously defames their character (see French 2015). At the same time, despite strong disapproval from much of the Brazilian middle class, the state now legally recognizes racial difference through affirmative action quotas that have withstood various legal challenges (Tavolaro 2008).

Brazil remains deeply ambivalent about how to deal with the idea of racial difference. It is not that some Brazilians were "duped" by oppressive dictators, nor that Brazilian racial inequality has ever really been a secret. Brazilians are paying constant attention to the racial hierarchy that they live within, which concentrates people of lighter skin at the top, in positions of power and in jobs requiring education and intellectual capacity, and rewards them with easier access to resources. At the same time, blackness continues to be seen as linked to manual and service labor, poverty, crime, and violence. Racial ideas help explain these connections between people and resources and their positions in society, even as one is asked to take pride in Brazil's racial mixture and spirit of racial tolerance. I turn next to explain how we can watch Rio residents work through this contradiction, which encourages them to "see" race even as they seek to ignore racial difference and avoid racism.[23]

RACE, LANGUAGE, AND THE BODY

Within the confines of the familiar Brazilian–North American comparison, race is determined either by *marca* or *origem* (Nogueira 1985), by the whiteness or blackness phenotypically displayed on the Brazilian body (D. Silva 1998) or by "blood," biology, and known racial ancestry in the context of the United States (F. Davis 1991). Yet the reading of racialized bodies has never been this self-evident or clear-cut. Looking at the U.S. antebellum South, Mark Smith insightfully points out that southerners inadvertently "acknowledged the visual instability of race by increasing their reliance on the one-drop rule, which, if anything, confirmed the argument that race could not, in fact, be seen" (2006:7). Researchers working in a range of national contexts and across different time periods have similarly argued that racial whiteness, in particular, is not reducible to or guaranteed by skin color or parentage (Bashkow 2006; Heneghan 2003; Stoler 2002; Weismantel 2001). In what follows, I take my inspiration from the work of Ann Stoler (1995, 2002), to show how race draws its coherence and stability not from biology or ancestry, but rather from the "interpretive space" between "the 'seen' and the 'unseen'" (Stoler 1997:187). In this book, I argue that visible phenotypical features, knowledge of ancestry, and embodied practices thought to "display" one's inner racial capacities are read together, forcing Rio residents to interpret themselves and others in terms of racial difference.

As is obvious to everyone, scholars and laypeople, Brazilians and North Americans alike, phenotype is critical to racial meaning, as physical attributes such as shade of skin color, hair color and texture, and facial features are heavily scrutinized (Pinho 2009), and they are readily assumed to provide insight into a person's character and racial capacity. And yet I illustrate how blackness and whiteness are both visibly significant and also powerfully imagined, ascertained from cultural and linguistic practices that do not always neatly "match" the bodies who engage in or embody them. Political scientist Michael Hanchard suggests that Brazilian(ist) researchers should pay attention to the "importance of the interpretive, as opposed to the phenotypical, criterion of racial differentiation" (1994:178). And historian Matthew Pratt Guterl argues that "discrimination is a shared practice of racial sight, of finding evidence of race on the body" (2013:209). I am therefore not the first to note that bodies need to be racially interpreted, but few have attempted to systematically analyze how people read bodies for signs of race in day-to-day interactions that occur both within and across race and class lines.

My approach, and my focus on reading "the body," is discursive on two levels. To begin with, I analyze how racial ideas (or racial "discourses") link observable qualities of bodies, including cultural and linguistic practices, to essentialized capacities that cannot be observed. To uphold the opposing racial poles of whiteness and nonwhiteness, racial discourses contrast bodies as clean or dirty, civilized or barbaric, controlled or undisciplined, restrained or violent, among other shifting criteria (Hall 1997; Inda 2000). The central idea here is not that these categories are predetermined or essentialized characteristics of individuals, but rather that through daily and repetitive performances, bodies come to be understood in these racialized terms. This performative approach to race, which is well articulated and illustrated by linguistic anthropologist Kristina Wirtz in her book *Performing Afro-Cuba* (2014), allows me to separate ideas of blackness and whiteness from the physical features that seem to ground them. Understandings of racial difference that hinge on assumptions of white superiority and black inferiority are connected to bodies based not only on the way they appear but also on their obligatory display of embodied practices. As I show in the following chapters, medium brown–skinned bodies can be read as "black" in Rio when they take up the racial stance of aggressiveness associated with politically conscious hip-hop. These same bodies can be read as "white" when they occupy exclusive private spaces such as social clubs and demonstrate "proper" restraint and decorum. Drawing on everyday interactions, I describe how Rio residents unavoidably draw on these racial discourses to make themselves interpretable, and to interpret others, as they interact in both comfortable private spaces among "equals" and as they move through more hotly contested public spaces.

On a second level, I focus on what linguistic anthropologists think of as "actual" discourse. This includes the things that people say to each other, the stories they tell, what they read in newspaper articles, and even the song lyrics fans memorize and recirculate among one another. Here my focus on daily linguistic practice relies on the concept of language ideologies (or the power-laden connections made between speakers and their speech) to show how language gets pressed into the service of racial discourse and how it helps uphold racial hierarchies (Bucholtz 2011; Hill 2008). For example, in my research I have paid careful attention to how speakers of what is commonly called *a norma culta*, or "standard" Portuguese, who more consistently display grammatical agreement, are said to sound more "proper." Their sense of linguistic discipline projects not only their level of education and their class standing but also their claims to racial whiteness.

By contrast, the "nonstandard" linguistic features associated with *gíria*, or "slang," come to suggest a racialized lack of discipline and control. The frequent use of slang (and certain types of slang in particular) is commonly understood to be a less "civilized" way of speaking, and it is readily linked to blackness and criminality. Here I treat language as a bodily practice, that is, as something that bodies "do" as an ongoing and performative display that shapes the body that is there to be "seen." My focus on how language helps racialize the body connects both levels of discourse: what is said—discourse in the sense of linguistic practice—helps construct how bodies, through appeals to racial discourse, come to be recognized as inherently different.[24] This approach helps us locate and better understand the ideas that back up racism and racial hierarchy. As linguistic anthropologist Susan Philips notes: "Ideas do not float in the air, and they do not exist only in the heads of individuals. Ideas live in discourse. They are configured by the social organization of face-to-face interaction and by the sequential structure of discourse. Analysis of the ecology of ideas in discourse practices contributes to an understanding of why and how cultural constructs not only change but also endure" (2004:248).

Throughout this book, I also explore how racial ideas move and how they compel movement. This movement includes the ways that racial meaning circulates, in the sense of traveling between spaces and different contexts, as when Brazilians imported North American hip-hop (as I discuss in chapter 6), or across generations, as when teachers and parents explain to children what blackness looks like and how to talk about it (as I discuss in the conclusion). I will also explore the way that race settles in and on bodies (Weismantel and Eisenman 1998) and the ways that people are forced to move toward or away from the racial poles of whiteness and nonwhiteness. Here a comparison with gender and the performative construction of gender may prove instructive. We have long understood that gender does not reside in the physical body and that bodies must engage in repeated gender practices to be "readable" as male or female (Butler 1990, 1993). While gender must be understood as embodied rather than as a simple biological "fact," its frequent and obligatory performances allow for slippage: men can be perceived (or self-identify) as feminine (and vice versa), and expressions of sexuality often hinge on conformity or play with gendered bodily practices, including language. This type of flexibility, which includes movement toward and away from idealized notions of masculinity and femininity, has not typically been embraced in discussions of people's daily experiences of race. One notable example of the racial flexibility made possible through embodied linguistic practices (what I have elsewhere described as *racial malleability*; see Roth-Gordon 2013) can be found in the work of Frantz Fanon. As he noted:

> The Negro of the Antilles will be proportionately Whiter—that is, he will come closer to being a real human being—in direct ratio to his mastery of the French Language. . . . What we are getting at becomes plain: Mastery of language affords remarkable power. . . . The Black man who has lived in France for a length of time returns radically changed. To express it in genetic terms, his phenotype undergoes a definitive, an absolute mutation. (Fanon 1967:18–19)

I have long been fascinated by the ways that speakers use language to manipulate racial readings of their bodies and the fact that they do not ultimately control the interpretations of others. Based on ethnographic research and recordings of everyday interactions, in this book I explore how Rio residents take up language and other cultural practices to orient toward or away from whiteness and blackness, linking themselves to racialized attributes (such as civility and upstanding citizenship, discussed in chapters 2 and 3), positioning themselves vis-à-vis racialized city spaces (chapters 4 and 5), and responding to their nation's pride in its racial mixture and its racial "cordiality" (chapter 6 and the conclusion). I will, at times, talk about how their linguistic choices relate to ideas about their racial identity, when speakers seek to make this explicit. But given the sociopolitical context that I have just outlined, in which racial difference is not supposed to be embraced or even noticed, I analyze how speakers and listeners are employing and listening for racial cues that do not always map neatly onto phenotype or identity. In line with my argument that bodies are "read" for racial meaning, which includes attention to phenotype and embodied practices, I attempt to refrain from pre-labeling the people in this book.[25] I offer phenotypical cues as they would normally be available for the seeing, but I do not label my participants as "black" or "white." The amount of blackness or whiteness that a body displays is exactly what is constantly assessed and reassessed in the interactions I analyze (D. Silva 1998).

Although I was intrigued by Brazilian race relations from the minute I stepped foot in the country, I was quickly cautioned by Brazilian sociolinguists, as soon as I expressed interest in this topic, that there were no racial "dialects" in Brazil akin to the African American English well documented in the United States (see, for example, Rickford and Rickford 2000). There were regional differences in speech, I was told, and definitely class differences that reflected levels of education, but these could not be related to race. Poor people were said to sound the same regardless of whether they were white, brown, or black—an idea with which many nonsociolinguist Brazilians would also agree (see Burdick 2013:87–88). In addition, sociolinguistic work at the time often suggested that racial mixture in Brazil made finding clear groups of "black" or "white" speakers an impossible task, and thus race was dismissed as a salient social factor of linguistic differentiation. My hastily thrown-together "matched guise" tests, in which the same speaker read scripts on the same topic but varied his or her language over separate recordings, in this case by adding lots of slang to one version, proved that things were more complicated than this quick dismissal suggested. Listeners, who could not see the speaker of the recording, were perfectly comfortable making guesses about their race, especially if the speaker sounded like a poor person from the geographically marginalized parts of the city. These speakers, and their use of slang in particular, were readily associated with blackness.

This book is based on "real" conversations (rather than the made-up ones I have just described), but I also relied on a related linguistic technique as I played for middle-class listeners some of the conversations that I had recorded in the housing project of Cruzada. These listeners' recorded reactions are equally "real," though they are no doubt influenced by the set-up of recording their commentary in the comfort of their living rooms. The point I wish to make here is a useful one for the framing of this book: Rio residents don't just see bodies. They hear them speak; they sometimes imagine how they speak; and sometimes they hear them speak without seeing them at all. All of these linguistic practices, from the speaking to the overhearing to the imagining of speech (Inoue 2003), are informed by racial ideas that oppose blackness and whiteness in a highly racially mixed but also sharply divided city. In short, we do not need to have clearly defined groups of "black" and "white" speakers who speak in radically different ways in order to talk about the connections between race and language in Rio. What I have found is that these imagined connections, in particular linking what is called "standard" speech to whiteness and associating slang use with blackness, are critical to the process of making sense of and participating in everyday linguistic interactions, both within and across race and class lines. In Rio de Janeiro over the past few decades, the need to see, hear, and perform racial differences as one traveled through and occupied public spaces has taken on a level of urgency, as I now turn to describe.

COMPULSORY CLOSENESS

I would be remiss to begin describing the urban politics of Rio without stating the obvious: Rio de Janeiro is a stunningly beautiful city. In terms of its natural bounty, of which *cariocas* (Rio residents) are justifiably proud, it boasts jagged mountains, lush tropical rainforest, and miles of sandy beaches all within an urban environment. Its hot and humid climate, which in the minds of nineteenth-century European colonizers threatened racial degeneration, continues to earn the city the scorn of its larger (and more temperate) city rival São Paulo, which believes that industriousness cannot be found within a city whose residents spend so much time at the beach. Within Brazil, Rio is thought of as the cultural capital and the place where fashion is born, a notion that draws on the fact that it was the actual capital of the country for nearly two centuries (from 1763 to 1960). Rio has long boasted an established international reputation, a fact that undoubtedly aided in its bid to be the first city in Latin America to host the Summer Olympics in 2016. Yet for all its glory, Rio is also a city of shocking contrasts. While Rio is best known for its beaches, it has also attracted global attention for its hillside *favelas*, where red brick shacks constructed by their residents seem impossibly stacked one upon the other as far up as the eye can see.[26]

As the price of having nature in its backyard, Rio's usable city space is severely restricted, especially near the beaches and near the city center, leading to high population density and vertical growth. Shantytowns in Rio are often euphemistically called *morros* (hills) because many of the city's most famous *favelas* climb the lush mountains that connect the wealthier areas of the city. Within the South Zone of Rio, a sharp distinction is made between those who live in shantytowns and those who live down on *o asfalto* (the asphalt, or the city's paved and well-maintained parts). Indeed, it is impossible to conceive of and discuss social relationships and social hierarchy in Rio without understanding these constant references to space. The majority of Rio's poor and working-class residents live in sprawling, flat, and equally infrastructurally challenged neighborhoods in the city's North Zone and suburbs. Here the meaning of "suburban" is literally "sub-urban." As anthropologist Roberto DaMatta notes, "In sharp contrast to the American urban experience, suburban dwellers are not the well-off in search of bucolic contact with nature but rather the poor who still lack basic municipal services" (1995:19). Residents of these communities often travel up to three hours or more *one way* to get to their minimum-wage jobs in the more central areas of Rio.

This book does not focus on daily life within Rio's hillside *favelas* or its suburbs, yet it is important to stress the role that these spaces play in urban struggles and in *cariocas'* understandings of their city. Despite the impressive views it offers in many spots, elevation in Rio can be a stigma, as most of the city's lush green hills and mountains were not developed by city planners but instead "occupied," initially by former slaves as early as the late 1800s. As in most of Latin America and the Global South (including cities in Africa and India), informal settlements, where approximately 20 percent of Rio's population lives, have long been an urban "fact of life." Within Brazil, these areas are often referred to as *a periferia* (the periphery), alluding to their social (if not physical) distance from the city's more cosmopolitan sections. These areas were once thought of as illegal and a blight on the city's reputation because of the squatting practices through which they were settled and the primitive living conditions of their inhabitants. Today, the main source of these neighborhoods' continued marginalization is their occupation by notoriously well-armed and violent drug gangs; recent efforts by the state to "pacify" these areas and remove the ruling drug gangs have had only mixed success (Arias 2006; Doriam Borges, Ribeiro, and Cano 2012; Larkins 2015; McCann 2014; Penglase 2014; Perlman 2010; L. Silva 2015).

Because of the international press that Brazil and Rio have received, the term *favela* now appears in many English dictionaries, defined as a Brazilian shantytown. However, I have chosen to italicize the term in this book, marking it as Brazilian Portuguese, because I want readers to keep in mind what this term means in Rio and to *cariocas*. A *favela* is not just a place where people live, and it doesn't simply mark specific geographic spaces as physically or socially distant. Living in a *favela* has long been a source of profound stigma (even if it is also sometimes a source of personal pride). Because the term carries such weight, and because it was used to marginalize and exclude the large population of city residents that lived there, it has now become more politically correct to refer to a *favela* as a *comunidade* or "community." This term is meant to offer dignity and respect to the *pessoas humildes* (poor, humble people) who live in these impoverished neighborhoods. Despite the euphemism (which I also occasionally use), there remains the pervasive belief that where you are from speaks volumes about the kind of person you are. Whether or not you live in one, all *cariocas* define themselves in relation to the *favela*.

Despite recent efforts to gentrify some of the more centrally located South Zone *favelas*, members of the middle class still rarely enter these spaces, except to attend the occasional baby shower or birthday party at the home of their *empregada* (domestic worker or maid). And yet *favelas* are all around them, climbing the hills behind their apartment buildings. It is impossible to live in the wealthy South Zone of Rio, where all of the middle-class families that I knew owned and rented apartments, without living in close proximity to a *favela*. Rio residents do not have to imagine urban poverty; they either live in it and make their way to wealthy neighborhoods to go to school, get to work, or access other basic city services, or they walk past it every day—without directly experiencing it but utterly unable to ignore its presence. I can think of no better way to describe daily life in Rio than Brazilian anthropologist Leticia Veloso's (2010) term *compulsory closeness*.

It was by happy coincidence that I met my research assistant CW when he was seventeen and attending his last year of high school at the public school where I began conducting research on slang. It was the introduction he gave me to the *comunidade* of Cruzada São Sebastião that allowed me to live (and write about) compulsory closeness from both sides. Although it did not look or feel like a hillside shantytown, residents and outsiders commonly referred to Cruzada as a *favela*. Its inhabitants shared many of the same experiences of poverty, employment in manual labor or service economy jobs for subsistence wages, discrimination, and cramped and

FIGURE 3.   A *cobertura* (penthouse apartment) with a pool
and barbecue space overlooks a nearby *favela*. Photo by
Marcelo Santos Braga.

unsanitary living conditions, all of which provided a sharp contrast to the
lives of Rio's middle class. As may be inferred from the term compulsory
closeness, Cruzada residents lived under the constant scrutiny of both the
police and their extremely wealthy neighbors. In what follows, I attempt to
address what Brazilian anthropologist Cecilia McCallum describes as "the
problem of how to study class ethnographically . . . in this kind of highly
divided setting" (2005:101). "Ideally," she explains, "an ethnographer must
find a way to appreciate the subtleties of all sides of these encounters"
(2005:101). As I describe life across Rio's social divide, I draw on my experi-

ence living in the middle-class and affluent neighborhoods of Copacabana and Ipanema and my time conducting research in Cruzada. To force some of the cross-race and cross-class interactions that were often difficult to catch in "real time," I played conversations that I had recorded in Cruzada for middle-class residents in metalinguistic interviews in which I asked them to react to the speech and the stories that they had just heard. Poor youth from the city's most stigmatized areas, including rappers and rap fans, needed less prompting to discuss their views of the middle class.

Although I offer a glimpse into the lives of predominantly dark-skinned poor youth, as well as snippets of conversations that occurred in the more comfortable homes of the whiter middle class, I had little contact with those living at the extreme ends of Brazilian society. None of the youth whom I met in Cruzada lived in absolute poverty, and none of the wealthier families that I knew would be considered by others or consider themselves part of the Brazilian elite, which, like the global elite, has access to incredible power and privilege, as well as international connections, and does not worry daily about money. Although there were, of course, differences among the families and among the youth that I studied, the largest gap was between the two groups. When I contrast "whiter and wealthier" families with poor dark-skinned community youth, as I often do, I am calling attention to the surprisingly clean lines between their everyday lives.

While they did share some city spaces—a fact that became a source of tension and occasionally provided an opportunity for friendships to develop (as I discuss in chapter 5)—all of the middle-class families that I knew lived in well-appointed condominium buildings with doormen and two sets of elevators. Elevators are socially significant in Brazil, as they enforce a separation between residents and "social" guests, as distinguished from "service" workers and residents who arrive dirty from the beach or encumbered by large packages (and are thus engaging in forms of manual labor). Being asked to use the service elevator instead of the social one was a common experience in middle-class apartment buildings for people of color, who were not assumed to be residents or guests (Hanchard 1994). Physical separation from poor nonwhite people was a common experience for members of the middle class, who often opted out of public spaces assumed to offer services of poor quality. They therefore sent their children to private schools (without exception) and visited private doctors, and they were often members of private social and athletic clubs (as I discuss further in chapter 4). They moved through the city mostly in private cars, though they also walked on city streets in the South Zone neighborhoods of Leblon, Ipanema, and Copacabana. As its service expanded, they occasionally rode the metro,

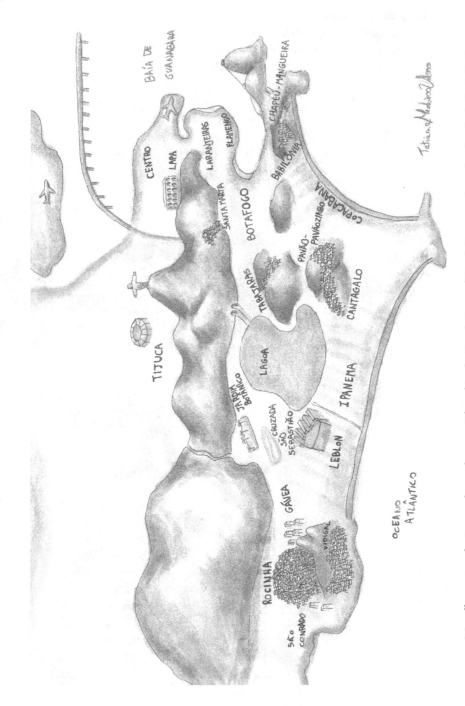

MAP 2. Map illustrating the "compulsory closeness" found in the South Zone of Rio de Janeiro, where *favelas* climb the hills that separate wealthier neighborhoods. Cruzada São Sebastião is a housing project located in Leblon just blocks from one of Rio's most famous beaches. Artwork by Tatiana Medeiros Veloso.

but they very rarely took public buses, which were considered more dangerous. They all employed at least some domestic help, sometimes more than just one person per household, including a nanny or driver in addition to a full-time maid. While they did worry about money, their concerns centered on what kinds of leisure activities (such as travel) or imported goods they could afford and never about basic necessities.

By contrast, the Cruzada youth with whom I spent time all attended public schools, if they had not dropped out of school already, and they were not college-bound. They often slept on cushions on the floor of the living room of their small, cramped apartments and climbed as many as seven flights of stairs to get home. They mostly hung out on the street in front of their buildings, and they had far fewer opportunities to enjoy city spaces, except for the beach. They rarely were able to travel outside Rio. Although they lived in a busy neighborhood full of shops and restaurants, they felt comfortable visiting only a small number of these establishments. While my research with middle-class families included multiple generations and both males and females, most of my time in Cruzada was spent with male youth, and thus my ability to discuss or make comparisons by gender is constrained by the data that I collected.

Given all that I have said so far about my chosen field sites, it should not surprise the reader to learn that Rio has been nicknamed both A Cidade Maravilhosa (the Marvelous City) and A Cidade Partida (the Divided City; see Ventura 1994). As I am about to describe in detail, developing everyday strategies for dealing with this highly diverse social mixture has taken on a palpable sense of urgency in the wealthy South Zone of Rio de Janeiro over the past few decades. Middle-class residents felt themselves to be "at war," "under siege," and "trapped" (encurralada) given unprecedented levels of (mostly drug-induced) crime and violence. Their fears, combined with the city's close quarters and the failings of a disorganized and corrupt Brazilian state, meant that they assumed responsibility for their own personal safety and the safety of their families. By contrast, the audible demands of whiter and wealthier city residents for their own protection subjected poor dark-skinned male youth (including CW and his friends) to additional state scrutiny and violence and compromised their status as legitimate Brazilian citizens (as I discuss in chapter 2).

During my first full year living in Rio de Janeiro, it became painfully clear to me that no one, neither the middle class nor the poor, felt safe. This situation has continually improved and regressed ever since, but one lives in Rio always on some level of alert, aware that experiences of crime and violence are possible and even probable. They are never understood as a distant reality. I do not believe that *cariocas* are the only ones engaged in the racial strategies that I am about to describe in this book, and I expect readers to make connections to other regional, national, cultural, and historical contexts with which they are personally familiar. And yet the obligatory situations of social contact across race and class borders and this shared level of insecurity help explain the constant vigilance on the part of Rio residents in reading race and racial capacity off of bodies, and in carefully manipulating those readings, as part of daily life in what is, by all accounts, a dense and dangerous city.

OVERVIEW OF THE BOOK

As I attempt to write ethnography "out of the bounds of particular communities or social groups and across race and class lines" (McCallum 2005:102), I weave back and forth between middle-class and *comunidade* experiences and perspectives. I have organized the chapters thematically, moving from examples in which *cariocas* attempt to embody or acquire whiteness, to situations that induce fears of racial contact and confirm the need to avoid blackness, and ending with the case of politically conscious rappers and rap fans who make visible the social imperative to be racially "cordial" through their defiant racial stances. The cultural and linguistic practices that I describe—taken from interviews, observations, recordings of daily conversations, and descriptions in magazine articles and popular songs—allow us to see how racial ideas are immanent and critical to daily interactions.

I begin, in chapter 2, by describing how poor dark-skinned male youth in the community of Cruzada turn to language to talk their way out of potentially dangerous and always uncomfortable encounters with the police. Here I argue that youth know that they must counteract the negative associations that accompany their "black" phenotypical features and place of residence by attempting to "improve" their racial appearance to look more like (white) upstanding citizens instead of (black) criminals. They must work to present *boa aparência* (literally a "good appearance"), a term that once was used euphemistically in job ads to suggest that only "white" applicants need apply, but that I pick up here to describe the continued social imperative to "whiten."[27] While *boa aparência* often entails careful grooming and "good" personal hygiene, it also includes cultural and linguistic practices associated with white, wealthy Brazilians, including polite and civilized speech, familiarity with standard Portuguese, and the avoidance of slang. Rappers also encourage youth to take up these linguistic strategies in critical situations such as job interviews in order to achieve what I refer to as "situational whiteness." This temporary racial status does not entail "feeling" or identifying as white, and it does not mean that poor dark-skinned youth are ultimately viewed as white. However, gaining situational whiteness improves their chances of acquiring citizenship rights and future employment in a society where blackness continues to be stigmatized and where black people continue to suffer from structural racism—earning less pay, completing fewer years of education, being sent to jail, and finding themselves targeted (and threatened) by police officers far more often than their lighter-skinned peers.

If Cruzada youth turn to language to gain access to basic civil and human rights (to work and to avoid being harassed by the police), the middle-class families that are the subject of chapter 3 embrace language to gain and secure privilege. Here I look at how experiences that often require access to financial resources (such as obtaining a private-school education, mastering standard Portuguese, and exposing oneself to "culture") are taken up by members of Rio's small middle class not only to mark their class status but also to resolve situations of deep racial anxiety. This chapter begins with a summary of global research on the instability of whiteness and on the failure of ancestry and skin color to guarantee whiteness, especially in Brazil. I argue that these families seek to cultivate a sense of "personal whiteness" for themselves and for their children that helps justify and make possible their sense of belonging and inclusion in private facilities, exclusive urban spaces, and global travel. I draw also on linguistic anthropology for the concept of language ideologies to examine not only how these families' beliefs about their own linguistic refinement and intellectual capacity are tied to the superiority of whiteness, but also how a lack of "proper" grammar and the extensive use of slang are linked to blackness and embraced in order to naturalize social inequality and racial difference. The ease and confidence that accompany whiteness can be achieved only through cultivation, training, and daily effort. Chapters 2 and 3 thus offer ethnographic examples of how Brazilian racial ideologies encourage Rio residents (across race and class borders) to embrace linguistic strategies in order to secure the privileges of whiteness.

In the following two chapters, I explore the experience of living within Rio's compulsory closeness, where city residents struggle over who belongs in prime urban spaces, including the beach and privatized shopping malls. In chapter 4, I draw on interview data, daily conversations, songs from popular culture, and media reports to interrogate experiences of and reactions to heightened crime and violence in Rio. Whereas a century ago, members of the whiter middle class used to avoid contact with the darker masses out of fear of contagious disease, today "dangerous social mixture" in urban public spaces entails the possibility of crime and violence. While these fears are not always explicitly articulated in terms of race or blackness, I show how Rio residents engage in the endless process of reading bodies for racialized signs of civility or disorder in an attempt to keep themselves safe and make sense of the violence. Here one's capacity for crime and lawlessness can be linked to the simple (but "uncultured") act of eating a bologna sandwich at the beach, a site where privileged lighter-skinned South Zone residents now worry they will be swept up in an *arrastão*, or beach theft or riot, amid the thousands of new darker-skinned beachgoers who arrive by bus and metro from the geographically distant and socially marginalized suburbs. The lack of confidence in the security offered by the Brazilian state, combined with the vast openness and lack of barriers restricting access to Rio's kilometers of postcard-worthy coastline, produces a rich and complicated system of symbolic segregation, one that relies on the opposition between cultural and linguistic practices associated with whiteness versus blackness.

In chapter 5, I build on these fears of racial contact to examine what I call the flip side of *boa aparência*: the avoidance of blackness. I show how middle-class youth and parents seek to secure the investment that they have made in their family's whiteness by avoiding contact with black people and black spaces. Stronger than the fear of physically "black" bodies, however, is the fear of embodied practices associated with blackness, practices that circulate independent of dark-skinned people while threatening to steal the whiteness of middle-class youth. Here I explore these fears, and the implicit rule that one should avoid contact with blackness, through the case of Bola, a *moreno* (brown-skinned) middle-class youth who boldly disregards established social and racial borders. He begins to hang out in the community of Cruzada, makes friends, and picks up their facility with *gíria* (slang), convincing outside listeners that he is from a *favela*. While his laid-back mother accepts his new companions and remains relatively unconcerned about his presence in the city's "peripheral" spaces, her reactions to recordings of his speech show that she also believes that too much blackness is dangerous. It is not black *people* that she fears so much as her son's acquisition of the embodied signs of blackness, which seem instantly to undo the years she has invested in training him in white middle-class sensibilities to help ensure his future success.

Chapter 6 focuses on the intentional and defiant displays of blackness by politically conscious Brazilian rappers and rap fans (including Bola) and the challenges they pose to Brazil's belief in racial tolerance. Mainstream Brazilian society previously mocked, scorned, and policed the importation of other North American black cultural movements, including the "black is beautiful" soul movement of the 1970s. By the time politically conscious hip-hop reached the peak of its popularity in the late 1990s, the nation was on the brink of engaging in a national debate concerning sweeping legislative changes that would work toward addressing some of the country's problems with structural racism, particularly through affirmative action quotas in higher education. But these changes would mark a dramatic shift in state policy and for the nation's reputation. Rather than celebrating race mixture and racial tolerance, the Brazilian state would publicly and officially admit to the visibility of blackness and to its racism. As reactions to politically conscious hip-hop make apparent, this public recognition of racial difference and the challenges to ideas of racial tolerance provoked strong racial anxiety. This chapter explores rappers' and rap fans' embrace of "imported" cultural and linguistic practices that allowed them to wear blackness visibly, and defiantly, on their bodies in order to challenge their assigned place in Brazil's racial hierarchy. Together, these chapters offer different snapshots of everyday life to show how Brazilians engage with three critical social and racial imperatives: (1) the need to display whiteness, (2) the desire to avoid blackness, and (3) the obligation to remain racially "cordial."

In the conclusion, I share a story of how five- and six-year-old children (including my daughter) learned about racial difference and appropriately "polite" racial terminology in the wealthy private school that my children attended in Rio in 2014. More embedded forms of racial hierarchy and the racialized belief system that still posits the superiority of whiteness never surfaced in these discussions of how and when to notice racial difference. I argue that we must look deeper, into the cultural and linguistic practices that are the "stuff" of everyday life, to find the connections that Brazilians have been trained to make between race, bodies, and the ongoing inequitable distribution of resources in their society.

2. "Good" Appearances

Race, Language, and Citizenship

Dinheiro embranquece. (Money whitens.)
Common Brazilian expression

Pergunta: Por que o negro que fica rico e famoso só quer casar com mulher branca?
Resposta: Por que mulher branca só quer casar com homem negro que fica rico e famoso?

Question: Why is it that black men who become rich and famous only want to marry white women?
Comeback: Why is it that white women want to marry black men only after they become rich and famous?

Recent Brazilian joke

Brazilians have been playing with the intersections of race and class for centuries. They have had a lot to work with: not only has Brazilian society exhibited significant racial mixture, but it also allowed for the more frequent manumission of slaves, meaning that millions of African slaves were freed before the end of slavery; some of the "mixed-race" children of slave owners and slaves acquired a European education; and some of Brazil's leading intellectual artists and elites (including ones who wrote about the dangers of miscegenation and racial degeneration) were themselves "mulattos" (Andrews 2004; E. Costa 1985; Daniel 2006; D. Davis 1999; Degler 1986 [1971]; Skidmore 1974). There are two trends that I wish to emphasize from this long and complicated history. To begin with, race and class have never really been understood as separate phenomena. The acquisition of attributes normally linked to socioeconomic class (money, education, professional standing, and celebrity) were often assumed to increase the whiteness of otherwise phenotypically "black" individuals (J. Dávila 2003:6). This fit in well with a national desire in the late nineteenth and early twentieth centuries to "lighten" the Brazilian population, which included facilitating (and financing) the migration of millions of European immigrants and encouraging individuals to intermarry (Skidmore 1974). Alongside racial "mixture," racial "improvement," or whitening, often turned on the acquisition of class-based traits. In studies of interracial marriages, for example, race appeared to be "traded" for attributes linked to socioeconomic status. In other words, lighter-skinned men were more likely to marry darker-skinned women when these women belonged to a higher socioeconomic class, and light-skinned women more often married darker-skinned men when these men had higher levels of education and professional titles (Azevedo 1975; M. Harris 1952; Hordge-Freeman 2015; Telles 2004; see also Burdick 1998). These patterns suggest that people pay careful attention to both race and class status.

In sharp contrast to the attention paid to both race and class differences, the second trend I wish to highlight is one in which researchers (and lay-people alike) point to the flexibility of race and class to argue that racism does not exist in Brazil. If money could, in fact, whiten, this seemed to suggest that race was not as strong a barrier to social mobility as class. As a noteworthy example of this thinking, here are the observations made on the connections between race and class by anthropologist Marvin Harris in the 1950s (1952:72; reproduced as a similar chart in Degler 1971:105; see also Pierson 1942):

A "Negro" is any one of the following:	A "White" is any one of the following:
Poverty-stricken white	White who is wealthy
Poverty-stricken mulatto	White of average wealth
Poor mulatto	White who is poor
Poverty-stricken Negro	Wealthy mulatto
Poor Negro	Mulatto of average wealth
Negro of average wealth	Negro who is wealthy

Harris's research was part of the UNESCO studies of Brazil's alleged racial democracy, studies commissioned by the United Nations after World War II to understand how Brazil had achieved racial harmony (see Maio 2001). In more rigidly defined societies, race was seen as nonnegotiable, often leading to situations of racial conflict. Under North America's "one drop rule," for example (see D. Davis 1991), legal segregation limited the social mobility of those with even one "drop" of black blood. The idea that darker-skinned individuals could achieve both money and a higher status in Brazil seemed to argue that class, rather than race, was the more significant factor in explaining social inequality. A few decades after the UNESCO studies, when quantitative research had separated out the effects of race and class to prove that race remained a relevant factor, Oracy Nogueira revisited the common belief that "money whitens" in Brazil to clarify: "'O dinheiro compra tudo, até status para um negro,' o que está longe de ser uma negação do preconceito ou da discriminação" ("[The expression] 'Money buys everything, even status for a black person' is a far cry from denying the existence of prejudice or discrimination"; see Nogueira 1985:21–22).

Quantitative studies conducted over the past few decades have repeatedly proven that race matters even when class is held constant in Brazil (Bailey 2009; Hasenbalg and Silva 1988; Telles 2004). Years ago, historian Carl Degler (1971) proposed a "mulatto escape hatch," an "informal social mechanism by which a few 'visibly' multiracial individuals, for reasons of talent, culture, or education, [were] granted situational whiteness in accordance with their phenotypical and cultural approximation to the dominant whites" (Daniel 2006:x). Sociologists have since examined whether a "middle group," identifiable as *pardo* (brown), rather than as *preto* (black), had been able to achieve the type of social mobility that Degler predicted, but they have fairly routinely found that this group statistically matches up more closely with "blacks" than with "whites" (Telles 2004).

As an anthropologist, I am more interested in, and better equipped to comment on, the everyday lived experiences of social mobility. In this sense, we might think of social mobility as the ability to temporarily negotiate for access to citizenship rights and rights to city spaces that are often denied based on racial ideas of the inferiority of blackness. For this reason, I adopt G. Reginald Daniel's (2006) term *situational whiteness,* which he used to describe Degler's theory and to argue that the successful presentation of a "whiter appearance," or what is called *boa aparência* (a good appearance) in Portuguese, can often grant even dark-skinned individuals temporary access to the privileges of whiteness. The need to look and act "white"—by taking on cultural and linguistic practices associated with intellectual capacity, rationality, and cultural refinement—offers a glimpse into how racial ideas of white superiority (and black inferiority) continue to permeate daily interactions in Rio de Janeiro today.[1] I turn first to describe in greater detail this social, cultural, and historical imperative to "whiten" one's body, often through the "managing" of stereotypically black physical features (Hordge-Freeman 2015; Sansone 2003), as well as the acquisition of traits or habits associated not only with whiteness but also with higher class status.

BOA APARÊNCIA AS A SOCIAL IMPERATIVE

Over the past few centuries, Brazilian racial ideology has suggested both implicitly and explicitly that nonwhiteness is something to be feared and minimized, not just within the body politic but also within the individual Brazilian body. Historian Darien Davis (1999) has described this as Brazil's desire to "avoid the dark," which also described racial thought and policy across much of the Americas.[2] Neither a long history of racial mixture nor the continued pride in racial tolerance (which can be taken quite literally, as in "to tolerate"; see chapter 6) negates this aversion to blackness. Along with its embrace of miscegenation, Brazil took up the racial logic of eugenics in the early twentieth century, which suggested that the nation could scientifically manage (and improve) the genetic quality of its population. Brazil was not alone in its interest in racial eugenics, and many countries were influenced by what scholars have called "soft" eugenics, which emphasized the role of education and environment in increasing whiteness (Borges 1993; J. Dávila 2003; Stepan 1991). As one dramatic example, the United States, Canada, and Australia all applied eugenic theories to racially "improve" indigenous children through boarding school programs designed to "Kill the Indian, [and] Save the Man" (see, for example, Cahill 2011 and Jacobs 2009). By contrast, "hard" eugenic policies included practices that controlled the reproduction of racially "inferior" groups by sterilization or extermination, as in Hitler's Germany. The horrors of World War II, which took eugenics to a state-supported extreme, largely put an end to the global interest in this specific type of racial thinking.

In the early twentieth century, however, racial improvement—for the nation and for the individual—was made possible in Brazil through instruction in "behavioral whitening: that is, discarding African and indigenous cultural practices" (J. Dávila 2003:27; see also Hanchard 1994). In *Diploma of Whiteness: Race and Social Policy in Brazil, 1917–1945*, historian Jerry Dávila describes how public schools sought to "furnish poor and nonwhite Brazilians with the tools of whiteness," including lessons in a whiter appearance and the demeanor, habits, and values associated with the white middle class (2003:10). Even today, darker-skinned Brazilians who have achieved higher levels of education and the behavioral refinement associated with white people are referred to as *negros de alma branca* (blacks with a white soul; as in the Amorim example with which I begin this book) or *negros embranquecidos* (whitened blacks; see Figueiredo 2002:103). Those who are almost fair-skinned but not quite white can be positively described as *socialmente branco*, or "socially white," in different regions of Brazil (including the heavily black state of Bahia; see Azevedo 1975). These terms reveal the eugenic ideal that "white is best and black is worst and therefore the nearer one is to white, the better" (Dzidzienyo 1971:5).

While more overt eugenic policies lost governmental support, beliefs in the superiority of whiteness persisted and continued to be publicly articulated. In a study of help-wanted ads in São Paulo in the early 1940s, Oracy

Nogueira (1942) surveyed those who had placed racially specific advertisements (the vast majority requesting white workers, especially as house servants). Their reasons for this explicit preference drew heavily on racial ideas
of black inferiority and "lack." Reasons for wanting white workers included
fears of theft; perceptions of black job candidates as lacking cleanliness or
responsibility; not wanting black maids in contact with one's white children;
and worrying about bad odor, carelessness, and laziness (see also Willems
1949:403–4). Examining ads over the decade after Nogueira's study, Caetana
Damasceno (2000) tracks the shift from overtly requesting whiteness to the
more covert request for *boa aparência* (literally "good appearance," meaning
a white appearance) in positions that entailed intimate relationships (as with
domestic help) and high visibility and contact with the public (including
receptionists, store clerks, and the like; see also Bento 1995; Burdick 1998).
The recognition that this term acted as a widely understood euphemism that
allowed for racial discrimination has resulted in cities and states banning the
use of the term in advertisements, with federal and additional state legislation still pending. And yet agencies that place domestic workers can still ask
employers for their preference as to "ethnicity" (*etnia*), even in online
forms, so that they can avoid "causing embarrassment" (*constrangimento*)
to either side when employer and employee meet.[3]

In this chapter, I examine how the legacy of *embranquecimento* (whitening) and the desire for *boa aparência* (a white appearance) work together to
form a social and racial imperative that impacts daily practice. Other scholars
have noted that Brazilians attempt to manipulate their racial appearance and
"manage" the stigma of blackness (Sansone 2003; see also Hordge-Freeman
2015; Pinho 2009, 2010). For example, studies have documented the ways that
individuals seek to improve themselves through practices and procedures that
alter the visual signifiers of race and provide an "alleviation of African traits"
(Edmonds 2010:161). Such efforts include the use of skin lighteners, hair
straighteners to improve what is commonly referred to as *cabelo ruim* (bad,
or kinky, hair; see Burdick 1998; Caldwell 2007; Figueiredo 1994; Hordge-
Freeman 2015), and cosmetic surgery operations such as rhinoplasty (to narrow what is referred to as a *nariz chato*, or a wide/ugly nose). In a recent
ethnography of black Bahian families, Elizabeth Hordge-Freeman recounts
the daily "pinching" exercises that one mother performed on her newborn
baby in order to narrow her nose (2015:44–45). This routine, practiced in
other families, is viewed as part of a mother's duty to minimize or eliminate
phenotypically black racial features in her children. Anthropologist Livio
Sansone also reports that some Brazilian politicians continue to "whiten"
their photos in campaign materials (2003:109). While these practices may be

regionally specific and more commonly discussed in private, they hint at the widespread (and culturally familiar) preference for whiteness.

While physically appearing white enough is critical to having *boa aparência*, this racial requirement alludes not only to appearance but also to proper bodily discipline (Damasceno 1999, 2000). As Cláudia Rezende and Márcia Lima note in their study of domestic workers who sought to "neutralize" their darker color, "Being black . . . presupposed negative characteristics such as physical and moral dirt, ignorance and dishonesty, which required being countered by 'good' behaviour," such as being especially clean, clever, and trustworthy (2004:768). Dress is another way to reduce stigma and negate racial stereotypes, as the following sayings imply: "Negro não pode andar mal vestido" (A black person cannot go out badly dressed); "Somos negros mas não somos porcos" (We are blacks but we're not pigs; see Cicalo 2012b:66). The ability to speak standard Portuguese (Edmonds 2010:45) and to control the so-called *cheiro de negro,* or "black smell" (Pinho 2010:108), have also been critical elements of one's ability to demonstrate proper forms of self-presentation. As anthropologist Livio Sansone similarly observes, dark-skinned Brazilians manage more than their visual appearance when trying to reduce the effects of racism, including "speaking intelligently, being polite, looking attractive, and showing off status symbols" (2003:107–8). "Whiteness is achieved through various means," historian George Reid Andrews notes: "through economic success, through cultivating white friends and acquaintances, through consciously adopting the norms and behaviors of white middle class life" (1991:177; see also Vargas 2011:264). The power and importance of whiteness is perhaps best summed up by a Brazilian expression: "Branco pode mais que Deus" (The white man can do more than God; see O'Dougherty 2002:180). What I describe in the following examples is the efforts of dark-skinned youth from a poor, stigmatized area of Rio to achieve "situational whiteness" through the use of linguistic strategies of *boa aparência,* by associating themselves with white spaces and white professions, speaking calmly and politely, demonstrating their familiarity with standard Portuguese, and avoiding the use of slang.

It is important to note that in these situations *boa aparência* does not rely on or create a white identity, nor is it about being or feeling white.[4] Instead, it hinges on one's ability to suggest the appearance of whiteness ("to look like white people"; see Willems 1949:405) and to outwardly display all of the positive attributes linked to whiteness (e.g., rationality, civility, refinement). True to its Brazilian context, the concept helpfully reminds us that the purity and absoluteness of whiteness are ideals, not lived or phenotypical realities. To illustrate how this imperative to display whiteness works, I draw on

deceptively simple day-to-day interactions in this and the chapters that follow: conversations among friends; narratives of experiences of crime, violence, or racism; elicited commentaries on the way that people speak or the
way that they should speak. As an anthropologist, I am interested in how Rio
residents navigate urban spaces, interact with people across race and class
divides, and strategize to improve their lives. I seek to reveal and denatural-
ize how deep-seated beliefs in the superiority of whiteness structure daily
life in ways that are often imperceptible and therefore frequently unacknowledged. The subtlety of this racial imperative to whiten does not imply,
however, that the effects of white supremacism are benign.

The everyday interactions that I draw on come from fieldwork that I conducted among poor dark-skinned youth in the neighborhood of Cruzada, in
Rio's South Zone, and also with rappers who lived in the more distant suburb
of Cidade de Deus (City of God). It is significant that none of these youth talk
directly about whitening in the conversations that I analyze, nor do they link
their linguistic behavior to boa aparência. However, they frequently point to
their blackness as a source of discrimination and stigma and as a social fact
that puts them at increased risk for police violence and unemployment. They
describe how they have to "manage" their appearance and self-presentation
in situations where their race makes them especially vulnerable.
Anthropologist Marvin Harris once commented, "Much has been made of
the expression . . . that 'money whitens.' The unstated corollaries: 'Whiteness
is worth money' and 'Blackness cheapens' also need to be emphasized"
(1952:64–65). I turn here to describe other clear benefits that accrue to those
perceived as racially whiter, such as citizenship rights and protection that
includes the recognized value of one's life and body (Alves 2014; Alves and
Vargas 2015; C. Smith 2015, 2016; Vargas 2011; Vargas and Alves 2010).[5]

CONTRADICTING THE STATISTICS

In the late 1990s I began conducting research on slang use, following my
skilled research assistant, CW, around in the community (a housing project)
of Cruzada. He spent a lot of time hanging out on the public street in front
of their buildings with his friends, all male youth from their young teens to
their early twenties. As the conversations that they generously let me
record were often filled with slang terms that I didn't understand, CW and
I had frequent work sessions back in my apartment, where he translated the
slang into the standard Portuguese that I had learned. A common topic of
conversation among the youth was the harassment that they experienced
from police. The police had a small station right where their ten housing-

project buildings ended and the fancy middle-class condominium buildings of Leblon began. Cruzada's location, on some of Rio's (and Brazil's) most expensive land, was largely advantageous, despite the scorn they suffered from their wealthy next-door neighbors. The proximity of the police limited the influence of drug gangs (though drug traffickers were still present and drugs were constantly being sold), and the visibility of their neighborhood meant that more egregious (and lethal) forms of police violence were kept in check. Police could physically and verbally harass residents, as they had for years, but they were unlikely to "disappear" youth, not an unknown occurrence in more isolated *favelas* (see, for example, Alves 2014).

At the time, the public street in front of Cruzada was part of their community. Youth spray-painted murals (sometimes of popular rap albums) on the walls that separated them from the private social and athletic clubs next door, and few cars were brave enough to pass through the road, crowded as it was with people escaping the heat and the cramped quarters of their apartments. Although there was an expensive dance club at the end of the block, middle-class neighbors most often walked in a big circle to get there, avoiding a space that they often referred to as a *favela* (Almeida 2010; C. Costa 2015). Cruzada did not consist of self-constructed homes or precariously climb a hill, but it was readily associated with poverty, crime, and blackness. The community suffered from lack of garbage collection (a sadly ironic fact, since many of the residents were city garbage collectors), and the buildings were for the most part poorly maintained by the city. In sharp contrast to neighboring middle-class condos, Cruzada buildings still have no elevators; seven flights of very steep outdoor stairs lead to the top of each. Residents thus are forced to engage in the socially meaningful act of climbing—just like their counterparts in hillside *favelas.* The neighborhood has changed over the past few decades and the community has lost more space. A high-end mall was built on land right behind Cruzada's buildings (see chapter 5), and construction for a metro stop in the surrounding neighborhood meant that their public street became the new connector into nearby Ipanema. When this change was made, Cruzada's Leblon neighbors complained bitterly about having to walk directly in front of the housing project and travel down a street they considered unsafe (Erika Robb Larkins, personal communication). Now there is constant car traffic, and the city has put up fences along the sidewalk, giving the impression that residents are caged in.

In previous published work, I gave this community the name Praia do Cristo (Christ's Beach), due to its privileged location only a few blocks from one of Rio's nicest beaches and with views of Corcovado, Rio's world-famous Christ statue. At the time, I sought to protect the identity of youth

FIGURE 4. Cruzada's colorful but poorly maintained buildings, in the foreground, are surrounded by stark-white luxury apartment buildings and the scenic Lagoa (lake/lagoon), only blocks from Rio's famous beaches. Photo by Marcelo Santos Braga.

who participated in my frequent recordings and interviews, as they often talked about drug use, criminal activity that they or others in their community engaged in, and their interactions with the police. Now that they are adults, many with children of their own, and given how recognizable the location is to anyone familiar with Rio, I have retained pseudonyms for the speakers, but not for the community.

Cruzada presents an excellent example of "compulsory closeness" (Veloso 2010) not only because of its location on some of Rio's most expensive real estate but also because it was readily perceived as a dangerous area in need of surveillance. For the poor male youth in this study, encounters with the police constituted their most direct experiences with racism. Those who have studied the need for a "good appearance" have often described how black women suffer on the job market, particularly when employers pay careful attention to the look of employees who will serve as the public face of their companies (Bento 1995; Burdick 1998; Caldwell 2007). A focus on *boa aparência* thus helpfully reminds us that gender also matters in people's daily experiences of race and racism. Anthropologist Livio Sansone points to employment, marriage and dating, and police interactions as three sites of "hard" race relations, which he contrasts with the comparatively

FIGURE 5.   Cruzada residents relax in the stairwell of their
seven-story walk-up, while a father plays soccer with his son
at the private athletic club right across the street. Cruzada
has been described as "uma favela vertical incrustada numa
das áreas mais nobres da cidade" (a vertical shantytown
embedded in one of the most exalted areas of the city; see C.
Costa 2015). Photo by Marcelo Santos Braga.

"soft" areas of leisure activities and socializing (2003:52–53). Although
Brazilians are known for their "racial cordiality" and interracial friendships,
racialized struggles over rights to occupy city spaces such as shopping malls
and public beaches suggest that racial ideas and racial inequality shape not
just how and where people work in Rio but also how and where they play
(as I illustrate in greater detail in chapters 4 and 5).

It is widely agreed, however, that interactions between dark-skinned male youth and the military police are particularly dangerous (Cano 2010; Goldstein 2003; Huggins 2000; M. Mitchell and Wood 1999; Santos 2006; Scheper-Hughes 2006).[6] And by *dangerous,* I also mean deadly. Despite the transition to democracy in the 1980s, Brazil retains a military police force (*Polícia Militar,* or PM) that is responsible for "public security" but is frequently accused of human rights abuses such as torture and extralegal killing, including by death squads (Alves 2014; French 2013; Holston 2008; C. Smith 2016). Officers enjoy high levels of impunity, as they can be tried only in military courts. It is a commonly cited statistic from the time that I conducted research in Cruzada, in the 1990s, that the Rio police killed just about as many people per year as the combined U.S. police forces did, though their populations were 5.5 million people and 250 million people, respectively (Cano 1997:32). More recent and equally chilling statistics on police violence show that between 2009 and 2013, Brazilian police killed an average of six people per day (Alves and Vargas 2015). This level of violence, and the lack of widespread protest against it, has been described by researchers and activists as an ongoing "black genocide" (Alves and Vargas 2015; C. Smith 2015, 2016).

Even those citizens who were not subjected to the daily threat of deadly encounters with the police held the general view that police were corrupt, disrespectful, and abusive (Caldeira 2000; French 2013; Holston and Caldeira 1998; Perry 2013; Zaluar 1994). One *favela* youth informed me that the military police's slogan was "Bandido eu mato. Trabalhador eu dou tapa na cara" (Bandits or criminals I kill. Workers I hit in the face.) While Cruzada youth never described themselves as intentionally pursuing *boa aparência,* they made very clear that their perceived blackness increases their vulnerability. In lyrics from Rio rapper MV Bill (1999), presented in example 2.1, police officers use racial insults and illegal searches to keep poor dark-skinned youth "in their place."

EXAMPLE 2.1: "A NOITE" (THE NIGHT)

Na saída da minha casa	Exiting my house
levo uma geral	I get frisked
Pra não perder o costume natural	To make sure I don't fall out of practice
Coisa normal no meu bolso	It's normal, there's nothing in my
não tem nada [sem droga]	pockets [no drugs]
Aí negão tá liberado	Hey *negão* [big black guy], you're free
rala!	now scram!
Tô acostumado isso não me abala	I'm used to it, this doesn't phase me

Brazil has been described as a *disjunctive democracy* (Holston and Caldeira 1998) and an uncivil political democracy, in which political rights for Brazilian citizens (such as the right to vote) are relatively secure, while civil rights (including rights to equal protection and equality) continue to be threatened. As poor youth from Rio's most marginalized communities explained eloquently in their descriptions of police harassment, the terms of their citizenship are up for grabs: while some citizens deserve protection, others are subject to constant surveillance. Fernando Rosa-Ribeiro explains that in Brazil "direitos (rights) are not something enshrined in legislation or pertaining to every single person so much as they are a quality that certain individuals (a chosen few, as a matter of fact) carry inside them. It is a highly moral quality" (2000:225; see also Holston 2008, 2011). This "moral quality" is readily associated with civility and whiteness, turning nonwhite Brazilians into "bearers of noncitizenship," individuals considered "without reason and rationality" (Hanchard 1994:166, 170; see also Alves and Vargas 2015). As anthropologist Patricia de Santana Pinho notes, the common assumption is that "blacks are always suspect" (2010:105). One criminal court justice wrote in 1996: "A century after this abolition [of slavery], the Negro has not adjusted to social standards and our *mestizo* [a person of mixed white and African ancestry], our *caboclo* [a person of mixed white and indigenous ancestry], is generally indolent, has a propensity to alcoholism, makes his living from primary tasks and very rarely is able to prosper in life. This is the *type* that normally . . . ends up involved in marginality and crime" (reported by H. Silva 1998:86, cited in Nascimento 2001:517).

Statistics on structural racism from the legal system seem to confirm these suspicions. While dark-skinned youth filled the courts and the jails, Brazil appointed its first black federal judge in 1998, its first black Supreme Federal Court justice in 2004, and in 2015, elected only twenty-two black legislators out of a total of 513.[7] Of the sixty-one current senators, none identify as black. The racialized assumptions that poor dark-skinned youth face—for example, that they are not upstanding members of Brazilian society, that they are lazy, that they are associated with the drug trade and crime—run through the narratives that I present here.

In example 2.2, a Cruzada youth nicknamed Mano (Black Brother) tells me the story of one of his run-ins with the police, in which an officer attempted to illegally search him. Although Brazilian citizens are required to carry identification, it is not obligatory within a certain distance of one's home, and few wealthy Brazilians carry their documents as they walk through Rio's South Zone on their way to the beach. Dark-skinned and poor community residents cannot afford to be so carefree and secure in their rights to walk the streets of their own neighborhoods. Youth from South Zone *favelas* and housing projects surrounded by wealthy areas are especially vulnerable, as their mere presence is read as a sign of an illegitimate encroachment of space. To avoid the humiliation and potential violence of a bodily search, Mano tells the police officer that he is a second-year law student at a well-known private law school. In fact, Mano is not a law student; he has just told me that he dropped out of school after the seventh grade.

Before I tell Mano's story, I want to pause briefly to explain some of my linguistic conventions for readers who may be unaccustomed to reading transcripts. The conversations and interactions from my research that are analyzed in this book were all recorded by me or my research assistant, and rather than just summarizing what they shared, I pay careful attention to the way they tell their own stories. Along with the English translation, I provide the original spoken version in Brazilian Portuguese, as is customary in the field of linguistic anthropology. Since I am interested not only in what people say but also how they say it, I include the types of linguistic details often edited out, particularly in written speech. These include, among other features, repetitions, false starts, emphasis, and hesitations, all of which offer clues to how things were spoken, but sometimes (on paper) do not seem like "natural" speech. (Listeners know how to interpret these features while someone is speaking.) I employ fewer transcription conventions than linguistic anthropologists and sociolinguists often do, and this is to balance out readability. Words given in brackets are notes to the reader, while those offered in parentheses indicate uncertain transcription. Ellipses indicate places where I have omitted words or whole sections that are unclear or unrelated to the story being analyzed. Expressions or sentences highlighted in bold are meant to draw the reader's attention and are analyzed in greater detail in the discussion that follows.[8] Speakers are also given pseudonyms, some in Portuguese, others in English, so that all readers can appreciate the lively Brazilian tradition of conferring creative nicknames.

In example 2.2, Mano narrates, for me and his friends CW and Cachaça, one of his encounters with the police.

EXAMPLE 2.2: "CONTRARIANDO AS ESTATÍSTICAS" (CONTRADICTING THE STATISTICS)

Mano:	O cara agarrando. Eu falei,	The guy was grabbing [me]. I said,
	"Vou botar advogado. Tô	"I'm going to get a lawyer. I'm
	fazendo meu segundo ano	doing my second year

	de advocacia da Universidade Gama Filho e pá. Sei todos dos direitos. Eu sei dos meus direito (?). Eu moro aqui na comunidade e a menos de cinqüenta metros da minha casa eu não sou obrigado a mostrar documento." [. . .] E aí o sargento, "Não, tá certo."	of law school at Gama Filho University and all. I know all of my rights. I know my rights (?). I live here in the community and less than fifty meters from my house I am not obligated to show my documents." [. . .] And then the sergeant [said], "No, it's okay."
Cachaça:	Caralho.	Shit.
CW:	Porra.	Damn.
Mano:	Não, é que eu tô certo não. Porque eles pensam, eles pensam que todo mundo que mora aqui é favela. Aqui não tem um intelectual, não tem um oficial, não tem um sargento, não tem nada. Aqui só tem o quê? A classe de burro. E não é isso. Aqui tem pessoas bem educadas. [. . .]	No, it's not that he thinks that I'm right. Because they think, they think that everyone who lives here is slum. Here there isn't an intellectual, there isn't an official, there isn't a sergeant, there isn't anything. What is there here? The class of idiots. And that's not right. There are very well-educated people here. [. . .]
Cachaça:	[Aplauso e risadas] "Vinte e oito anos contrariando as estatísticas."	[Applause and laughter] "Twenty-eight years contradicting the statistics."

Based on research conducted in Bahia, anthropologist Christen Smith finds that Brazilian police work to *produce* blackness through acts of humiliation and violence (2016: 168). It is this process of victimization that Mano must spontaneously work against in this interaction with the police officer. Mano's strategy of self-defense (citing relevant laws about carrying identification) illustrates a growing public awareness not only of legal and human rights, particularly since the Brazilian constitution of 1988 was ratified, but also of "the right to the city and the right to rights" (Holston 2011:337; Veloso 2008). After he receives applause for his defense of his community, one of his friends quotes from the popular Racionais MC's (1998) song "Capítulo 4, Versículo 3" (Chapter 4, Verse 3). As I describe it in greater detail in chapter 6, not only does this politically conscious Brazilian rap group recount frequent experiences of police harassment in its songs (describing the members' own experiences in the city of São Paulo), but they also explicitly link these experiences to racial inequality and attempt to spell out how the decks are stacked against poor black youth. The song from which Mano's friend quotes was one of the group's biggest hits, and many of the rap fans I met had memorized it in its entirety. The song opens dramatically: as a discordant low F sharp sounds on a piano, invoking a bell tolling ominously, Primo Preto (Black Cousin) recites a list of statistics on structural racism in Brazil, provided in example 2.3.

EXAMPLE 2.3: "CAPÍTULO 4, VERSÍCULO 3" (CHAPTER 4, VERSE 3)

60% dos jovens de periferia	60% of youth from the periphery
sem antecendências criminais já	without criminal records have
sofreram violência policial	already suffered police violence
A cada 4 pessoas mortas pela	Of every 4 people killed by the
polícia, 3 são negras	police, 3 are black
Nas universidades brasileiras	In Brazilian universities
apenas 2% dos alunos são negros	only 2% of students are black
A cada 4 horas um jovem negro	Every 4 hours a young black person
morre violentamente em São Paulo	dies violently in São Paulo
Aqui quem fala é Primo Preto,	This is Primo Preto here,
mais um sobrevivente	another survivor
[...]	[...]
Mas não, permaneço vivo	But no, I stay alive
Prossigo a mística	I follow the mystic
Vinte e sete anos contrariando	Twenty-seven years contradicting
a estatística	the statistics

To "contradict the statistics" and not become another victim of police violence, Mano plays the part of an upstanding citizen in his encounter with a police officer, suggesting that he is someone who is productively contributing to Brazilian society and therefore (in theory) not associated with drugs or crime. But he also strategically aligns himself with Brazilian citizenship through his invented affiliation with the elite white space of Gama Filho University, which was at the time one of the most important and expensive private universities, not just in Rio de Janeiro but also throughout Brazil. Interestingly, Gama Filho University, which has since closed, was located in the North Zone of Rio in a working-class area, and wealthy white kids would drive in from the South Zone to acquire their *ensino superior* (higher education). Mano's act of pretending to be a college student is significant on multiple levels. At the time of this narrative, prior to the passing of affirmative action laws, few poor and black shantytown or suburban residents had access to a college degree. Mano also chooses a well-known university and a prestigious program of study, as law has long been associated with a white, wealthy student body (Cicalo 2012a, 2012b). But beyond the suggestion that he is intelligent and well educated, Mano is (intentionally or unintentionally) also hinting at legal privileges accorded individuals with a college degree. As recently as 2015, the Supreme Federal Court had yet to rule on whether it would declare *prisão especial,* or "special prisons," discriminatory and illegal. The law establishing *prisão especial* has been on the books since 1941 and affords preferential treatment by police and the prison system (in the form of separate cells until one is tried) to the select minority of Brazilian citizens who have achieved a college degree.[9]

I have no doubt that part of Mano's "success" at getting the officer to let him go has to do with his allusion to lawyers and his knowledge of the law. However, it is impossible to separate these legal references from associations with white people and white spaces. Mano embraces language to attempt to manage how he appeared to the officer. Does he look like a black criminal suspect or more like a (white) upstanding citizen who could potentially have important personal connections? His linguistic strategy is one of several that Cruzada youth appeal to in order to talk themselves out of situations where their bodies attract unwelcome attention from the nearby military police. Language is a readily available resource, and youth are aware of the weight that it carries. Criminals and upstanding citizens do not *sound* the same, and this is something that Cruzada youth have some amount of control over. They cannot (at a moment's notice) change what they are wearing, nor can they change the damaging racial associations of the space where they live and hang out. The facts of their actual relationship to criminality are also irrelevant; innocence and distance from the drug trade do not protect "workers" from police harassment or violence (see also Larkins 2015). All Mano has is his ability to act the part of an upstanding white citizen who deserves some respect, along with his ability to sound like one.

"SHOW ME YOUR DOCUMENTS"

When Cruzada youth share their stories, they juggle multiple and conflicting needs. In telling a story to an audience of peers and a North American white researcher (who is recording their tale), CW and his friends perform a version of what happened in their encounters with the military police, a version that must balance their desire to look tough (and less vulnerable) to their friends with the need to tell a story of clear harassment in which their civil rights have been unfairly violated. I was never present for any of these police stops, which would likely have proceeded very differently if I had been there. However, it's not important to me whether their version of these events is "objective" or even if their memories are accurate. What they present to us in these stories are distilled and carefully crafted versions of events that combine their understanding of what happened alongside their current concerns in this particular "for the record" moment (Tannen 1989).

What this distinction helps us see are the points that they *think* are important, even if these represent things that they wish they had said (or said more forcefully) rather than things that they actually said. This becomes clear in example 2.4, in which a youth named KLJ suggests that he withheld critical information from the officer questioning him "to see what he would say." Whether he was so bold with the officer in person, I cannot say, but linguistic anthropologists would be interested in his concern over a positive face-threatening act and his desire to sound tough and "save face" in the retelling—what Marcyliena Morgan calls presenting a "cool social face" (2002:40). More critically, what KLJ reveals as he and my research assistant, CW, jointly construct this narrative are the strategies that they feel they can use to try to stay safe during these potentially dangerous and undoubtedly uncomfortable situations. Their shared focus on linguistic strategies reveals how they work to manage their racial appearance by means of whatever resources they have available to them.

Here is KLJ's story of being stopped by the military police in Cruzada, right outside his home:

EXAMPLE 2.4: I'M NOBODY: KLJ'S STORY

KLJ: Aí, o PM [Polícia Militar]   So, the PM [military police]
        veio assim pra perto de mim.   came up real close to me.
        "Me apresenta os   "Show me the
        documentos no   documents from your
        bolso." [. . .] Eu tava—   pocket." [. . .] I was—
        eu tava— eu tava até   I was— I was even ready
        com os documentos no   with the documents in my
        bolso. Já pronto pra quando   pocket. Ready for when
        vi— visse eu chegar assim, né?   they sa— saw me arrive, right?

Jennifer:	Mas eles querem ver os documentos por quê? Tá procurando o quê? Em ver um documento?	But why do they want to see your documents? What are they looking for? In seeing your document?
CW:	Não, pra ver se você é alguém na vida. Pra ver se você é— é alguém na vida.	No, to see if you are somebody in life. To see if you are— are somebody in life.
Pitbull:	Tanto o lado mau, quanto o lado bom.	As much from the bad side, as the good side.
KLJ:	Se ver o lado mau, e já vai querer—	If they see you are from the bad side, they will want to—
CW:	De repente, ele conhece o sobrenome de um bandido. Aí ele olha assim, se tiver assim, ele pode, sabe? "Pô, tu é da família de não sei quem? Não sei o quê lá." Só essas coisas. Aí, ele te pergunta, "Tem documento aí?" Mas não é obrigado. Entendeu? Aí, a gente tem que amostrar de noite. Ninguém quer apanhar. Ninguém quer tomar tapa na cara.	Maybe, he knows the last name of a *bandido* [criminal]. So he will look like this, if it's like, he can, you know? "Damn, you are from the such-and-such family? And whatever." Things like this. So, he asks you, "Do you have ID?" But it's not obligatory. Understand? Then, we have to show them at night. Nobody wants to get beaten. No one wants to get hit in the face.
KLJ:	Aí— aí, eu tô voltando, aí— aí o— o— policial fez assim . . . "Ô, cidadão."	So— so, I'm going back, then— then the— the— cop goes like this . . . "Hey, citizen."
Jennifer:	Falou o quê?	What did he say?
KLJ:	"Ô, cidadão." Aí, eu parei . . . e falei assim: "Boa noite." Aí, ele falou assim mesmo, "Boa noite."	"Hey, citizen." So, I stopped . . . and said: "Good evening." So, the cop said just like this, "Good evening."
CW:	Sabia que— tá certo assim. Você já quebra o PM já no "Boa noite." Sabia?	Did you know that— that's right like that. You already break the officer with "Good evening." Did you know that?
KLJ:	Eu sei disso.	I know that.

CW: Primeiramente, "Boa noite." Aí ele já fica meio, sabe?

First, "Good evening." Then he gets kind of, you know?

KLJ: Mais light. [. . .] Aí, poxa. Ele chegou. [KLJ falou:] "Boa noite. Posso te ajudar em alguma coisa?" [o PM falou:] "Você mora aqui mesmo?" "Caralho, hum . . . Eu moro tanto aqui dentro como do lado de fora." [Voz alta] "O que é que você é pra poder ter duas casas?" Eu falei, "Não—"

More light. [. . .] So, damn. He came up to me. [KLJ says:] "Good evening. Can I help you with something?" [The cop says:] "Do you really live here?" "Shit, um . . . I live as much here inside as I do outside." [Voice raised] "What are you to be able to have two houses?" I said, "No—"

CW: Escutou? "Que é que você é pra ter duas casas?" Só porque ele é preto. [. . .]

Did you hear that? "What are you to be able to have two houses?" Just because he is black. [. . .]

KLJ: Aí, eu falei, "Não, eu tô no lugar comum porque . . . a casa é aqui e a outra é ali." Eu não quis esclarecer logo assim que era minha mãe . . . tá ligado, e meu padrinho no outro bloco. Já deixei logo um mistério pra ele— ver que— o que é que ele iria falar. Aí, "Não porque numa casa eu durmo e na outra eu fico assim, escutando som ou então eu vou comer." [o PM:] "Quem você é?" "Ah, não sou ninguém. Você não tá vendo o meu documento? Eu sou esse rapaz aí." [. . .] [o PM:] "Você tá querendo tirar onda com a minha cara?"

So, I said, "No, I'm just out here because . . . one house is here and the other is there." I didn't want to clarify right away that it was my mother . . . you know, and my godfather on the other block. I left it a mystery at first for him— to see what— what he would say. So, "No because in one house I sleep and in the other I hang out, listening to music or else I eat." [The officer:] "Who are you?" "Oh, I'm nobody. Aren't you looking at my ID? I am that guy there." [. . .] [The officer:] "Are you trying to show off to my face?"

| CW: | Qualquer coisa— se ele te perguntar, a gente tem que ficar quieto. Se a gente responder, é um— já quer ficar mais ignorante, entendeu? Quer— pô, se for possível, ele dá até tapa na cara. | Whatever— if he asks you, we have to stay calm. If we respond, it's a— he'll want to get more ignorant, understand? He'll want— damn, if it were possible, he'd even hit him in the face. |
| KLJ: | Aí, eu já vi que ele já tava ficando meio estressado. Aí eu, "É porque— eu não sou ninguém. Eu—" [o PM:] "Você trabalha?" [KLJ:] "Eu saí do quartel há pouco tempo, mas no momento eu não trabalho." [o PM:] "E tem duas casas? Não, tem alguma coisa errada. Calma aí. Aguarda um momento aí." | So, I saw that he was getting a little stressed. So I was like, "It's because— I'm not anybody. I—" [The officer:] "Do you work?" [KLJ:] "I just left the army, but right now I don't work." [The officer:] "And you have two houses? No, there is something wrong. Hang on. Wait here a minute." |

Privilege in Brazil has typically meant being above the law, so that elite members of society could respond to a request for identification with a challenge of their own: "Você sabe com quem esta falando?" (Do you know who you are talking to?). A common Brazilian aphorism proclaims, "Aos amigos tudo! Aos inimigos a lei!" (For my friends, anything! For my enemies, the law! See DaMatta 1991).[10] The military officer's hailing of KLJ as a *cidadão* (citizen) thus implies KLJ's lower status, as someone who is accountable to (but not protected by) the law. In a book on police violence in the Americas, Paul Chevigny reports that the Rio government ordered police to begin referring to all individuals as *cidadão* instead of using other (likely racialized) derogatory address terms (1995:151). Indeed, Cruzada youth often use the term *negão* (big, strong or intimidating black guy) in their retellings of how they are addressed by the military police (see also French 2013). As they narrate these events, racial difference is made doubly significant: not only has the police officer paid careful attention to their blackness, but the youth are aware (and want to make others aware) of how the police have singled them out because of their race. In this particular recording, KLJ and my assistant, CW, interrupt the narrative several times to make sure that I realize that this is just one everyday example of a widespread pattern of the denial of their citizenship rights and also their rights to move freely within their own city and neighborhood. They want to make sure that I understand that rights are unequally distributed according to race and class positions, in what anthropologist James Holston (2008) has described as an "entrenched regime of differentiated citizenship" and what Vargas and Alves (2010) call a "racialized regime of citizenship." As anthropologist Christen Smith notes, "Even if Brazil is a disjunctive democracy, blackness still sits symbolically outside of this reality" (2016:82).

KLJ is at a disadvantage during this particular police encounter because he is not currently employed and cannot produce evidence that he is on the right side of the *trabalhador-bandido* (worker-bandit) divide.[11] Instead, he points to his possession of citizenship documents and his army service. He must perform the role of the legitimate citizen because this position is not automatically granted to him. Drawing on the work of anthropologist Mariza Peirano, Roberto DaMatta notes: "In the Brazilian case, it is the possession of a document that confers citizenship, not the other way around" (1995:39). KLJ must also work against the assumption, due to his race, that he merits only second-class citizenship (or noncitizenship). As the police constantly remind Cruzada youth of their "place" as racialized subjects in need of surveillance and discipline, they must think carefully about how they react physically and also how they choose to linguistically react. Language is one tool at their disposal. In their retelling, both KLJ and CW call my attention to their linguistic strategies of politeness ("Good evening. Can I help you with something?"), intended to signify their upstanding status. In a world where violence is associated with black criminals and where innocence is linked to white victims (as I have discussed in Roth-Gordon 2009b), this is a fundamental—and racialized—distinction. In the absence of necessary (but often insufficient) documents, language has the potential to suggest both race and class status. Someone who follows the rules of standard Portuguese and demonstrates calm and civil politeness places himself in opposition to, and at a distance from, law-breaking, uncivilized, and dangerous criminals. This kind of respectful behavior seems to demand respect in turn, and KLJ points out that this is initially the case in his encounter: when he responds to the officer calling out to him with a courteous "Boa noite," he reports that the officer responds in kind: "Good evening."

Throughout the nineteenth century, and across the Americas, "citizenship implied the acquisition of fine and affable manners, as well as a 'correct' language; being a citizen meant having a body and a language adjusted by rules, patterns, and laws" (González Stephan 2001:319). As I explain further in chapter 3, KLJ's linguistic style is at its most formal here, and he likely employs forms of standard language to point to and call upon "socio-economic (and other) entitlements, to images of national unity, to ideals of rationality, beauty and other types of social essence" (Agha 2007:147). As KLJ appeals to strategies of *boa aparência* through his use of exaggerated politeness, he seeks to counteract the assumptions made of his phenotypical blackness with the "racial respectability" (Carbado and Gulati 2013) associated with polite, "proper" speech. Writing about the U.S. context, legal scholars Devon Carbado and Mitu Gulati explain that what distinguishes "good blacks" from "bad blacks" is not actual criminality, but "perceived criminality," which is read through how one speaks, acts, and dresses (2013:99). Along similar lines, a Brazilian manual for lawyers notes, "O bem-vestido e bem-falante terá sempre mais chances, frente à Justiça, do que o negro com cara de bandido" (The well-dressed and well-spoken will always have a better chance in court than the black person with the face of a bandit; Frederico Abrahão de Oliveira 1996, quoted in H. Silva 1998:85; see also French 2013; Ramos and Musumeci 2005). Language is thus used as a way of linking oneself not only referentially (through what one talks about) to white spaces and white resources (such as a law school education) but also to whiter speakers, through the "borrowing" of white speech, a topic I now turn to.

"USE THEIR PORTUGUESE"

CW and his friends introduced me to politically conscious hip-hop, which was at the height of its popularity in the late 1990s. They listened mostly to "domestic rap" (in Portuguese), and it was through them that I began paying more attention to the racial politics of rappers and rap fans (see chapter 6). The Rio rappers whom I got to know well, including Rio's MV Bill and DJTR (not pseudonyms), viewed themselves as actively engaged in the struggle to raise racial consciousness and revalorize "black practices" in Brazil. But they needed to balance their simultaneous desire to raise the prestige of blackness and to reject whitening strategies with dominant racial ideas that associate whiteness with modernity, link blackness with overall deficiency and inferiority, and justify the continued marginalization of poor black youth (see also Sansone 2003). Thus, despite their anti-assimilationist and racially empowered stance (Pardue 2008), there were times when rappers felt compelled both to use and to encourage their fans to engage in linguistic accommodation by embracing the language associated with *boa aparência*.

My visit in 1998 to the rappers' community radio station in Cidade de Deus while they broadcast a live hip-hop program provided an elegant illustration of their struggle to reconcile their racial ideals with the reality that racial ideas of white superiority and black inferiority still pervade everyday interactions and justify the distribution of resources in Brazilian society. A "visit" to a community radio station most often entails a live interview, as I quickly learned, and DJTR took the opportunity to ask me to publicly explain my research. As he introduced me to his audience, he began by describing, in positive terms, my interest in Brazilian Portuguese slang. Example 2.5 shows how DJTR started out my impromptu radio interview:

EXAMPLE 2.5: A NOSSA FORMA DE FALAR (OUR OWN WAY OF SPEAKING)

E ela veio de longe e	And she came from far away to
tá fazendo uma— um estudo em cima	do this— this study about
dessa questão, que é importante	this question, that is important
e pra gente muito interessa, né?	and very interesting to us, right?
Mostrar que a gente também tem	To show that we also have
nossos dialetos, a nossa forma de	our dialects, our way of
falar, nossa forma de	speaking, our way of
comunicação, e a gíria, ela é	communicating, and slang, it is
muito importante pra isso.	very important for this.
Tem gente que até discrimina	There are people who discriminate
a gíria, né Bill? Mas a gíria é	against slang, right Bill? But slang is
importante, porque é uma	important, because it is
forma da gente se comunicar	a way for us to communicate
dentro da nossa minisociedade	inside our minisociety
que é a comunidade.	that is the community.

When I interviewed people in the hip-hop community, many rappers similarly professed their belief in using slang as a form of language that everyone could understand—as a show of solidarity and lack of pretention and as a way of affirming a shared motto: "Ninguém é mais que ninguém" (No one is better than anyone else).[12] When I spoke with KLJay, the DJ for Racionais MC's, for example, he noted that the group began to achieve success only after it had "assumed" the language of the street; this theme parallels the group's stance on *assumindo a sua negritude* (assuming one's blackness), as I discuss further in chapter 6. This support for slang directly contradicts linguistic ideologies that uphold the prestige of *a norma culta* (standard Portuguese) and suggest that nonstandard speech, including slang, is an impoverished, uncultured, and uneducated language, when it counts as language at all. Following DJTR's lead, which accurately represented my respect for slang, I spoke at length, praising *gíria* (slang) and suggesting that it was linguistically sound and important. But to my surprise, DJTR concluded the interview with the following warning to his listeners:

EXAMPLE 2.6: A GÍRIA É SÓ PROS DE CASA (SLANG IS JUST FOR THE PEOPLE AT HOME)

Eu só queria só dar um conselho pro pessoal do outro lado [os ouvintes] que gosta de falar . . . muita gíria. Infelizmente não é o nosso vocabulário que dá emprego. Não é o nosso vocabulário, a nível de gíria que dá— que põe comida dentro da nossa casa. Então a gíria é só pros *manos*. Mas quando você for batalhar aí— correr atrás de emprego, cara, use o português deles mesmo. Porque se não, você vai ficar sem emprego. A gíria é só pros de casa.	I just want to give some advice to the people on the other side [the listeners] who like to speak . . . a lot of slang. Unfortunately it is not our vocabulary that offers employment. It's not our vocabulary, on the level of slang that gives— that puts food on our tables. So slang is just for the *manos* [black brothers]. But when you want to try and— go after a job, man, use their Portuguese. Because if you don't, you'll wind up without a job. Slang is just for the people at home.

This exchange illustrates DJTR's awareness that practices associated with blackness remain stigmatized and that poor black male youth need to pay special attention to their bodies to "tame [their] black characteristics" (Pinho 2010:111). As Pinho explains, "Manipulating appearance thus becomes a necessity, a means to control the threat, the fear, or the repugnance associated with black bodies, avoiding . . . the gaze of disgust toward one's own body" (2010:110). While this often entails meticulous attention to dress and hygiene (just as it did in the earlier part of the twentieth century), it also means thinking about language and how a body sounds. In the United States, Signithia Fordham (2008) has found that black youth can take up white practices (including speech styles) in order to achieve success in school, accepting the "burden" of racial management that DJTR alludes to in example 2.6. Phenotypically "black" bodies (displaying a trio of dark skin, tightly curled hair, and "broader" facial features) carry an especially high risk of being misread: as criminal, as lazy, and as untrustworthy. In a job interview, just as in an encounter with the police, individuals who bear this stigma must try to quickly display *boa aparência* and an orientation toward whiteness, if they wish to alleviate hasty but dangerous racial assumptions about their body's innate capacities (though such attempts do not guarantee success).

Both familiarity with standard Portuguese and a careful avoidance of slang work together to imply education, an intellectual ability to follow rules and be "orderly," and a law-abiding stance. DJTR demonstrates his own metalinguistic knowledge that these linguistic styles are racialized: one linguistic variety should be used to impress a (white) superior in order to obtain a job; the other is what will impress the *manos* (black brothers) back at home. It is important to realize too, that DJTR, like Mano, is drawing on critical but often unspoken associations between race, space, and language. Slang, as I was often told, is the "language of the *favela*." Mano symbolically connects himself to the white elite space of a private prestigious law school, while DJTR encourages his listeners to carefully avoid subtle linguistic ties to the *favela*. They both recognize that "meanings and values are attached to urban spaces [and that] these meanings rebound on the significance of bodies" (McCallum 2005:102).[13]

The linguistic strategies of *boa aparência* employed by Cruzada youth are attempts to create symbolic but fleeting connections between racial ideas and bodies. These strategies play upon the very superficial nature of race itself. As Ann Stoler (1995, 2002) has critically illustrated in her work on colonial regimes, racial ideas conveniently link what is seen and what cannot be seen (see also Collins 2007a, 2015). That is to say, racial ideologies claim to have already worked through one-to-one connections between phenotypical features and innate capacities. This racial "cheat sheet" is especially useful for police officers and employers who are required to make fairly quick decisions about a person's character and their trustworthiness. More than just convenient, however, the ready availability of these signs gives both the reader and the one being "read" more material to work with. Racial signs can be found in what people wear, where people are, what they are doing, and how they sound. But if one is savvy enough, it is possible to manipulate these readings, as anthropologist John Collins similarly finds. Collins (2015) analyzes the complicated struggles over racial meaning that take place as the Bahian state remakes its now highly visible historic Pelourinho district. Most relevant to the discussion at hand, Collins describes how one resident in a highly surveilled area kept religious radio sermons playing loudly throughout the halls of his building as a way of sonically associating himself with morality and upstanding Brazilian citizenship. Through these cues, he attempted to "soften 'the men' up" in the face of repeated police intrusions (2007b:390).

In this chapter, I suggest that language offers vulnerable male youth an especially affordable, portable, and renewable set of resources. There is flexibility built into both what one chooses to talk about and how one chooses to talk. In his encounter with the police, Mano cannot run home and change his clothes or grab a briefcase to present a more respectable, law-abiding and citizen-like appearance, nor can he literally transport himself out of the racializing space of his community to associate himself with whiter neighborhoods or establishments. But as he confidently demands that his rights be respected, and as he talks about his (imagined) connections to elite universities, he plays the part of a white, wealthy, and upstanding citizen—all attributes that seem to negate, or at least mitigate, the criminality and danger that can be read off his phenotype. As KLJ and DJTR consciously modify their linguistic behavior (and encourage others to do the same) through strategies of politeness and appeals to standard Portuguese, they take up a temporary racial stance that orients them toward the norms of whiteness. They don't consider themselves to *be* white, nor do they assume that they will be seen as white, and yet achieving a "situational whiteness" is critical to their personal safety and to their ability to gain a foothold in a racially hierarchical society that relegates people like them to the bottom. They are "borrowing" whiteness, along with the security, confidence, and entitlement that it offers only to a select few. In this way, as Fordham also found in the United States, "'acting White' can be an act of protest" (2008:236).

The narratives that I analyze in this chapter provide a critical contrast to the examples that I am about to describe, in which middle-class residents of Rio de Janeiro who range in phenotype work to secure the status of whiteness for themselves and for their children. These research participants do not rely on situational whiteness, though they too must continually negotiate racial readings of their bodies. Instead, they seek to invest in whiteness, to accumulate whiteness within their bodies, and to radiate it through an "ease" (Khan 2011) that comes from constant exposure and familiarity. Whiteness, as it turns out, is not only a situational and interactional accomplishment; for some, it is also something to be acquired through years of careful bodily training and repetition (Bourdieu 1994; Bourdieu and Wacquant 1992; Mauss 1973). I am about to jump over Brazil's race and class divide into a place where whiteness and blackness retain similar meanings, but daily life, daily strategies, and daily practices look very, very different.

3. Investing in Whiteness
Middle-Class Practices of Linguistic Discipline

> Quanto mais branco, melhor; quanto mais claro, superior, eis aí uma
> máxima difundida, que vê no branco não só uma cor mas também
> uma qualidade social: aquele que sabe ler, que é mais educado e que
> ocupa uma posição social mais elevada.
>
> The whiter, the better; the lighter, even better. Here is a well-worn
> saying that sees in the white person not just a color but also a social
> quality: one who knows how to read, who is well educated and who
> occupies a higher social position.
>
> SCHWARCZ 1998:189

Whiteness in Brazil is not a straightforward sort of thing. It is quite common for middle-class *cariocas* (Rio residents) to avoid describing themselves as "white," preferring, even if they are light-skinned, to see themselves as *moreno* (light brown or tanned; see also Norvell 2002:258), which is often understood to be the "true" or "ideal" color of a racially mixed Brazil (E. Nascimento 2007). In fact, very fair skin can also be stigmatized as unattractive, allowing one to be described as *branquela* or *branco azedo* (the color of sour milk). The difference between color and race is critical here, as these do not neatly align to produce a coherent definition of whiteness: lightness is desirable, but true whiteness entails a certain "social quality," as Lilia Moritz Schwarcz notes in the epigraph. Social psychologist Lia Vainer Schucman (2014) helpfully distinguishes between "lightness" (the phenotypical features associated with whiteness, such as light skin, narrow facial features, and straight hair, that she calls *brancura*) and "whiteness" (the racial privilege accorded to "white" people in a racially hierarchical society, or *branquitude*). Indeed, as we will see, light skin neither guarantees nor is required for racial whiteness in Brazil, making the cultural and linguistic practices associated with whiteness all the more important.

Illustrating the way that these two forms of whiteness do not always overlap, several middle-class families that I knew had at least some members with medium or even fairly dark skin, and while they might identify as *pardo* (brown, or mixed race) on a census form, they all agreed that they would put "white" if they were required to give racial information for a travel visa. The fact that travel, as a practice that requires money and offers class status, has the ability to "whiten" (and, conversely, requires whiteness) is also documented in the literature. Marvin Harris and colleagues report that one of the authors has known her travel agent to change her race from *parda* (which appeared on her birth certificate) to *branca* (1993:453). By these examples, I do not mean to suggest that some Brazilians are "really" brown and that they reclassify themselves as whiter when it counts. Instead, these examples suggest that middle-class Brazilians find themselves subject to the social and racial imperative that encourages them to "whiten," as I discuss in chapter 2 (see also Mitchell 2016). In addition to asking how they racially identify, I explore how middle-class Brazilians seek to display whiteness and actively participate in what they recognize to be a global racial hierarchy that privileges whiteness. In what should prove to be a useful counterbalance to scholarship on the normativity or "possession" of whiteness in the U.S. context (Lipsitz 1998; see also C. Harris 1993; Pinho 2009),[1] Brazilians remind us that whiteness is always relative, imagined, produced, and insecure.

Because Brazilians do not understand race to be fixed or static, we can sometimes watch them overtly work through their relationships to whiteness in their day-to-day lives. In example 3.1, one of my light-skinned middle-class friends emailed me about her doubts in 2010 concerning how to racially classify herself:

EXAMPLE 3.1: MARQUEI PARDA (I CHOSE BROWN)

Jennifer,	Jennifer,
No dia do seu aniversário, fui recenseada (quando o governo manda contar a população).	On the day of your birthday, I was given another census (when the government counts the population).
O questionário (eletrônico) pergunta o nome dos moradores da casa, idade, quanto ganha por mês e a cor.	The questionnaire (electronic) asks the names of all of the residents of the home, ages, how much you make per month and your color.
Aí é que é engraçado, porque vale o que a pessoa disser.	And here is the funny thing, because it matters what the person chooses.
O rapaz do censo não pode dar opinião. Eu perguntei as alternativas: branca, preta, parda, amarela [origem asiática] e índio.	The guy from the census can't give his opinion. I asked what the choices were: white, black, brown, yellow [of Asian descent] and Indian [of indigenous descent].
Pensei: não sou preta, e brancos	I thought: I am not black, and white

são meus amigos Jennifer	is the color of my friends Jennifer
e Derek [o marido da autora]	and Derek [the author's husband]
(e definitivamente, eu não	(and I am definitely not
sou da mesmo cor deles).	the same color as they are).
Marquei parda.	I chose brown.

My friend Gabriela is closer in skin and hair coloring to me than she is to her brothers, who have much darker skin than she does. (They would also presumably mark *pardo* on the census, as they do not have curly hair or what are recognized as black facial features.) What is interesting is that Gabriela's idea of the "ideal" white is a North American, even though she undoubtedly knows Brazilians who are blond and fairer-skinned than I am. Here, whiteness takes on a transnational reality (Seigel 2009), and her own whiteness becomes relative.[2]

In this chapter, I examine the complicated and sometimes anxious relationship that members of Rio's middle class have with whiteness. Picking up the thread from the previous chapter, I suggest that all Rio residents, across race and class lines, are encouraged to orient toward whiteness. And yet there is a useful distinction to be made between how this orientation toward whiteness is experienced and what it can achieve. As I describe in chapter 2, poor dark-skinned youth attempt to show evidence of whiteness *on* and *through* their bodies, embracing, for example, standard Portuguese and other forms of respectful, civilized behavior to temporarily and situationally gain access to the privileges of whiteness. By contrast, the middle-class families that I knew, including Gabriela's, seek to accrue and accumulate whiteness *within* their bodies as something they can casually and even "naturally" exude, due to their familiarity and comfort in white spaces and with white practices (such as travel). Rather than a "situational" whiteness, these middle-class families invest in what we might describe as a "personal whiteness," which facilitates and justifies their inequitable access to everything from resources and privileges to rights to occupy exclusive urban spaces. Here I work to reconcile the twenty-first-century context of Rio de Janeiro, Brazil, with W.E.B. Du Bois's famous statement, "The discovery of personal whiteness among the world's peoples is a very modern thing, a nineteenth and twentieth century matter indeed" (Du Bois 1920:29–30).

I thus dive back into the complicated nexus of race and class to suggest that when middle-class families invest in expensive private-school educations, when they insist on proper grammar from their children, and when they take pride in their cultural refinement, they are doing more than just performing and securing their status through markers of class "distinction" (Bourdieu 1984). Indeed, socioeconomic insecurity is an undeniable part of their everyday experience: as their collective financial situation changes based on what can be a highly volatile Brazilian economy, they have often had to resort to symbolic strategies to justify and maintain their positions within the small Brazilian middle class and to distance themselves from "the masses" (O'Dougherty 2002; Owensby 1999). The situation of the middle class has felt even more precarious of late, as increases in the minimum wage and the extension of consumer credit (as just two examples) have facilitated social mobility for the poor and working classes, affording them increased opportunities to consume more expensive goods and rights to occupy middle-class spaces. At the same time, governmental programs expanded under the Brazilian Worker's Party (Partido dos Trabalhadores, or PT) opened up opportunities for higher education to Brazilians of African descent and poor Brazilians, thus reducing the number of spaces in free, public, and prestigious universities (and increasing competition for private-school spaces) previously occupied almost exclusively by middle- and upper-class children. Members of the Brazilian middle class, like many of their counterparts across the globe, worry constantly about their finances and their children's futures. In what follows, I argue that the middle class seeks to acquire and display "refined" linguistic and cultural practices because neither their racial whiteness nor their class status is guaranteed. I turn next to explain more about the instability of whiteness, before focusing on what this means for members of Rio's middle class.

PERSONAL WHITENESS

It might be helpful to begin updating W. E. B. Du Bois's 1920 observation on the "discovery of personal whiteness" by adding that it was in the nineteenth and twentieth centuries that people all around the globe discovered—and began to worry about—their relationship to whiteness. Once whiteness was something that you could have, it became something that you needed to work to acquire, as well as something that you could lose, and reinforcing it became an endless and daily task (Stoler 2002). The idea that whiteness, particularly for North Americans, is just "normal" and "taken for granted" has received much scholarly attention (see, for example, Frankenberg 1993). And yet, even in the U.S. context, neither phenotype nor personal ancestry nor connections to the Caucasus region (from which the term *Caucasian* is derived) solidly guarantee one's whiteness. Studies of "off-whiteness" (Brodkin 1998), "probationary whiteness" (Gualtieri 2009; Jacobson 2001), and "honorary whiteness" (Haney-López 2006; Tuan 1998) have discussed the constant renegotiation and reorganization of (North American) whiteness to include and exclude different groups of immigrants over time.

Race scholars have documented that whiteness is threatened not only through the possibility of external racial "contamination" but also through internal racial failure. Describing the tenuous situation of poor whites in the postbellum U.S. South, for example, Dreisinger asks, "If, after all, a mere drop of black blood could turn white black, then just how vulnerable was white blood?" (2008:21). And yet, in the case of so-called "white trash," described as "a distinct figure of degraded and contemptible poor whites . . . [who] threatened the stability and future of the white race at large" (Hartigan 2005:60), blackness was not to blame for white people's failed attempts to uphold racial whiteness (see also Wray 2006). Indeed, the popularity of "positive" or "soft" eugenics in the early 1900s, required the racial "improvement" even of white families and populations through behavioral modification in order to save an "endangered" white race (Cogdell 2004; J. Dávila 2003; Dorey 1999; Fender 2006; Rafter 2006; Stepan 1991). As John Hartigan notes of the North American context: "With the eugenical family studies . . . race is conceptualized as more than simply an epidermal fate or a matter given at birth, and increasingly becomes a matter of internalized, disciplined bodily orders, actively maintained through attention to class distinctions" (2005:98). Even in the United States, then, racial whiteness has been understood as fragile and something one has to work at.

Within colonial studies, several provocative investigations into white racial anxiety have been spurred by Ann Stoler's fascinating work (1995, 2002) on the surveillance of Europeans in the colonies, including their intimate relationships and daily practices within the domestic sphere (see, for example, W. Anderson 2003; Boddy 2005; Brown 2006). Here again, whiteness could not be assumed or taken for granted, but could be threatened in different ways, from the contact one had with nonwhite Others to one's inability to display specific social qualities and "proper" forms of bodily discipline. Various bodily practices took on racial meaning, especially in the colonial era: one's claims to whiteness could be determined by whether one sat comfortably in chairs or preferred to rest on one's haunches (Stoler 2002:120); whether one became accustomed to air conditioning or survived in the hot tropical sun (Van Leeuwen 2011:214); and even whether one knew how to properly dispose of one's own bodily waste (W. Anderson 2006; Collins 2015). Studies such as Stoler's (2002) also focused explicitly on the question of child rearing, reminding us that whiteness was not merely given as one's birthright but also required training in the "proper" behaviors associated with "good breeding."

Together, these studies help shed light on the situation of whiteness in Brazil, which, as historian Jerry Dávila notes, has always been precarious: "In the societies analyzed by [Ann] Stoler, whiteness was a threatened commodity and colonial officials preoccupied themselves with the task of shoring it up. For Brazilian elites, the problem was even more urgent—they believed their racially mixed nation already lacked the whiteness it needed to sustain its vitality. The task at hand, then, was to find new ways of creating whiteness" (2003:5). Although Brazil has never really aspired to racial "purity," given its foundational belief in and history of racial mixture, the possibilities for true Brazilian whiteness are a constant source of racial anxiety. Liv Sovik (2009) entitled her study of Bahia *Aqui Ninguém é Branco* (There Are No Whites Here), and anthropologist Rita Segato confirms the continued preoccupation with the racial status of Brazil's elite: "For a variety of reasons involving either biological or cultural contamination, no Brazilian white is ever fully, undoubtedly white" (1998:136). "Whiteness in Brazil," she observes, "is impregnated by blackness. Whiteness, in Brazil, as a sign of safe, uncontested status, is never fully achieved, never certain" (1998:147). Along similar lines, sociologist Guerreiro Ramos (1995) writes:

> Os elementos da minoria "branca" no "Norte" e no "Nordeste" são . . . muito sensíveis a quem quer que ponha em questão a sua "brancura." Por isso exibem a sua brancura de maneira tal que não suscite dúvida. . . . Este traço paranóico não caracteriza somente o comportamento do "branco" baiano, mas, em grau maior ou menor, do "branco brasileiro," em geral.

> The members of the "white" minority in the "North" and the "Northeast" are . . . very sensitive to those who would question their "whiteness." For this reason, they exhibit their whiteness to leave no doubt. . . . This trace of paranoia does not just characterize the behavior of the "white" Bahian, but, to a greater or lesser extent, the behavior of the "white Brazilian" in general. (227)

A lack of strict racial segregation or legal definitions of racial status has also meant that whites could racially fall into the category of blackness through scandalous or inappropriate behavior (Fischer 2004), while blacks could be racially "improved" to near-whiteness (J. Dávila 2003). At the same time, as Denise Ferreira da Silva found, all individuals have had to manage the situation of their potential blackness:

> In the United States and in the colonial situation, the racialised Other was defined as part of a distinct group; in Brazil there is a laundry-list of traits that serve to classify a person in situations of contact. Thus, it is the body that needs to be known, to be described, to be spoken of

endlessly. Only through this inexhaustive, continuous definition of the amount of blackness a body displays is it possible to separate races. Yet, the "Other" is the "Other-within," within anybody, any-body; any body is more or less black, more or less white, more or less both. (1998:228)

Given this ongoing monitoring and the constant need to read bodies for signs of race, members of Rio's middle class invest heavily in the training of their children so that their personal whiteness is readily recognizable (and less impeachable) to those around them.

GRAMMAR AS DISCIPLINE

To illustrate the ways Rio residents constantly seek to "create" whiteness, as Jerry Dávila (2003) suggests, I examine the ever-changing set of cultural and linguistic practices on which the historical (in)stability of racial privilege is based. Prior to the 1920s, *cariocas* who wanted to be considered white used lightening creams on their skin and took umbrellas when they bathed in the sea (Barickman 2009:179). At that time, a darkening of the skin could suggest *um pé na cozinha* (literally "a foot in the kitchen," or a black ancestor), a reference to slavery and stigma. And yet, ever since the 1920s, tan has been the ideal Brazilian color (Barickman 2009; Farias 2006) and one has had to demonstrate one's whiteness through other means. Bridget Heneghan's (2003) study of the antebellum U.S. South explains how whiteness could be displayed through the care one took of refined "white things," which included material goods and consumption patterns that extended the white body. Taken together, these white things signified one's whiteness through the demonstrated care one lavished upon them: teeth needed to be brushed; houses needed to be freshly whitewashed; white porcelain tea cups needed to be kept clean and free of chips or cracks. As Heneghan explains, "One might have been born with a biological whiteness, and earn or inherit it in the upper-class goods delimiting class, and display it upon the body and throughout the house, but one also had to maintain it—clean it and polish it and take care not to break it—in order truly to achieve whiteness" (2003:132). Cleaning, polishing, and taking care not to break things revealed the inner discipline that only white people were thought to possess and be capable of. Whiteness implied civility and cultivation, as well as rationality and expertise.

Along similar lines, as Pinho explains, daily hygiene practices have constructed racial difference over the centuries: "Over three hundred years of slavery in Brazil was enough time to reinforce and expand negative images of blackness. In addition to being considered ugly and rough, black bodies of the enslaved were associated with filth and stench. . . . The alleged smell of the slaves' bodies became an additional excuse for classifying them closer to animals than to humans" (2010:105). Racial difference has thus been predicated on all sorts of bodily regimens that serve to uphold concepts of superiority versus inferiority and reify the biological basis of race. The idea that black bodies "smell," for example, is a common and deeply naturalized belief, not only in Brazil but elsewhere (Guimarães 2003; Nogueira 1942; M. Smith 2006). The concept of race and the superiority of whiteness thus rely on distinctions made between bodies and one's ability to discipline and control them.[3]

Middle-class parents in Rio invest heavily in private-school education for their children as a site where they can acquire linguistic discipline (among other skills). Children often begin this training around age two, when they are enrolled in preschool, while daily instruction in the grammatical rules and formal description of standard Portuguese begins at age six. The general assumption is that these children should attend good schools in order to get into a good university, get a good job, and become productive, upstanding members of Brazilian society. (This idealized trajectory is obviously shared with members of the middle class around the globe.) Poor and working-class Rio residents who do not follow this path seem to fall outside all formal institutions. They often live in informal housing settlements (shantytowns or suburbs); they attend public schools that, due to lack of teachers and resources, often fail to provide formal instruction; they may leave school without graduating to work in the informal economy (as domestic workers or in manual labor); and they may even wind up involved in illegal activities (drug use, theft, and the like). As a perfect example of linguistic ideology (Irvine and Gal 2000; Kroskrity 2000; Schieffelin, Woolard, and Kroskrity 1998; Woolard 1998), connections are made and naturalized between "rule breaking" of all sorts: people who have not learned and do not speak a rule-governed standard Portuguese must also be prone to criminal activity and societal law-breaking (see also Cameron 1995).

The idea that certain people disregard rules and have no discipline in any aspect of their life, from language to bodily conduct, also illustrates "the powerful symbolism in which language stands for other kinds of order— moral, social and political" (Cameron 1995:25). People who fall outside this societal order are racialized as nonwhite due to their inability to demonstrate proper bodily control. In this chapter, I present examples of the daily speech that I recorded during my research in the South Zone housing

FIGURE 6. Early training in linguistic and personal discipline. Photo by Marcelo Santos Braga.

project of Cruzada, where young people are known to use (and actively choose to employ) nonstandard speech that includes *gíria* (slang). I will show how these linguistic differences are taken up by the middle class in order to create whiteness and class distinction. Members of the middle class have plenty of opportunities in public spaces to hear their poor and often dark-skinned next-door neighbors speaking, and in what follows, I present their private reactions to this speech. With the permission of my Cruzada research participants, I played excerpts of their conversations for several middle-class families in their own homes, and I recorded the discussions that followed in what could be described as "metalinguistic interviews."

FIGURE 7.   Spelling and grammar drills begin at an early age for middle-class children. The common assumption is that public schools, which are poorly funded and subject to frequent school strikes, barely teach anything. Photo by Marcelo Santos Braga.

Before I offer examples of the language that the poor dark-skinned male youth in my study spoke when they were socializing with peers in their neighborhood, I explain how sociolinguists and linguistic anthropologists think about this kind of linguistic "difference." The idea that there is only one "correct" variety of speech has been described by sociolinguists as "the standard language myth" (Lippi-Green 2001:55–63) or the "suppression of optional variability" (Milroy and Milroy 2012:6). Outside the academy, the desire to adhere to linguistic (and grammatical) correctness is widespread and deeply embedded, particularly among more educated speakers (Cameron 1995). Linguists, however, have documented that so-called "nonstandard" varieties have their own grammaticality and that all linguistic varieties are socially evaluated based instead on the prestige of their imagined speakers: the most highly valued forms of language are always associated with speakers who have other forms of social and cultural capital (Bourdieu 1994), including money, education, and social status. Within the field of linguistics, then, there exists clear consensus that perceived "correctness" is not based on matters of grammaticality, but rather offers insight into those who are the most (and least) powerful members of a particular society.

In Brazil, sociolinguist Marcos Bagno (1999, 2003) has written both academic and popular books trying to debunk common "myths" such as "Brasileiros não sabem português" (Brazilians do not know how to speak Portuguese) and "É preciso saber gramática para falar e escrever bem" (One needs to study grammar to speak and write well), both of which work to disparage the Brazilian "masses" with limited access to education. Given the discrepancy between what linguists and nonlinguists think about the value of speaking "correctly," I pay careful attention to the beliefs of middle-class speakers at the same time that I attend to the fact that they are obviously heavily invested in the linguistic forms and rules of grammar in which they have been trained (often at great personal cost and effort). Linguistic anthropologist E. Summerson Carr has coined the term *metalinguistic labor* to describe the "work to protect, patrol, and produce such highly naturalized assumptions about language" (2011:125). I also seek to demonstrate that members of the middle class have been taught to view language as a form of bodily practice (Bourdieu 1994; Bourdieu and Wacquant 1992; Mauss 1973), one that helps them display (and further invest in) their own personal whiteness.

Whereas sociolinguists and linguistic anthropologists hear creativity and innovation from less educated speakers in what they would describe as straightforward (and expected) linguistic variation among social groups, members of the middle class are likely to hear chaos and lack of personal discipline that they readily associate with nonwhiteness. Sociolinguist Penelope Eckert has refuted the notion that speaking "casually" and "informally" requires less concentration or skill by speakers: "While formal style certainly involves greater attention to speech, and while speakers have to pay careful attention when they're speaking in the most extremely standard end of their stylistic repertoire, there is every reason to believe that a similar effort is required at the extremely non-standard end of their repertoire as well" (2000:18). Thus as I turn to present the speech of Cruzada youth, and middle-class reactions to their speech, it is important to remember that language, like hygiene, offers endless possibilities for "creating" whiteness.[4] It is not that bodily cleanliness or linguistic "correctness" are natural and proper; they are, in fact, highly relative concepts that require both implicit and explicit training to acquire in culturally appropriate ways. What it means to be "clean" and what it means to speak "correctly" are judged in relation to constantly shifting norms. Most important, those norms serve as taken-for-granted (or naturalized) cultural ideals that helpfully allow people to invest in, and then demonstrate, the orderly discipline and civility associated with whiteness while they afford opportunities for justifying racial hierarchy based on the comparison with nonwhite and "undisciplined" others.

SLANG: THE LANGUAGE OF THE *FAVELA*

Slang is notoriously hard to define (even for linguists), as it includes many linguistic features beyond the lexicon that both speakers and listeners consider nonstandard. In their daily talk with one another, Cruzada youth typically incorporate a range of innovative slang terms that not only invent new words and new meanings for old words but also create new discourse rules that alter the rhythm of their speech (Roth-Gordon 2007b). In addition to the frequent use of profanity, they pepper their speech with what linguists call pragmatic markers, or optional words and expressions that help organize their speech. Some of these markers play with sounds (like *bum*, meant to represent the sound of a gunshot) and are considered highly nonstandard. In example 3.2, a Cruzada youth nicknamed Feijão (or "black bean," a common racialized nickname in Brazil) narrates for my research assistant, CW, and an audience of Cruzada peers the only time that he thought he was going to be robbed. He had been sitting at a local bus stop, wearing a showy watch, which is often the target of theft, and listening to a personal music player, when two *favela* (shantytown) youth attempted to intimidate him with references to their gun collection, the kind of veiled threat that often precedes robberies in Rio.

EXAMPLE 3.2: THE ONLY TIME I THOUGHT I WAS GOING TO BE
ROBBED: FEIJÃO'S STORY

Feijão:	Aí **na moral,** sou doidinho pra ser— [. . .] O dia— o único dia que eu ia— eu ia ser— eu <u>senti</u> que ia ser roubado foi ali no Flamengo. **Bum. Sentadaine, maior relojaine**. Aí ele **bum.** "Ô, o moleque . . . aí formas as horas aí?" Eu falei, "Porra, . . . uma e brau." Aí começou a falar o negócio	So **seriously,** I'm a little crazy to be— [. . .] The day— the only day that I was— I was going to be— I <u>felt</u> that I was going to be robbed was there in Flamengo. ***Bum*** [boom]. [I was] **All seated,** [with a] **huge watch**. Then he ***bum.*** "Oh, kid . . . hey ya got the time there?" I said, "Shit, . . . one and change." Then he started to say some stuff

	de arma pra me intimidar aí.	about guns to intimidate me.
	[Ele falando com o amigo:]	[He says to his friend:]
	"Porra, cadê a pistola,	"Shit, where's the gun,
	cumpadi? Porra, tem que	buddy? Shit, we have to
	arrumar aquela pistola. Tô com	get that gun. I only have
	uma aqui só, mas pô . . .	one here, but damn . . .
	tá ligado?	you know what I'm saying?
	//Perdemos pro PM."	//We lost it to the police."
	[. . .]	[. . .]
Judô:	//Caralho.	//Shit.
CW:	//Tem que mandar— [Risos]	//You had to— [Laughter]
Feijão:	Eu tava de Walkman,	I had a Walkman
	[aparelho]	[personal music player]
	mas já de::sliguei.	but I had already turned it o::ff.
CW:	É!	Yeah!
Feijão:	Aí **bum**. Balançando a	So **bum**. [I'm] Bouncing my
	cabeça [para fingir que ainda	head [to pretend he is still
	está escutando o som]. Aí, ele	listening to the music]. So, he's
	falando altã::o, né?	practically shou::ting, right?
	Bum. Aí começo a comentar.	**Bum**. So I start to respond.
	Aí vem o 433 [ônibus]. Porra.	Then the 433 comes [bus]. Shit.
	Eu falei, "Pô, não vou	I said, "Damn, I'm not going
	deixar o 433 passar, só pra—	to let the 433 pass, just to—
	sabe, demonstrar	you know, show him
	medo pra ele." Falei, "Pô."	I'm not afraid." I said, "Damn."
	Fui pegar o 433. Aí **bum**.	I got on the 433. So **bum**.
	Entrei no ônibus. Aí ele foi—	I got on the bus. So he goes—
	fez assim pra mim [gesto],	went like this to me [gesture],
	pensando que eu tinha	thinking that I had
	peidado. Aí cara deu vontade	chickened out. So man I wanted
	de— porra— [Risos]	to— shit— [Laughter]
Judô:	Vem cá, como é que eu vou ter	Come on, how am I going to
	pena de te bater?	feel bad about beating you up?
	Tu não tava com pena	You didn't feel bad
	de me roubar, arrombado.	about robbing me, asshole.
	Eu da cor. [. . .]	Me, a person of color. [. . .]
Feijão:	Não sabe o que é que fez,	You don't know what you did,
	rapá. Roubar pobre.	buddy. Rob a poor person.

Feijão's story is filled with innovative slang terms that generated very different reactions from listeners. While his friends found these terms amusing (there is much laughter as he recounts his harrowing tale), outside listeners described his narrative as confusing and ungrammatical. The non-standard slang terms that Feijão embraces range from local, in-group forms such as the rhyming suffix *-aine* ("Sentadaine, maior relojaine"), used instead of the standard aggrandizer *-ão* (big), to better-known slang terms such as *na moral* (seriously). Throughout his narrative, Feijão employs the loud and emphatic pragmatic marker *bum!* (boom!) to attract attention and dramatically parse his narrative, focusing his listeners on the key parts of his story. *Bum* comes from a class of Brazilian Portuguese slang terms that I call "sound words" due to their onomatopoeïc effect. Working on a similar class of words in Greek, Deborah Tannen (1983) notes that they might also be referred to as "sound non-words," an observation that rings especially true for standard Portuguese speakers who would not recognize these sounds to be a productive part of the linguistic system. Feijão himself described them as a kind of verbal comma. Emphatic sound words were used frequently in daily conversation among Cruzada male youth, and they appear in the lyrics of politically conscious rap groups such as Racionais MC's, from São Paulo, that intentionally use slang to connect with the youth of Brazil's social and geographic *periferia* (periphery; see chapter 6). Although his peers view Feijão as a skilled and entertaining storyteller, these sound words attracted considerable attention—and scorn—from members of the middle class.

PRIDE AND PREJUDICE

Slang is said to trickle down the hills of Rio de Janeiro, and members of the middle class are quick to contrast what they perceive as nonsensical slang terms and grammatical errors with their own competency in standard Portuguese. The spatial contrast, between the modern and orderly *asfalto* (including the paved and more developed parts of the city) and the self-constructed and poorly maintained shantytowns, maps neatly onto this linguistic contrast. "Modern" and "orderly" speakers receive proper training and linguistic development through expensive private-school education; in the absence of this formal training, "disorderly" and "self-constructed" speakers appear to just make up words. When I played Feijão's narrative for middle-class listeners who did not know him, and recorded their reactions, they invariably turned to discuss his use of slang and the pragmatic marker *bum*. In example 3.3, parents Bernardo and Isabela and their children, Manuela and Francisco, explain the social and linguistic salience of the pragmatic marker *bum*.

EXAMPLE 3.3: *BUM BUM* IS *BUMBUM*

Bernardo:	Para mim, bum bum é bumbum.	For me, *bum bum* is *bumbum*.
Isabela:	[Risos] Bumbum. [bunda]	[Laughter] *Bumbum.* [literally "butt, rear end"]
Bernardo:	Bumbum. Os caras falam bum. Fui aqui bum. Fui lá bum. Eu não entendo nada disso. [. . .]	*Bumbum.* The guys say *bum.* I went here *bum.* I went there *bum.* I don't understand any of this. [. . .]
Jennifer:	Que é que vocês não entenderam dessa conversa?	What didn't you understand in this conversation?
Manuela:	Esse bum para mim é um detalhe tem que ser riscado. Não entendo nada do bum. [. . .]	This *bum* for me is a detail that has to be crossed out. I don't understand anything of this *bum.* [. . .]
Fernando:	Agora esse bum é bem gente de morro [favela].	Now this *bum* is really from people of the hill [a *favela*].
Isabela:	Esse bum eu nunca escutei.	This *bum* I've never heard.
Fernando:	Esse bum é bem gente de morro.	This *bum* is really from people of the hill.
Jennifer:	É?	Really?
Bernardo:	É. Super.	Yes. Very much so.
Jennifer:	Por quê?	Why?
Fernando:	A maioria não usa bum.	Most people don't use *bum.*
Manuela:	Não existe. Não existe.	It doesn't exist. It doesn't exist.

Example 3.3 illustrates what linguistic anthropologists call the enregisterment of slang (Agha 2007), as specific linguistic features seem to group together to point directly to particular city spaces, select speakers, and their imagined characteristics. Note that this middle-class family talks about Cruzada as a *morro* (hill, a euphemism in Rio de Janeiro for a *favela*), even as they are familiar with its location and know that it is a housing project comprised of multistory buildings located on a paved city street just like theirs. This "slip" between housing project and hill casts a shadow of illegitimacy over the speakers, their language, and their rights to occupy contested city spaces. *Favelas* still do not exist on many city maps, an erasure that reinforces Manuela's dismissal of Feijão's use of *bum*, suggesting

that it needs to be crossed out and that it does not actually exist. Bernardo's initial reaction, likening the emphatic pragmatic marker to the word *bum-bum* (butt or rear end), similarly trivializes not only Feijão's linguistic style but also the force of his narrative. Members of the middle class have long used the physical space of the *favela* to reinvent themselves as whiter, more modern, more cosmopolitan and upstanding urban dwellers (Leeds and Leeds 1970:261). It is their pride in their ability to display proper Portuguese, and to define which linguistic features *count* as "real" Portuguese, that leads to their prejudice. Indeed, it is significant that though Feijão shares a story that most *cariocas* can relate to, describing his fears of being the victim of a robbery, members of the white middle class for whom I played this excerpt actively worked against this implicit connection, choosing instead to racialize and criminalize Feijão because of his language, as this family does when our conversation continues in example 3.4:

EXAMPLE 3.4: HERE IT'S FUNNY. BUT IF I'M ON A BUS . . .

Isabela:	Agora uma coisa. Aqui eu tô achando engraçado [bum]. Mas se eu tô no ônibus, e eu escuto dois— duas pessoas tendo . . . esse diálogo, que eu não ia entender que era roubo nem nada, falando eu não ia entender, mas se eu escuto esse tipo de coisa—	Now one thing. Here I am thinking it's funny [*bum*]. But if I'm on the bus, and I hear two— two people having . . . this dialogue, that I wouldn't be able to understand that it was about a robbery or anything, speaking I wouldn't be able to understand, but if I hear this type of thing—
Bernardo:	Linguajar.	Dialect.
Isabela:	Eu trocaria de lugar ou— ou tentaria saltar do ônibus.	I would change places or — or try to get off of the bus.
Bernardo:	Eu também ia ficar . . . apreensivo.	I also would be . . . apprehensive.
Isabela:	É.	Yes.
Bernardo:	Se escutasse dois ou três caras dentro do ônibus—	If I heard two or three guys inside of a bus—
Isabela:	Conversando assim—	Talking like this—
Bernardo:	Com esse linguajar, eu ia ficar na maior atenção que ia ser assaltado.	With this dialect, I would be paying a lot of attention that I was going to be robbed.

	[...] Sem virar	[...] Without turning my
	a cabeça, eu vou—	head, I would—
	eu vou dizer assim—	I would say—
Isabela:	A intonação—	The intonation—
Bernardo:	"Ih, tem negão	"Eee, there are big black guys
	atrás. Tem assaltante.	behind me. There are muggers.
	Tem cara de morro.	There are guys from the hill.
	Tem bandido atrás	There are criminals behind
	de mim."	me."

Freely ignoring the content of the story (as Isabela herself acknowledges), respondents feel no sympathy for a near-victim of crime. Invested in creating social distance and safety in a city of uncomfortable proximity (as hypothetical passengers on a shared public bus), the people I interviewed foregrounded their own positions of vulnerability. Indeed, Isabela and Bernardo invent a scenario in which Feijão and friends are the unintelligible slang-speaking criminals, and they are the innocent victims. For the middle class, Brazilian Portuguese *gíria* (slang) has long symbolized disorder, and people who speak with gunshots (*bum!*) are made to represent people who use guns (Roth-Gordon 2009b). These connections between slang, *favelas*, blackness, and crime seemed obvious to many of the middle-class listeners, even though they would occasionally stop to acknowledge that not all of the people who live in *favelas* are criminals.

Beyond the fact that Feijão and his friends were understood to be black, and despite the reality that their actual bodies could only be imagined, far more foundational ties were being stitched together between notions of superiority and inferiority, whiteness and blackness, and the (in)ability to speak and understand slang. I interviewed about a dozen middle-class individuals, in several group interviews, and I played about a half-dozen different recordings for them. The families spoke for hours about the "problems" with the speech they had heard from Cruzada male youth. To them, these speakers did not just demonstrate stylistic difference or the creativity of youthful slang; they suffered from linguistic difficulties that impeded their ability to communicate. As Bernardo commented:

Ele formou uma frase pelo menos. [...] É uma das poucas horas que ele forma— que ele forma uma frase. [...] Que às vezes você ponha bum e não quer dizer nada mesmo. Só está ajudando ele a formar a frase. Deu sentido na frase dele. Que é a coisa mais difícil, deles aí, é formar a frase com sentido da gente, né?

He formed a sentence at least. [. . .] It's one of the few times that he formed— that he formed a sentence. [. . .] Because sometimes you put *bum* and it doesn't mean anything at all. It's only helping him to form a sentence. It gave his sentence meaning. Which is the most difficult thing, for them, to form a sentence with the meaning that we have, right?

Parents from other families that had young children came quickly to the same sorts of conclusions. This type of language, which included the heavy use of slang, demonstrated the speakers' cognitive difficulties and lack of personal discipline:

Muito pouca concentração . . . no que fazem. [. . .] Não conseguem se concentrar numa frase inteira, num pensamento com começo, meio, e fim e dá essa ordem. [. . .] Não constrói uma frase . . . com verbo, predicato, com alguma coisa, até o fim. Não conseguem ter um pensamento de uma frase. Uma.

They have so little concentration . . . in what they are doing. [. . .] They can't concentrate on one complete sentence, one thought with a beginning, middle, and end and give that sense of order. [. . .] They don't construct a sentence . . . with a verb, a predicate, with something, until the end. They can't have one thought of one sentence. Not one.

The speakers' lack of rationality, order, and intellect seemed obvious to middle-class listeners, despite the fact that they were telling complete stories that their peers received well and clearly understood. When I followed up on the consensus that Cruzada youth had "difficulty expressing themselves" and pointed out that they seemed able to understand one another quite well, Isabela and Bernardo's teenage daughter, Manuela, explained that the inability to express oneself was shared and that this fact must somehow facilitate communication between them:

Acho que um não consegue explicar [. . .] e pelo fato— pelo fato de não conseguir expressar, o outro, como também acho que não tem essa capacidade de se expresser, já entende mais fácil.

I think that one person doesn't manage to explain [. . .] and because— because one of them can't express himself, the other, who I think also doesn't have this capacity to express himself, manages to understand more easily.

The youth's engaging stories were thus understood only in terms of lack: "falta de cultura, falta de conhecimento, falta de vocabulário" (lack of culture, lack of knowledge, lack of vocabulary). Indeed, I would argue that through this metalinguistic commentary, middle-class speakers worked not only to criminalize these youth but also to dehumanize them and to question their ability to be productive Brazilian citizens.[5] As Ann Stoler has noted of the colonial context: "Language was seen to fix the parameters of children's perceptions, enabling them to think certain sentiments and not others. Linguistic fluency was a necessary, not sufficient, condition for citizenship rights and, without the appropriate moral referents, of little use at all" (2002:129).

This lack was occasionally linked explicitly to blackness. As Bernardo noted, "O preto no Brasil, infelizmente em comparação com Estados Unidos, realmente é um cara pobre, de nível baixo, de pouca instrução" (The black person in Brazil, unfortunately in comparison with the United States, really is a poor guy, at a low level, with little instruction). The storytellers' lack of standard Portuguese also denied them any individuality or recognizability. When I asked which speaker had used the most slang in one particular conversation, one mother responded: "Isto para mim é uma massa única. Que eu não diferencio [. . .] uma pessoa da outra" (This to me is a singular mass. I don't distinguish [. . .] one person from the next).

By way of comparison, many of the middle-class families emphasized their own linguistic competence, the value they give to their language, and the emphasis they placed on speaking "properly" (and demanding that their children do the same). Manuela, for example, compared her Cruzada contemporaries' lack of instruction and their inability to express themselves with her own (private-school) training:

> Porque eu tendo uma noção— eu tenho um vocábulario legal. Porque? Eu conheço <u>milhares</u> de— de palavras diferentes. Sei o que é que elas dize— o que é que elas significam. Eu sei como empregar os verbos. Eh— eu sei usar os verbos. Então eu tenho uma quantidade maior de— de palavra, de recurso da língua, para explicar o que eu estou sentindo, o que é que eu quero dizer. Então, e eles não têm toda— toda— vamos dizer assim . . . todas essas ferramentas. Eu tenho muito mais ferramentas do que eles.

> I do have that notion— I have a good vocabulary. Why? Because I know <u>thousands</u> of— of different words. I know what they say— what they mean. I know how to employ verbs. Uh— I know how to use verbs. So I have a larger quantity of— of words, of linguistic resources, to explain what I am feeling, what I want to say. So, and they don't have all this— this— let's say . . . these tools. I have many more tools than they do.

What I wish to convey here, through the uniformity of these responses, is not only the ways that members of the middle class emphasized a linguistic contrast that explained Rio's social divide, but also how deeply racialized their confidence in standard Portuguese is and how easily it allows them to justify social and racial inequality. Here another speaker clearly articulates her understanding of the connections between language and a person's place in society, using references to Europe to emphasize the racial and class contrasts:

> Eu dou importância à minha lingua. Eu acho que é uma língua riquíssima que a gente pode se expressar muito bem, contar histórias, e tudo mais. Agora não é o— hoje em dia o que é importante. Eu acho até que eu sou uma patrícia em Roma na época do Cristo. Eu falando Latin e a negrada toda já está falando italiano na rua, entendeu? E eu estou mantendo o meu Latin dentro de casa. [. . .] Eu vou falar a minha lingua, e eles vão falar a deles. A gente só tem que se entender no balcão de McDonald's. Eles do lado de cá e eu do lado de lá.

> I give importance to my language. I think that it's a particularly rich language through which people can express themselves well, tell stories, and everything else. Now it's not— what's important today. I think I am an aristocrat in Rome in the epoch of Christ. I'm speaking Latin and the black masses are already speaking Italian in the streets, understand? And I'm maintaining my Latin inside the house. [. . .] I'm going to speak my language, and they are going to speak theirs. We only have to understand each other at the counter at McDonald's. They will be on one side and I'll be on the other.

Beyond the obvious references to the production of race and class differ-ence, I am interested in understanding how this comment reveals the work that must be done to acquire personal whiteness and to pass it on to one's children. Constant vigilance inside the home is required to demonstrate and maintain one's status as "civilized." In an article describing protests against inequality and exclusivity within Brazilian shopping malls (see chapter 5), Brazilian academics Rosana Pinheiro-Machado and Lucia Mury Scalco (2014) quote a description of Brazil as a type of

> apartheid brasileiro que separa, como se fossem dois planetas distintos, o espaço de sociabilidade dos brasileiros "europeizados," da classe média verdadeira, e os brasileiros percebidos como "bárbaros," das classes populares.

> Brazilian apartheid that separates, as if they were two distinct planets, the spaces of sociability of Brazilians who are "European," the true middle class, and the Brazilians perceived as the "barbarians," from the popular [or working] classes. (Souza, quoted in Pinheiro-Machado and Scalco 2014)

This distinction thus upholds both class status and racial thinking: to be educated is not only to have had access to better training, cognitive development, and linguistic refinement, but also to value this knowledge, to practice and employ it in daily speech, and to demand its display from the people around you. (This recalls Heneghan's [2003] discussion of the whiteness conveyed through the display and proper care of white porcelain teacups.) Father and daughter Bernardo and Manuela could not imagine living amidst speakers like the youth that they had heard in my recordings. They described it as "pobreza Cultural" (cultural poverty, referencing high culture), that "se limita" (was personally restrictive), and noted that these were people who do nothing to improve themselves ("são umas pessoas que não trazem nada para acresentar como pessoa"). While the lack of access to better education for Cruzada youth was lamentable and explained much of what the middle-class families had heard, there was an underlying idea that such uncultivated and "primitive" speakers contributed nothing to society but their ability to engage in manual and service labor. In the current climate, they posed an even greater threat as the lack of opportunity and their own lack of self-discipline predisposed them to crime. These brutally honest reactions, given in the absence of the people they are speaking about, suggest how language helps solidify what is in Rio a staggering divide between people who live right next door to each other. With a quick and dismissive wave, Bernardo commented, "Ele falando todo dia ... deve ser uma coisa muito cansativo" (Having to listen to him speak every day ... must be very tiring). The social and racial distance between them, I was made to understand, felt insurmountable.

"WITHOUT CULTURE"

Brazilian anthropologist Cecilia McCallum laments that the difficulty of studying class in Brazil has produced a static understanding of the situation of middle-class Brazilians: "Class outside the favela comes across as a thing, rather than a social relation" (2005:101). My goal in forcing reactions to their poor and working-class neighbors has been to better understand how the position of Rio's middle class is built in constant comparison—racial, social, and linguistic—to those around them. This includes their daily contact with hired help inside their homes. It is not unusual for close bonds to develop between domestic workers and their employers; some *empregadas* spend nearly their whole lifetimes working for the same family (though this is increasingly rare). Yet despite the camaraderie and the closeness, the symbolic distinctions between them are often perpetuated through language. In her study of domestic workers, Donna Goldstein found this to be a near-constant:

> The idea that these workers are a bit stupid because they cannot "tell a story" or are not very articulate, or speak *errado* (wrong), is so common that I came to expect these comments in my conversations with middle- and upper-class Cariocas. The "innate" inability of the working classes to function in what is considered to be everyday, ordinary, middle-class society is a common theme among them, a complicated discourse in which their class privilege is implicitly protected as "natural." (2003:87–88)

In the interviews I conducted, these differences are rarely overtly racialized (as is true in Goldstein's description); they are thought to reflect class distinction and class discrimination, and they are euphemized in various ways. It is quite common to find that poor and working-class people are described as *sem cultura* (literally "without culture") or *mal-educado* (uneducated, ignorant, and impolite). Maureen O'Dougherty, in her study of São Paulo's middle class in the early 1990s, also stresses *cultura,* which folds together ideas of education, manners, refinement, and interest in high culture (2002:14).

Throughout Latin America and the Caribbean, racial ideas contrasting whiteness and nonwhiteness are often discussed as differences in the amount of "culture" one has, which implies not just varying levels of access to cultural refinement (which requires financial resources) but also an innate (in)ability to acquire culture in the first place (see, for example, Roland 2013). I appreciate Daphne Patai's translation of the term *gente sem cultura* as "people with no breeding" (1988:4), as it helpfully ties "culture" to racialized capacity, a connection more clearly articulated amidst the global popularity of eugenic theory in the 1930s (Dorey 1999). "Having" culture is not just about knowledge and familiarity; it is a way of being in the world, an "ease" (Khan 2011) and a sense of entitlement that comes from extensive cultivation, training, and constant effort (what some might call good breeding). Although few members of the middle class would acknowledge a connection between the training that they provide for their children and the development of their whiteness, Brazilians on the other side of the divide are well aware of the racialized incapacity for *cultura* (in the Brazilian Portuguese sense of the term) that they are thought to embody. One of Brazil's earliest and most visible black empowerment groups, TEN, or Teatro Experimental do Negro (Black Experimental Theater), engaged in various political activities but also focused its efforts on involving black people in *cultura fina* (fine arts), such as theater, in order to fight against the stigma of their "lack of culture" (Alberto 2011:164). And the youth whose conversations I played for middle-class listeners were quite aware of how they would be interpreted: "Vai achar que somos indiciplinados" (They are going to think that we are undisciplined).

The distinctions made between those "with" and those "without" culture discretely draw on racial ideas that link whiteness to "civility" and discipline and blackness to incapacity and lack, even as they do not neatly map onto phenotype. These distinctions and subtle euphemisms offer yet another example of how Rio residents can rely on racial difference, and can justify and explain racial hierarchy, without openly breaching the spirit of racial tolerance. How can Brazil be racist when race and color map so poorly onto class in people's everyday experiences and when it all boils down to differences of "culture"? To demonstrate the problems with looking only superficially at phenotype to determine race and ignoring the way that whiteness must be cultivated through cultural and linguistic practices, I return to my friend Gabriela, who sent me that email the day after she had been chosen to complete the longer form of the census. When I emailed to ask if I could include our correspondence in my book, she helpfully elaborated on the situation and all its complexities. I had asked what racial category the other members of her family had chosen and how her *empregada* (housemaid) had been classified. Example 3.5 gives her (emailed) response:

EXAMPLE 3.5: ANOTHER STORY ABOUT COLOR IN MY FAMILY

Eu respondi pela minha casa: papai [Gustavo], Guilherme [filho] e eu. Teresinha [a empregada] respondeu na casa que ela morava com o namorado. Eu não sei, mas Teresinha deve ter respondido "branca" e ela realmente é mais clara que nós, além de ser uma questão de status. Papai achou muito engraçado eu dizer "pardo" sobre ele também, afinal ele sempre fez parte da elite "branca" desse país. Aí eu digo para ele se comparar com os "brancos" que conhecemos, inclusive vocês [a autora e o marido] e ele concorda. Aqui eu sou branca, mesmo que tenha gente mais clara. Tenho olhos verdes,

I responded for my household: Dad [Gustavo], Guilherme [her son] and me. Teresinha [the maid] responded at her house, where she lives with her boyfriend. I don't know for sure, but Teresinha must have responded "white" and she really is lighter than us, despite it being a question of status. Dad thought it was very funny that I had said *pardo* [brown] for him too; after all he has always been a part of the "white" elite of this country. Then I told him to compare himself with the "whites" that we know, including the two of you [the author and her husband] and he agreed. Here I am white, even though there are people who are lighter. I have green eyes, cabelo liso castanho claro. Quem é branco mesmo (e temos muitos portugueses para provar) chamamos de "branco azedo," como leite quando fica ruim.

Outra história sobre cor na minha família. Depois da Copa do Mundo de Futebol de 1994, Guilherme tinha 4 anos e achava que Portugal, Itália, Alemanha, Camarões, Estados Unidos, era times de futebol. Ele não entendia que eram países. Eu peguei um mapa-múndi e mostrei a ele. Apontava os países, o Brasil e dizia que os times representavam os países. Aproveitei mostrei a África e disse: - Aqui é a África de onde vieram as pessoas pretas para o Brasil. Na hora ele falou: - Eu sei, meus tios Daniel e Bruno nasceram lá.

straight light-brown hair. Someone who is really white (and we have lots of Portuguese people to prove this), we call them "sour milk," like [the color] when milk goes bad.

Another story about color in my family. After the soccer World Cup in 1994, Guilherme was four years old and he thought that Portugal, Italy, Germany, Cameroon, the United States were all soccer teams. He didn't understand that they were countries. I got a world map and I showed it to him. I pointed out the countries and Brazil and said that the teams represented countries. I decided to take advantage of the situation and show him Africa, and I said: "Here is Africa, where the black people came to Brazil from." Right away he said: "I know, my uncles Daniel and Bruno were born there."

These two stories encapsulate much of what we need to consider when we think about race and class in Brazil. A maid can be white, and lighter-skinned than her *patroa* (boss), but because of her "status" this poses no threat. In academic terms, she possesses *brancura* (lightness), but she does not exude *branquitude* or racial whiteness (Schucman 2014:169; see also Sovik 2009:50). By "status," Gabriela means that she is not cultured, not well educated, not wealthy, and not a professional; she has light skin, but she is not racially "white," especially as she is an immigrant from the poor and stigmatized Northeast of the country (see Weinstein 2015). By contrast, a member of the former white Brazilian "elite" (this descriptor really better explains the status her father's family held in the past) finds it amusing when he is labeled brown by his daughter on the census, even though that does not accurately represent how he would describe himself. It does not bother him to be considered *pardo,* because his racial whiteness is made obvious to everyone through his daily practices and the spaces he occupies.

Gabriela's family's apartment, in the "old money" neighborhood of Flamengo, with a stunning view of Pão de Açucar (Sugarloaf Mountain) is filled with hundreds upon hundreds of old books, stacked in floor-to-ceiling bookshelves, and her father has a collection of tens of thousands of coins from around the world that point to his ability to travel and his global connections. His family's former status, his current "comfortable" financial situation (what Brazilians call having *condições,* or "means"), his own education and professional training as an architect, his hobbies, and his home all demonstrate that he is cultured, well traveled, and refined. He retains a membership, handed down through his family, to the Iate Clube do Rio de Janeiro (Rio's yacht club, founded in 1920, a private social and athletic club), which allows him gated access to socializing with Rio's upper-middle class. He does not require *brancura* (lightness), as the continual display of his culture, good breeding, and "bourgeois sensibilities" (Stoler 1995, 2002) help shore up his *branquitude* (whiteness). Basking in this comparative racial security, the whole family loves the story about Gabriela's son, Guilherme, believing that his two uncles were born in Africa.

This is a story that family members tell frequently because it successfully mocks the two brothers for their darker skin (which continues to be stigmatized in Brazil), but it cannot be considered really offensive, since it came out of the mouth of a four-year-old whose uncles possess no other trappings of blackness (phenotypical, cultural, or linguistic). To suggest that class, rather than race, explains their difference from the maid who worked for their family for twenty years is to miss the ways that racial ideas uphold (and work with) class status, even as they can blatantly ignore phenotype. Cultured, well-educated, and well-spoken professionals are readily considered racially white, even if they are brown. Their identities are built on the sharp contrast between themselves and their poorly educated immigrant maids, who work in the service economy and have illiterate family members in the "backward" region of the Northeast. These domestic workers do not possess or display the racial attributes of whiteness, even if they have the lightest skin around. Centuries of racial thought inform and explain the hierarchies in which and with which they all live, both within the comfortable space of the domestic sphere and outside it. Given Brazil's ambivalent relationship with racial mixture, personal whiteness is not guaranteed by skin color or ancestry, and it can sometimes be found lacking, especially when placed within transnational comparisons. Because of this instability, it must be cultivated and continuously displayed, usually through great effort and expense.

In this and the previous chapter, I have explored the ways that poor dark-skinned male youth and more privileged middle-class families temporarily lay claim to—or more diligently invest in—whiteness through the demonstration of linguistic discipline. In the following two chapters, I examine threats to one's whiteness that include fears of racial contact and the potential loss of personal whiteness. I take up a corollary to the social and racial imperative to whiten (and to display whiteness), or what we might also describe as the flip side of *boa aparência:* the need to avoid blackness.

In "Fear of a Black President," Ta-Nehisi Coates (2012) describes how U.S. experiences of slavery, Jim Crow, and segregation united white people under a banner of "unblackness." In chapter 4, I examine how middle-class Brazilians seek to limit their contact with blackness, which only sometimes entails a fear of black people. Within an urban context of heightened crime and violence, whiter and wealthier *cariocas* "read" bodies for signs of blackness in order to reduce their risk and ensure their safety. In the situations I describe, their acquired whiteness does not guarantee their protection; it is only their constant vigilance for signs of a lack of order and discipline *on other people's bodies* that seems to keep them safe. Blackness, and the lack of discipline and predisposition to crime and violence that it signifies, is no longer just a stigma or a source of national embarrassment; it is a source of potential personal danger to oneself and one's family and something to be actively avoided. Experiences of Rio's compulsory closeness have only increased over the past few decades due to infrastructural improvements that now allow residents of the distant suburbs to access Rio's wealthy South Zone and its famous coastline. Increased social mixture and the continued desire to ignore racial difference as a show of racial tolerance have meant that those who live on the white and wealthy side of Rio's staggering social divide resort to a complicated racial calculus of reading bodies for signs of cultural and linguistic difference. In short, race and class anxiety have increased as physical barriers that kept people apart have seemed to disappear entirely, especially at the beach.

4. Fears of Racial Contact

*Crime, Violence, and the Struggle
over Urban Space*

On my very first day in Rio, in June 1995, I accompanied my host mother, Maria, and her six-year-old daughter, Louisa, to a Festa Junina performance at Louisa's school. As we walked the few short blocks to her private school in Ipanema, through one of the wealthiest neighborhoods in Rio, Maria gave me a list of "street smart" tips to protect myself against crime: (1) do not wear fancy jewelry or watches in public; (2) separate your cash into different pockets; (3) look around you at all times and don't display any money on the street; (4) if someone tries to rob you, give whatever you have visible, and do not resist or look as if you are holding anything back, which might turn a robbery into a more aggressive mugging. When I visited the high school English class that Maria taught and asked about experiences with crime, I found that the vast majority of the young teens had been robbed or had someone in their immediate family who had been robbed (see also Zaluar 1993). As I spent more time in Rio, I learned that several friends had even been robbed or carjacked at gunpoint. Most of the middle-class people whom I met lived in fear of the gunshots between drug gangs and the police that sometimes flew from hillside *favelas* (shanty-towns) into the wealthy condominium buildings on neighboring streets.

These more affluent city residents were well aware that the dangers were far greater for the low-income Brazilians who lived in *favelas*. And yet daily life within a context of *compulsory closeness* (Veloso 2010), and in a city with staggering levels of peacetime violence, meant they never felt safe. Maria also explained that Hospital Municipal Miguel Couto, the hospital closest to Rio's (and Latin America's) largest *favela*, Rocinha, often hosted international doctors and residents looking for medical war training without having to go to a country currently at war. Public hospitals in Brazil were not known for their quality, but this one was different. To prove her point, Maria continued: "So when my doctor friend received the call that all mothers fear: 'Your teenage son has been hit by a stray bullet,' that's where she told them to take him." As other anthropologists working in Rio have documented, insecurity has become "a permanent feature of life" (Larkins 2015:11) and, especially among the middle class, there exists the sense that "crime finds virtually no boundaries" (Veloso 2010:260; see also Penglase 2007).

Over the past two decades, security in the city has waxed and waned, in particular with the advent of Unidades de Polícia Pacificadora, or Pacifying Police Units (UPPs) and the police takeover of some of the city's *favelas* (Doriam Borges, Ribeiro, and Cano 2012; L. Silva 2015), but middle-class fears and experiences of crime and violence are ever present. On more recent trips to Rio, I found that smartphones and similar electronic devices had become the most common target for theft, and new protective strategies had developed. In addition to separating money into different pockets, middle-class residents sometimes walked around in public with two cell phones: the trendy expensive one they used when it was safe, and an older one that they could give up in the event of a robbery. Teenagers were given strict instructions as to when they could and when they could not use their cell phones in public. Cell phone theft, particularly in front of private high schools, was a new fact of life, and everyone among the middle class knew someone who had had one stolen, if it hadn't already happened to them personally. Whereas wealthier *cariocas* (Rio residents) of the early twentieth century worried about cross-class and interracial contact due to their fears of contagious diseases (Caldeira 2000; Fischer 2014; Pino 1997), one hundred years later, interactions in mixed public spaces brought about fears of crime and violence. The racial ideologies that explained these fears have not changed. White, disciplined, and upstanding bodies were put at risk by contact with what were understood to be undisciplined and dangerous nonwhite bodies. Learning to read bodies for signs of their racialized capacity for violence was thought to be an essential life skill, particularly for urban residents.

In this chapter, I transition away from the previous two chapters, in which I discuss how both poor and middle-class Rio residents work to display linguistic and cultural practices associated with rationality, civility, and discipline. Whereas chapters 2 and 3 describe the social and racial imperative to embody whiteness, chapters 4 and 5 illustrate the related desire to avoid blackness. Middle-class *cariocas* seek to protect themselves in this dangerous climate through complicated strategies that include retreating to private spaces (which remain predominantly white) and engaging in the careful racial reading of the people around them. Having money (which can be euphemized as *condições*, or financial means) does allow them access to additional safety and protection. Just as they point to the failures of the Brazilian public education system to justify their huge investment in private schools, members of the middle class turn to private services whenever possible to ensure their own physical safety and the safety of their children. Almost all private condominium buildings have doormen and fences, and stores, private schools, and private social clubs are equally well guarded and gated (see my discussion of Teresa Caldeira's work [2010] in the following subsection). Some condominium building residents even split the added expense of a private security guard to watch *outside* their buildings, to increase the security of the public street that they are forced to share with nonresidents. At the end of the day, however, the retreat to private spaces and services in the population-dense neighborhoods of Rio's South Zone offers only a limited sense of security. As Brazilian anthropologist Leticia Veloso's concept of compulsory closeness suggests, "Rio's residents live both physically close to each other and symbolically segregated" (2010: 261).

To explain the racial logic behind this "symbolic" segregation, I draw on narratives taken from spontaneous conversations and interviews, as well as examples from popular culture and the media. I argue that in order to ensure their own safety in public spaces, members of Rio's middle class actively look for signs of blackness that they associate with danger and disorder. However, in a cultural climate where blackness is heavily stigmatized and feared but racial difference is not supposed to be noticed, attention paid to blackness cannot be overtly articulated.

RACE, CRIME, AND BODILY PROTECTION

My analysis of fears of crime and violence in urban Brazil in the late twentieth and early twenty-first centuries necessarily draws on *City of Walls* (2000), Brazilian anthropologist Teresa Caldeira's extensive study of the relationship between crime, citizenship, and city spaces. Based on hours of interviews with São Paulo residents across various social classes (from the working class to the wealthy), Caldeira describes a narrative genre, "the talk of crime," through which city residents attempt to impose order on their fears and experiences of crime and violence. This discursive practice, which includes jokes, stories, daily conversations, and constant repetition of the theme of crime, attempts to assuage their feelings of vulnerability. And yet, as Caldeira makes clear, the open discussion of fear inescapably generates more fear, which then transforms urban public spaces and threatens Brazilian democracy. To "feel safe," the middle and upper classes who reside in São Paulo build walls around houses, apartment complexes, and commercial

areas, limiting their physical contact with outsiders and increasing segregation and inequality. As Holston and Caldeira (1998) found in their study of
Brazilian democratization in the 1980s and early 1990s (after twenty years
of military dictatorship), a context of heightened crime and violence fed the
denial of citizenship rights to the poor as São Paulo residents voiced strong
public support for the death penalty (which has never been legal in Brazil)
and condoned extralegal physical violence by both private security guards
and the military police. As Caldeira explains, "The talk of crime works its
symbolic reordering of the world by elaborating prejudices and creating categories that naturalize some groups as dangerous. It simplistically divides
the world into good and evil and criminalizes certain social categories"
(2000:2).

In expressing their animosity for *bandidos* (bandits, robbers), few São
Paulo interviewees mentioned race explicitly. It was widely assumed that
criminals were *nordestinos* (people from the Northeast of Brazil) who lived in
cortiços (akin to U.S. tenements) and *favelas*. Social discrimination against
these marginal spaces was readily admitted, along with the view that "their
inhabitants, potential criminals, are people from the fringes of society, humanity, and the polity" (Caldeira 2000:53). Despite a long history of associations
between blackness and criminality within Brazil, none of the São Paulo residents whom Caldeira interviewed ever talked specifically about fears of black
people. In part, this may be because São Paulo has a smaller percentage of
black residents: 6 percent, compared to 12 percent in Rio de Janeiro.[1] And yet
historian Brodwyn Fischer analyzed hundreds of criminal court records from
the early to mid-twentieth century in Rio de Janeiro and also finds that race
was rarely mentioned explicitly. In the few situations in which race arose, it
was generally mentioned when racial expectations of class and behavior were
breached. Fischer suggests that lawyers, judges, and prosecutors instead "sub-
stituted racially tinged social language for open racism" (2004:48).

In her study, Caldeira attributed this lack of racial reference to her interviewees' desire to distance themselves from the racist thoughts that circulate
in Brazilian society, as talking overtly about racial difference was commonly
understood to be indelicate or impolite (and is now widely recognized as
illegal). She remarks, "The art of discriminating while denying it ought to be
full of ambiguities. But it is an art at which Brazilians excel" (2000:89). In
my own research, I found that one way Rio residents successfully juggled
discrimination and denial was through correlations. Thus, black people were
not so much all criminals, or even "naturally" criminals, as they were the
ones commonly committing crimes. To be concerned about dark-skinned
youth sitting near you on a bus or walking together in large groups at the

beach, or the situation of police routinely searching darker youth, became a matter of common sense and practicality. My discussion in this chapter seeks to reveal how connections that are global and centuries old continue to be made between blackness and danger and whiteness and civility. I argue that these connections are critical to middle-class perceptions of crime, violence, and urban contact—even as overt mentions of race are carefully avoided.

Illustrating what we might call the *art of correlation*, which allows one to mention race without mentioning it, by linking attributes and categories that carry racial meaning, one discussion of race with a middle-class family turned quickly to sports. "Torcida do Flamengo é uma bandidagem" (Flamengo fans are a bunch of criminals), the father, Bernardo, stated confidently. His daughter, Manuela, jumped in to explain her father's strong opinions on the subject:

> Uma coisa que a gente fica impressionada, meu pai então que adora futebol, ele não gosta do Flamengo. Todo assalto, arrastão, aí prenderam uns dez. Um tava com a camisa do Flamengo. [Risos da família] É impressionante. De tanto ele falar, você— sem querer, você presta atenção. Filmaram o arrastão. Pelo menos um tava com a camisa do Flamengo.

> One thing that we are always impressed with, my father who loves soccer, he doesn't like Flamengo. Every theft, *arrastão* (group theft on the beach), they arrest ten people. One is wearing a Flamengo shirt. [Laughter from her family] It's impressive. He says this so much that, you— without wanting to, you pay attention. They filmed an *arrastão*. At least one of them was wearing a Flamengo shirt.

Although the Flamengo soccer team boasts somewhere around 40 million devoted fans worldwide, it is very popular among *favela* residents and readily associated with dark-skinned male youth, and thus with criminality. Recently, Flamengo fans of all backgrounds have taken up slogans and celebratory chants aligning their team directly with shantytowns, singing "Favela. Favela. Favela. Festa na favela!" (*Favela. Favela. Favela.* Party in the *favela*!) when they win. Manuela's reluctance to make the connection between Flamengo fans and criminal activity provides evidence of how discrimination is supposed to be avoided. As she points out, it is her father who first articulated this observation, and though she works hard not to notice it ("without wanting to"), she is left realizing that he must be right ("There is always one"). Later in the conversation, Bernardo summarizes this stereotype in his own succinct truism: "Nem todo Flamengo é bandido, mas todo bandido é Flamengo" (Not all Flamengo fans are bandits, but all bandits are Flamengo fans). His family laughs, and no one objects. The damaging connection is thus firmly established, even as it is simultaneously denied. The

FIGURE 8. Youthful Flamengo fans. Their chosen soccer team often links them to residence in a *favela*, blackness, and criminality. Photo by Marcelo Santos Braga.

"fact" of the problem of race is asserted, in the absence of individuals who are intentionally racist (see also Bonilla-Silva 2014; Hill 2008).

This example illustrates how social discrimination works through correlation and rarely includes explicit racism, even as racial connections between blackness, criminality, and violence are recirculated. Bernardo did not say "Not all Flamengo fans are black, but all black people are Flamengo fans," nor did he publicly declare the stronger, more face-threatening stereotype that circulates widely in Brazilian society: "Most black people aren't criminals, but most criminals are black." As Fischer (2004) suggests, "racially tinged social language" that describes criminals in terms of their preferred soccer team, a team associated with shantytowns, poverty, and blackness (Beaton and Washington 2015), is used to link residence, class, and race with criminal activity. Here, soccer fandom—which is understood to be a personal choice for which one can reasonably be held accountable, rather than a "natural" or biological attribute—explains a proclivity for crime.

As this Flamengo example suggests, "The lie at the heart of the myth of racial democracy was not necessarily in the overwhelming prevalence of open and purposeful racial discrimination, but rather in the fallacy that social discrimination could be practiced free from racial implications" (Fischer 2004:59). The list of racially tinged language is long and often regionally specific. While Caldeira's informants talk about *nordestinos,* who may have light skin but are readily associated with racial nonwhiteness, poverty, and "backwardness" (see also Weinstein 2015), Rio residents more frequently talk about people *do morro* (from the hill, or from a *favela*) which includes both descendants of slaves and poor immigrants from the Northeast. Across Brazil, residence in shantytowns and discussions of *marginais* (marginals) imply strong connections to blackness (see, for example, French 2013).

While Rio residents rarely mention race explicitly, they cannot avoid the implicit racial logic that links whiteness to bodily control, cultural refinement, and law and order while connecting nonwhiteness with dirt, violence, and dangerous disarray. As I illustrate below, ubiquitous attention to bodily conduct is both informed by and compels fears of racial contact and potential contamination (Penglase 2007) and structures understandings of perceived danger. I turn now to describe how middle-class *cariocas* reacted to situations of crime and violence, how they were dismayed by their own relative lack of security, but rather quickly dismissed the vulnerability of *favela* residents affected by violence. Thus even as middle-class Rio residents can avoid direct mentions of race, their assessments of situations of actual (or potential) crime and violence rely on the presence or *immanence* of racial ideas that circulate through society and dwell within these interactions.[2]

LIVING WITH CRIME: THE MIDDLE-CLASS EXPERIENCE

Like São Paulo residents, middle-class *cariocas* did engage in frequent "crime talk"—relaying both personal experiences and stories that they had heard from friends—to process their experiences of living in a dangerous city. For example, Maria's in-laws Gustavo, in his early sixties, and his daughter Gabriela, in her late thirties, had been carjacked at gunpoint in front of their upper-middle-class apartment building in the old-money neighborhood of Praia de Flamengo. As I learned on my very first day in Rio, it is a common convention to give whatever is demanded in the event of a robbery, without resisting, in an attempt to ensure one's physical safety. On the night of the carjacking, Gabriela was therefore furious with her father, who quickly got out to give up his car, but refused to surrender his wallet because he had finally received his new driver's license two weeks prior and did not want to get a new one. (Dealing with Brazilian bureaucracy is not for the faint of heart.[3]) After the thieves took their car, Gustavo and Gabriela managed to attract the attention of a police car down the block, which followed the men but returned rather quickly and without success. Meanwhile, another police car had been following the assailants because of a previous car theft. This police car began shooting at the men, who dumped the car next to a police station and escaped by climbing a hill into the neighboring *favela*. Gustavo and Gabriela successfully recovered the car from the police station, though without the cartons of light bulbs they had purchased (which they assumed had been stolen by the police).[4] The next day, Gabriela explained the gunshot holes in the car by telling her seven-year-old son that they had hit a metal fence. This particular family had had multiple cars stolen from in front of their apartment building, as it was located on a central street (with a fabulous view of Pão de Açucar, or Sugarloaf Mountain) but near a dark corner.

Although Gabriela had previously told me this story, it came up again in the context of one of my group interviews, in which I played for their family the story of Feijão's near-robbery experience, presented in chapter 3. Although Feijão, a youth from the housing project in which I conducted research, recounted to his friends a time when he had almost been robbed, my middle-class listeners were more impressed with the language he used than with the tale he told. Even though Feijão talks about being a near victim of the theft of his watch in the neighborhood that they themselves lived in, middle-class listeners who did not know him, including the grandfather Gustavo, heard the voice of a criminal (Roth-Gordon 2009b). In particular, the slang that Feijão used to narrate this story for his friends in his community jumped out at them. Another research participant, unrelated to Gabriela and Gustavo, artfully "correlated" the use of slang and presumed criminality for me: "Gíria assusta bastante. . . . Não que toda pessoa que fale gíria seja bandido, mas o bandido com certeza fala gíria." (Slang is pretty frightening. . . . It's not that everyone who speaks slang is a *bandido* [thief, bandit], but a *bandido* definitely speaks slang.)

Looking carefully at the transcripts of Feijão's speech, Gustavo returned to the first line:

EXAMPLE 4.1: THE ONLY TIME I THOUGHT I WAS GOING TO BE ROBBED: FEIJÃO'S STORY

Aí **na moral,** sou doidinho pra ser— [. . .] O dia— o único dia que eu ia— eu ia ser— eu <u>senti</u> que ia ser roubado foi ali no Flamengo. [bairro nobre, cujo nome virou time de futebol]	So **seriously,** I'm a little crazy to be— [. . .] The day— the only day that I was— I was going to be— I <u>felt</u> that I was going to be robbed was there in Flamengo. [an old-money neighborhood, for which the soccer team is named]

In Rio, the slang term *na moral* (seriously) draws on its more traditional definition (literally "morals") to indicate that something was done well, helpfully, or urgently. Used in an utterance-initial position, the term serves as a pragmatic marker that commands attention, and Feijão likely chose this common slang expression to take up the conversational floor and tell his story. Reading this phrase aloud, Gustavo reflected on the event of their carjacking: "'Aí na moral, na moral'—that's what the guy who carjacked me said. He stuck a gun in my face, 'Na moral, na moral' (Let's go, hurry up), and I thought to myself, 'Que moral é essa?' (What kind of morality is this?)." Gustavo's reaction brings into sharp relief an observation made by sociologists Anthony and Elizabeth Leeds (1970) more than forty years ago: "The language of the favela slang is an impropriety to the stiff and stolid middle class which defines its users as *brutos* (rude people), *assassinos* (murderers), *ladroes* [sic] (thieves), *maconheiros* (pot-smokers), [and] *malandros* (people up to no-good)" (Leeds and Leeds 1970:261).

I had played this particular recording for Gabriela and Gustavo to get their reactions both to the language used, which I knew was different from the far more standard Portuguese that they spoke, and to the story itself, which should have evoked their sympathies given their own frequent experiences with theft. Yet their reactions (which matched those of other middle-class listeners) forced me to examine more closely what people said as they participated in these real and imagined encounters across race and class lines, as well as to think carefully about what they did not explicitly say. Slang speaking and slang speakers were readily linked to crime and violence and were interpreted as clear signs of danger. All of the social oppositions at play here evoke and are based on racial differences—criminals versus victims, slang speakers versus non–slang speakers, thieves versus law-abiding citizens. Yet race was rarely mentioned in these interviews, even as it was always there to help participants make sense of these common experiences of crime and violence.

"THIS IS NOT MY LIFE": MIDDLE-CLASS REACTIONS TO CRIME AND VIOLENCE IN THE *FAVELA*

Members of the middle class were aware that far more serious incidents of crime and violence occurred largely within poor suburbs and *favelas*. One day while recording in the housing project of Cruzada, my research assistant spotted an acquaintance from the community who happened to be catching up with someone he had met while they were both serving time in prison. One of them, nicknamed Tiger, had just been released, and "Frank" (short for his nickname, Frankenstein) was bringing him up to date on people they knew. Eager to present me with an example of serious slang use (readily associated with criminal activity), CW asked if we could record a brief bit of them speaking to each other. Their conversation was unlike any other I recorded or observed in Cruzada, as it engaged with a level of crime and violence directly experienced by only a small percentage of community or *favela* residents. And yet this short conversation captured a neatly wrapped package of the social "ills" readily associated with impoverished, marginalized communities. Here heavy, ungrammatical, and at times (even for my research assistant) nearly incomprehensible slang terms were used to discuss direct connections to drugs, teenage pregnancy, crime, violence, guns, gang warfare, and even murder. Although they agreed to the recording, Tiger and Frank's conversation was brief and at times stilted, as the two friends wanted to leave and go smoke marijuana. In the example that follows, my research assistant worked hard to keep them talking for a little longer, asking them a follow-up question about the death of a drug dealer they had just mentioned:

EXAMPLE 4.2: O KIKO FOI EM CASA MESMO? (WAS KIKO REALLY KILLED IN HIS OWN HOUSE?)

CW:	Vem cá— mas aí o Kiko . . . o Kiko foi [morreu] em casa mesmo?	Wait— but about Kiko . . . with Kiko it was [he was killed] in his own house?
Tiger:	Foi. Eu tive na Roça [a favela Rocinha] um dia antes. Aí, eu falei, "Qual é Kiko?" Aí ele tava com um oitão [arma]. Eu falei, "Qual é compadre? Amanhã?" Aí, ele falou, "Pô, Tiger, amanhã tu vem aí que a gente pega o neguinho lá na . . . no campo, tá ligado? Na cachanga dele." Aí no dia que eu vim brotar, mané, eu ia lá na terça-feira. Na segunda-feira o neguinho de manhã	Yes. I had been in Roça [the *favela* Rocinha] one day before. So, I said, "What's up Kiko?" So he had a big eight [gun]. I said, "What's up buddy? Tomorrow?" So, he said, "Damn, Tiger, come here tomorrow so that we can get the guy there in the . . . field, you know what I'm saying? At his house." So the next day I came [slang unclear], man, I was going to go there on Tuesday. On Monday the guy was sleeping in the

	dormindo com a filha dele	morning with his daughter
	é dentro da casa também.	inside the house too.
	Os caras tiraram, botaram	The guys shot, put bullets
	nas costas, dormindo.	in his back, while he was
	Aí chegou ainda vivo	sleeping. He was still alive
	no hospital.	when he got to the hospital.
	Não resistiu não.	But he didn't make it.
Frank:	Os cara lá, os	The guys there, the
	alemão [os inimigos].	Germans [slang for enemies].
Tiger:	Eu sei que é ele, mas tinha que	I know who it is, but I had to
	ter um parceiro pra fechar,	have a partner to close the
	pra pegar ele, mané.	deal, to get him, man.
	Pô, eu sozinho, vou	Damn, me alone, I ain't
	lá nada. Os cara tão	going there. The guys have
	de fuzil, amigo,	machine guns, buddy,
	na Roça.	up there on Roça.
CW:	Kiko também sabia dessa	Kiko also knew that this wasn't
	parada não era pra ele	a time for him to be
	ficar de bobeira.	fooling around.
Tiger:	Pô, não era pra ele	Damn, it wasn't time for him
	ficar de bobeira dormindo.	to be fooling around sleeping.
	Ele deu um tiro também no	He also got a shot at the
	neguinho também. Voltou e	guy. He turned around and
	brá, brá [barulho do tiro],	*brá, brá* [sounds of gun shots],
	tá ligado.	you know what I'm saying.

As the conversation continued, the reunited friends began to discuss their own situations, and they left open the possibility that they might work together in the future:

EXAMPLE 4.3: TÔ COM UMAS PEÇAS AÍ (I HAVE SOME STOLEN GOODS HERE)

Tiger:	Tô com umas peças aí.	I have some stolen pieces here.
Frank:	Tá com umas peças?	You have some pieces [stolen
	Porra, parceiro! Tu caiu	goods]? Shit, partner! You fell
	do céu legal, mané!	straight out of the sky, man!
	Tu caiu do céu!	You fell out of the sky!
	A gente vai conversar.	We are going to talk.
	A gente vai conversar	We are going to talk
	seriamente.	seriously.

Tiger:	Eu quero pegar o bagulho [arma]	I want to get the stuff [gun]
	chegar e brum [assaltar alguém]	go up and *brum* [rob someone]
	e tá ligado?	and you know what I'm sayin'?
	. . . Comprar uma motinha	. . . Buy a little motorcycle
	pra mim e ficar como—	for myself and chill—
Frank:	É isso, irmão!	That's it, brother!
Tiger:	Tô com um filé aí. Minha mina	I have a hot girl. My girl
	tá grávida também, mané. Três	is pregnant too, man. Three
	meses. Dezessete anos.	months. Seventeen years old.
	Maior— aquela mesmo que eu	Best— that same one that I
	falava que ia lá me visitar.	said was coming to visit me.
	Tá comigo aí ainda, mané!	She's still with me, man!
CW:	Não pode largar essa	You can't give up a
	mina de fé.	faithful girl.
Tiger:	Tô a fim de fumar	I really want to smoke some
	maconha. Fumar	marijuana. Let's go smoke
	uma maconha. Tô carente.	marijuana. I'm dying.
Frank:	Então a gente vai fumar. Tá	Then let's go smoke. Is that
	bom aí? [a gravação]	good like that? [the recording]
	Tá bom, tia?	Is that good, auntie? [to me]
Tiger:	Tá bom. Tá bom. Tá bom.	It's good. It's good. It's good.

While my research inside communities was a constant source of surprise and interest to middle-class friends and acquaintances, this particular conversation provided a window on a world that they were somewhat familiar with (from daily reports on television and in the newspaper) but also found akin to life on another planet. When I played this conversation for middle-class friends, I expected that they would find it shocking and disturbing. Stuck on the image of a father dying while sleeping with his young child, I thought they might also find it sad. Instead, for many, it was surreal and even patently absurd: "Não tinha nada que tá dormindo!" (He shouldn't have been sleeping!), Gabriela said as she burst into laughter. In a separate group interview, Manuela commented not only on the linguistic differences but also on the differences between her life and theirs:

> Enquanto eu tô preocupada com passar no vestibular, com namorado . . . com sair, com os amigos, eles estão preocupados com amigo, parceiro, pode morrer no dia seguinte que ele tem que se- Nossa! É uma coisa muito longe. Demais. Impressionante.

While I am worrying about passing the college entrance exam, with boyfriends . . . with going out, with my friends, they are worried about a friend, their buddy, who could die the next day that they have to— My God! It's very far from my reality. Too much. Impressive really.

Gabriela's brother summarized this reaction by responding simply: "A minha vida é outra" (This is not my life). Their social and emotional distance was notable, especially given their physical proximity. It became very clear that the people in this story were considered *bandidos* (criminals), and this meant that they could not, at the same time, be understood as victims, innocent or otherwise. As Gabriela commented flat out, "Eles matam eles mesmo . . . que se dane!" (They are killing themselves . . . Let them!). Here the referential content, which included talk about crime and murder together with a cryptic linguistic style filled with vague references to stolen goods and criminal activity, seemed to justify personal experiences of violence and even death. The reactions that I received gave clear evidence of "the ordinary letting-die practices" (Alves 2014:147; Smith 2016) that belie lives of privilege within a "racialized regime of citizenship" (Vargas and Alves 2010). And yet, through it all, race is never mentioned.

The two narratives of crime and violence that I have shared here bring into sharp relief larger questions of social order in Rio de Janeiro during Brazil's slow process of democratization. Which city residents were in danger and in need of protection? What happened when people from very different (but proximally near) parts of the city occupied the same city spaces? What kinds of behavior and language made public and private spaces safe or dangerous? And how did race inform the answers to these questions? For many members of the middle class, safety and protection were not understood as basic human rights applicable to everyone, in large part because these were not rights the state could guarantee for anyone. Given the presumed incompetence of the Brazilian state at all levels of governance, from policing, to the prosecution of crimes, to the very laws enacted, worrying about safety became a costly and time-consuming affair, and it was a job left in the hands of individuals. For the Brazilian middle class, then, the indignation of living in a city and country where extreme acts of violence— including murder—constituted daily life for some did not match the indignity of random acts of crime and violence inflicted on the decent, responsible people they knew (see also Alves and Vargas 2015). As I explain in greater detail in the following sections, one of the ways to protect oneself and one's family was to rely on an intricate system of reading bodies for signs of discipline. I turn to describe how these fears of crime, deeply ingrained beliefs about race and bodily discipline, and unavoidable racial contact played out on the most valuable and exposed of all public spaces in Rio: city beaches.

RACIAL CONTACT ON THE BEACH

In the mid-1980s, then-governor of Rio de Janeiro Leonel Brizola allowed buses to access the Túnel Rebouças, offering a still-long but more direct route from impoverished suburbs to the city's prime beaches. While South Zone beaches had been accessible to nearby *favela* residents who were also poor and nonwhite, infrastructural improvements brought about a radical change, as millions of Rio's most physically distant and socially marginalized residents were introduced to the most sophisticated and urbane parts of their own city and allowed to partake in the "delícias do mar," or "sensual pleasures of the sea" (Paixão and Leite 1996:72). These new beachgoers were not readily accepted, however, and their geographic and social differences were highlighted in the description of them as *freqüentadores além-Túnel* (beachgoers from beyond the tunnel; see Farias 2006:63). In 1985, drawing on the controversy and panic that ensued from this rift, a São Paulo cover band, Ultraje a Rigor, released the song "Nós Vamos Invadir sua Praia" (We are going to invade your beach), which became a megahit. The song title was meant as a double-entendre, suggesting first that a São Paulo rock group would take over the Rio airwaves. Its catchy title and refrain includes the expression *sua praia*, commonly used to mean one's space, scene, or set of interests, as in the saying "Não é a minha praia" (That's not my thing/scene). At the same time, the group offered a social critique of the growing fear of crime and violence on some of the country's most prominent beaches—all located in Rio de Janeiro—including Copacabana, Ipanema, and Leblon.

As historian Bert Barickman documents, ever since the 1920s, when it became fashionable to tan and sun oneself on the sand, these beaches have easily been recognizable as a "white space" (2009:200). Thirty years after buses began shuttling in North Zone residents and poor suburbanites, a sharp contrast remains between what these scenic beaches look like midweek and off-season, when only nearby residents with leisure time can afford to lounge on stretches of sparsely populated sand, and the frenetic scene of hot summer weekends, when up to hundreds of thousands

FIGURE 9.　On a winter day, South Zone beaches are sparsely populated with light-skinned and affluent city residents who treat the beach as their backyard. Photo by Marcelo Santos Braga.

FIGURE 10.　On sunny summer weekends, more remote city residents travel long distances by bus or metro to enjoy Rio's most famous South Zone beaches. Photo by Marcelo Santos Braga.

FIGURE 11.   Dark-skinned youth play soccer on the shore of a crowded Ipanema beach. Photo by Marcelo Santos Braga.

of scantily clad bodies turn the beach into a standing-room-only affair. The photos included here help illustrate ongoing struggles over social mobility and deeply naturalized patterns of inequality, as infrastructural improvements have not altered established patterns of residential segregation (Telles 2004:214) and rights to belong in the city's most privileged locations.

Because of the popularity of this particular song, the expression *invadir sua praia* (invade your beach) is still used when someone puts themselves where they do not belong (as in "Não quero invadir sua praia," meaning, "I don't want to intrude"). The song offers a nice introduction to how manners and "proper" bodily comportment came to stand in for concerns over new experiences of unavoidable social and racial contact and fears of crime and violence. The song's story is told through the perspective of poor shantytown residents who have recently been granted beach access. The full lyrics are presented (with permission of the copyright holder), in example 4.4:

FIGURE 12.   Police are often stationed at Arpoador, the part of Ipanema Beach known for frequent robberies and *arrastões* (beach sweeps). A nearby *praça* (city square), where metro and bus stops are located, makes this a popular spot for those traveling from more distant parts of the city. Photo by Marcelo Santos Braga.

EXAMPLE 4.4: "NÓS VAMOS INVADIR SUA PRAIA" (WE ARE GOING TO INVADE YOUR BEACH)

Daqui do morro	From here on the hill
dá pra ver tão legal	we can see so well
O que acontece	What's going on
aí no seu litoral	down on your coastline
Nós gostamos de tudo,	We like it all,
nós queremos é mais	what we want is more
Do alto da cidade,	From the height of the city,
até a beira do cais	to the ports
Mais do que um bom bronzeado	More than a good tan
Nós queremos estar do seu lado	We want to be by your side
Nós 'tamo' entrando	We're comin'
sem oleo nem creme	without oil or lotion
Precisando a gente se espreme	If need be, we'll squeeze ourselves in

Trazendo a farofa e a galinha	Bringing manioc flour and chicken
Levando também a vitrolinha	Taking also our Victrola
[fonógrafo ou toca-discos antigo]	[phonograph or old record player]
Separa um lugar nessa areia	Make space for us on the sand
Nós vamos chacoalhar	We are going to shake up
a sua aldeia	your neighborhood
[Refrão] Mistura sua laia	[Chorus] Get mixed up with our breed
Ou foge da raia	Or leave the ring
Sai da tocaia	Get out of your hideaway
Pula na baia	Jump over the fence
Agora nós vamos invadir	We are going to invade
sua praia	your beach now
[Refrão de novo]	[Chorus repeats]
Agora se você vai se incomodar	Now if this is going to bother you
Então é melhor se mudar	Then it's better for you to move
Não adianta nem nos desprezar	It won't help to despise us
Se a gente acostumar	If we get used to it,
a gente vai ficar	we will stay
A gente tá querendo variar	We're looking for a change of pace
E a sua praia vem bem a calhar	And your beach seems to suit us
Não precisa ficar nervoso	You don't need to get nervous
Pode ser que você ache gostoso	It could be that you actually like it
Ficar em companhia tão saudável	Being in such healthy company
Pode até lhe ser	Could even be
bastante recomendável	recommended for you
A gente pode te cutucar	We might poke you
Não tenha medo, não vai machucar	Don't be afraid, it won't hurt

In the music video that accompanied this song,[5] members of the band portray themselves as the invaders, but in order to stage their invasion (since they are racial and socioeconomic equals to Rio's South Zone beachgoers), they dress themselves in army fatigues. The video juxtaposes images of state violence and war (boats and tanks attack the beach from the ocean, band members jump out of a plane with parachutes) with scenes of "normal" and relaxing Brazilian beach life, including beach volleyball, swimming, and fraternizing on the sand. The military presence hints at the increasing use of actual military police to patrol city beaches: the large deployments of police at the beach on weekends are currently given names like Operação Verão (Operation Summer). In the video, the tranquil scenes of frivolity are disturbed not only by the rock group's physical invasion but also by the members' offensive behaviors (as described in the song). They bring the wrong foods, are accompanied by large dogs, and play loud music.

Race is never mentioned in the lyrics directly or overtly displayed in the video. And yet many subtle references run through both. During the verse that threatens physical contact and "poking," a blond beachgoer in a bikini is manhandled by a chimpanzee wearing a white T-shirt. The only visibly dark person on the beach is an older woman who feeds a parrot on her shoulder. This combination—a "black" woman with a parrot for a pet— alludes to a common expression (not directly quoted in the song) that people from the *favela* bring too much to the beach: "até o papagaio" (even a parrot). Bringing too much to the beach violates strong cultural taboos. One is supposed to live close enough that few supplies are required for spending time there; South Zone residents rarely bring towels. And one is supposed to know exactly what items are beach appropriate; a parrot marks one's ignorance and lack of sophistication, as well as breaching the divide between public and private spaces through the introduction of a house pet that is also associated with poor people.

The band does not intend to mock those who treat the beach as private space. Indeed, members of the middle class have long viewed Brazil's coastline as their own personal backyard, walking to and from home through crowded city streets in nothing more than a speedo. Reading, napping, and even intimate displays of public affection among couples are all acceptable. But displaying proper beach behavior requires a level of casual confidence and familiarity (Khan 2011), as well as the right cultural capital. In her study of Rio's beach culture, Patrícia Farias refers to this type of beachgoer as "o habitué ... aquele ser totalmente treinado nas técnicas corporais da praia" (the habituated ... one who is totally trained in the corporal techniques of the beach; 2006:121). To further humiliate the "new" suburban residents who do not demonstrate the right bodily habitus (Bourdieu 1984), the band members include in the lyrics their desire to bring along a record player, which was an anachronism even in 1985. In addition to the uncultured individuals interspersed with the tanned, trim, and fashion-savvy crowd, the band members open the video in their fatigues while rushing into a public bathroom. When one of them cannot get into a stall in time, the camera pans to urine streaming down his pant leg. Part of this play on crassness is no doubt important to their overall image as irreverent rock stars. Their group name, Ultraje a Rigor, is a play on words, taking the expression *traje a rigor* (dress clothes or formal attire) and changing it to *ul*traje *a rigor* (severe outrage or insult/offense). Their own intrusion into the physical space of Rio's coveted beaches and their violations of cultural norms while there are laminated on top of allusions to the "real" intruders that more privileged Rio beachgoers began to encounter in greater numbers in the 1980s. These new beachgoers were seen to be dirtying public space by their practices and their very presence.

The lyrics of the song display a nice blend of Fischer's "racially tinged social language" (2004:48). In the first line of the song *o morro*, meaning "hill," refers to the fact that several of Rio's largest *favelas* climb the hills close to the famous South Zone beaches. The group then sings "Mais do que um bom bronzeado, nós queremos estar do seu lado" (More than a good tan, we just want to be by your side), which implicitly suggests that even poor people of color should have the right to "tan" on the beach next to the white and the wealthy. Lines in the chorus tell listeners to "mistura sua laia" (get mixed up with our breed), and offer the tongue-in-cheek critique that this mixture might even be *saudável* (healthy) for the middle class. The *favelas* and suburbs where dark-skinned people live are still associated with disease and a lack of health (and health care). Ideas about blackness freely circulate in the absence of visibly dark-skinned Brazilians in the video and without overt racial references in the lyrics.

That this is possible, and also more culturally appropriate, should not be surprising: these are lighter-skinned middle-class Brazilians from São Paulo poking mild fun at other lighter-skinned middle-class Brazilians from Rio de Janeiro about their fears of contact with the poor black masses, who need not be present (and who, in fact, cannot be present) for this conversation to proceed. As in other satires of this type, there remains a central ambivalence. The song and the video suggest that people "with" culture should not be engaging in direct conflict or mockery of people "without" culture (as discussed in chapter 3). Then again, no one questions the validity or the significance of these opposing social and racialized categories. The intended addressees of this song are the white and the wealthy with their reactionary fears that social mixture necessarily leads to danger and violence. But the connections drawn between race and manners make poor black people the real targets of the joke and serve to justify their exclusion from desirable city spaces.

"WAR IN THE SAND"

Fears that increased cross-class and interracial contact on the beach would result in experiences of crime and violence were dramatically realized with the first televised *arrastão*. On the first hot summer Sunday in 1992, with reports of 600,000 people packed into the eight kilometers of sand shared by Ipanema and Copacabana beaches, several fights broke out among suburban youth. Panicked, middle-class beachgoers left the sand and ran to the sidewalk and city streets while a camera-crew filmed, and groups of youth stole bags left behind amidst the chaos. The event was nicknamed the *arrastão*, the term alluding to a large net swept over water to collect anything in its path. In an *arrastão*, a group of youth run down the beach grabbing valuables as if "sweeping" the beach, causing mass panic. As Geert Banck explains, "The metaphor of *arrastão* conveniently condenses the fear for a total clash, for something massive and violent that will sweep everything away" (1994:53). I have never personally experienced one, and I have heard many debates over how often these mass robberies actually occur and over whether fear of these male youth just drives a massive exodus from the beach. The experience of being among so many people crowded into such a small space between street and ocean adds to the anxiety, particularly for parents accompanied by small children. Regardless of how often they actually occur, *arrastões* have taken on a clear social reality, and videos, often filmed by spectators on cell phones, are frequently televised showing panicked beachgoers fleeing the beach while large groups of brown and black male youth take over the shore and police (sometimes brutally) drag off dark-skinned suspects.[6] As Patricia Farias (2006) notes, "the rare cases of collective violence (*arrastões*) signal, as critical events, the ever present threat of racial conflict."[7]

The Brazilian press continues to feed the desire to reflect on beach, body, and racial politics, its appeals couched within a broader concern over public safety. I now analyze one especially rich feature article on "Brazilian life" that was published in the respected Brazilian magazine *Veja* (a Brazilian version of *Time* or *Newsweek*), which catered to the well-educated and fairly politically conservative middle and upper classes. In a four-page spread filled with photos, maps, and a "slang" sidebar, authors Roberta Paixão and Virginia Leite (1996) rehashed in colorful detail the critical themes of crime, violence, and social or racial conflict and their connection to bodily comportment. Entitled "Guerra na Areia: O Subúrbio Invade as Praias da Zona Sul do Rio e Expõe o Muro Invisível do Preconceito" (War in the sand: The suburbs invade the beaches of the South Zone of Rio and expose the invisible wall of prejudice), the article invokes the expression *invadir sua praia*, made famous by the offbeat São Paulo rock band. Unlike those in the music video, however, the "war" images in this article are very real.

The very first photo showcases police officers with clubs patting down a line of brown- and black-skinned male youth who wait spread-eagled against the wall that separates the sand from the sidewalk. Images of invasion accompany the police violence: a photo taken from above shows a section of the beach that is wall-to-wall people, with hardly any space left to forge a path to the water (similar to the photo presented earlier in this chapter of a weekend summer day at Ipanema beach), and a computer-generated map captioned "Atalhos para o mar" (Shortcuts to the sea) foregrounds the new highways linking the suburbs to Rio's coast with colorful directional arrows. I include here an illustrated map, updated with the new metro lines, to show how public transportation now allows easier access to the city's most famous beaches, even for more distant city residents. Just a generation ago many suburban *cariocas* grew up without ever visiting the South Zone or going to the beach because of the difficulty of transportation and the distances involved.

Unavoidable social and racial contact pervades the remaining images in the *Veja* news spread. One large photo zooms in on the black face of an adolescent boy. A wide grin beams out from below mirrored sunglasses that reflect the images of the dark-skinned friends and family who accompany him. This happy image is labeled with the incongruous caption "José Marcos, Ipanema, 'A polícia só revista pobre'" (Police search only poor people). On the last page, a light-skinned mother described as an education specialist, who is accompanied by a friend and her children, quips "É muito tumulto" (It's a lot of confusion). A sidebar next to the photo of the mother with young children is entitled "O idioma da galera: Algumas expressões usadas pelos novos freqüentadores das praias da Zona Sul" (The language of the gang: Some expressions used by the new regulars of South Zone beaches). Together, the images link implied crime and violence and the necessity of police intervention with images of blackness, invasion, and signs of cultural and linguistic difference. Although I can only describe the images here, I am most interested in analyzing the article itself.

Like the rock group Ultraje do Rigor, the authors take an ambivalent stance toward the recent changes. On the one hand, they seem to mock the fears of privileged beachgoers unable to calmly share the beach:

> O contato entre peles de matizes tão diferentes gera um clima de instabilidade e atrito cultural. Um olhar atravessado, um esbarro ou uma simples guerra de areia bastam para detonar a multidão bronzeada: bate em fuga, histérica.

> The contact between such different shades of skin creates a climate of instability and cultural conflict. One sideways glance, a jostle, or a simple sand fight is all it takes to set off the tanned crowd: they run away, hysterical. (Paixão and Leite 1996:72)

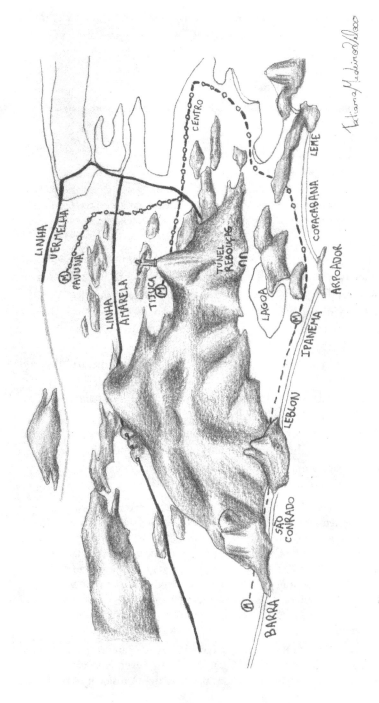

MAP 3.   Bus access through the Túnel Rebouças, new highways, and metro lines, all opened over the past three decades, have broken through the physical barriers that kept the South Zone sheltered, greatly reducing travel times and granting beach access to residents of Rio's "periphery." Artwork by Tatiana Medeiros Veloso.

And yet Paixão and Leite also explain this "war in the sand" by pointing to starkly different realities that, they suggest, have created dramatically different types of people. The opposing lifestyles of fellow *cariocas* that are offered as examples recall the distanced and often apathetic middle-class reactions I collected to situations of *favela* violence:

> Em areias [as praias] democratizadas à força, mauricinhos e patricinhas guardados em edifícios e condomínios cercados de grades por todos os lados convivem lado a lado com funkeiros acostumados ao dia-a-dia violento das favelas. É um choque.

> In areas [the beaches] democratized by force, privileged sons and daughters guarded in buildings and condominiums surrounded on all sides by fences now live side-by-side with funk fans who are used to the violent day-to-day reality of the *favelas*. It's a shock. (Paixão and Leite 1996:72)

The *choque* (shock) is not that some Rio residents live amidst such terrible violence, but rather that Rio's wealthier residents now share the beach with them. Along similar lines, the slippage between youth raised within a climate of violence and a youthful (more innate) disposition toward violence (suggesting that those brought up in a climate of violence must necessarily be violent themselves) is facilitated by discussion of the stigmatized and racialized youth culture of "funk" music. The authors carefully explain this different "culture" to their readers, emphasizing the relationship between funk dances and the drug gangs that control *favelas*, where territories are demarcated and deadly enemy battle lines are drawn. Funk music, gangs, and *favelas* are all subtle references to or stand-ins for blackness, though race is not directly mentioned here. Paixão and Leite interview both youthful beachgoers and hardworking ambulatory beach vendors to prove their point that violence is normalized for these individuals:

> "Se eu for sozinho para a Barra, saio com o corpo todo dolorido, cheio de hematomas," conta César Luís Coelho Lopes, 17 anos, freqüentador do Recreio dos Bandeirantes. Morador do Morro da Chacrinha, na Zona Oeste, ele só pode ir à praia nos pontos da sua galera. "Cada um tem uma parte da praia para ficar. É igual ao pessoal dos condomínios, que não se dá um com o outro," compara o vendedor Alex Santana Vieira, 19 anos, que mora na longínqua Vila Kennedy, bairro criado nos idos dos anos 60 com a remoção de algumas favelas da Zona Sul.

> "If I went alone to Barra [beach], I would leave in pain, with a body full of black-and-blues," explains César Luís Lopes, seventeen years old, who frequents the beach at Recreio dos Bandeirantes. A resident of the Ranch

Hill [the name of a *favela*], in the West Zone, he can go to the beach
only at the bus stops of his gang. "Everyone has their own part of the
beach to hang out on. It's the same as the people in the condominiums,
who don't get along with each other," compares the vendor Alex Santana
Vieira, nineteen years old, who lives in the remote Vila Kennedy, a
neighborhood created way back in the 1960s with the removal of some
of the South Zone *favelas*. (Paixão and Leite 1996:73)

The comparisons offered by the interviewees are intended to speak for
themselves. As in the crime narratives provided earlier in this chapter, the
gap between two starkly different realities should be obvious to the reader:
middle-class *cariocas* who live in condominium buildings may not know
their neighbors at all; they certainly do not worry about physical violence
should they choose to sit down next to the wrong middle-class crowd. There
are, of course, many ways that the beach is divided up by social groups
(Farias 2006), but "civilized" residents do not resort to physical violence to
negotiate their place in the sand. As the authors also emphasize, *favela*
residents have already been removed from these spaces—decades ago—as
their neighborhoods were destroyed and their residents were dispersed to
the far ends of the city to make way for upscale development. That they are
back, and bringing daily experiences of violence with them, is set up for
readers as clear cause for concern.

But, as in the Ultraje song, fears of crime and violence reveal more
entrenched concerns about interracial contact. There is the risk of physical
contact for exposed and vulnerable bodies and the dismay over aesthetics
and offending behaviors. Increased access to the beach means that those
from the far ends of Rio still travel hours each way to get to the beaches
that are mere blocks away for others. But their remoteness has shrunk with
the infrastructural improvement of new highways, and the authors remind
readers that these man-made wonders cannot improve upon the limitations
set by Mother Nature herself: the beaches aren't getting any bigger to
accommodate additional visitors, and in some places, such as Leblon, Rio's
bounty has shrunk, along with the shore. Less sand and more bodies means
increased risk of undesirable contact:

"Eu só venho à praia com amigos e, mesmo assim, abro bem a canga
para os suburbanos não se aproximarem muito," conta a professora
Gabriela Raphael Cabral, 24 anos, moradora no condomínio Alfa Barra,
a menos de 100 metros das areias da Barra da Tijuca. . . . "Cresci no
Arpoador mas nos domingos não vou mais à praia. Não se vê mais gente
bonita. Só dá suburbano," queixa-se o professor de educação física
Frederico Mello, 33 anos.

"I go to the beach only with friends and, even then, I open up my
blanket wide so that suburbanites don't get too close," says the teacher
Gabriela Raphael Cabral, twenty-four years old, a resident of the
condominium Alfa Barra, less than one hundred meters from the sand
in Barra da Tijuca. . . . "I grew up in Arpoador, but on Sundays I don't go
to the beach anymore. You don't see beautiful people anymore. You
only find suburbanites," complains physical education teacher Frederico
Mello, thirty-three years old. (Paixão and Leite 1996:74; see also Corrêa
2009:145)

This connection between beauty and the beach is not superfluous.
Beyond the imagery of war and invasion and amidst the fears of crime and
violence, there is much discussion amongst the middle class of cultural
"clash," experienced as a violent assault to their senses. Local beach deni-
zens must now listen to the loud sounds of funk music and *favela* slang;
they smell the foods brought to the beach to sustain those who cannot
return home for a proper meal; and they visually endure the breaching of
the latest fashion trends from *brega* (tacky) suburbanites (Paixão and Leite
1996:72). Indeed, the *Veja* article reads in part as etiquette or advice column,
in the vein of popular socialite and advice columnist Danuza Leão (see, for
example, Leão 1992). Offending behaviors include shaved heads, shirtless
men, mirrored sunglasses, Rastafari necklaces, big watches, the use of tanning oils, and the bleaching of body hair from head to toe (Paixão and Leite
1996:74). As the authors relay the insult of it all, here on Brazil's most
renowned beaches, in the birthplace of cosmopolitan fashion and style (see
also Banck 1994), they simultaneously draw on racial ideas that are centuries old and were well defined, especially during the colonial era. Then, as
now, privileged people believed that behaviors and bodily comportment
revealed inner, invisible (in)capacities for cultural refinement (Stoler 2002).
Their concern over providing a "civilizing influence" for the nonwhite
natives included "moral understanding of how to inhabit a place with propriety" (W. Anderson 2003:4). The *Veja* article is quite clear about the distinction between those with and those without culture (*sem cultura*):

Demonstração eloqüente da zoeira é o som ensurdecedor de seus
megarrádios sintonizados a todo o volume em programas de funk.
Doa a quem doer, repetem estribilhos ingênuos: "Cabelo, bebelo, bebelo,
elo, elo, elo." Roqueiros, amantes de MPB, jazz ou clássico escondem a
careta ou o sorriso de desdém. "Incomodados? Que se mudem," pensa a
galera.

An eloquent demonstration of the commotion is the deafening sound of
their mega-radios tuned in high volume to funk programs. Hurting

whomever it hurts, they repeat the ingenuous choruses: "*Cabelo, bebelo, bebelo, elo, elo, elo.*" Rock fans, lovers of MPB [Popular Brazilian Music], jazz, or classical music hide their grimace or smiles of disdain. "Bothered? Then move," thinks the gang. (Paixão and Leite 1996:73)

As McElhinny notes, racial discourse links lack of sophistication, cultural imitation, and racial inferiority, suggesting that nonwhites are "highly impressionable, unable to reflect on their own conditions, and capable only of mimicking those above them" (2005:184). These ideas are also well established within the history of Brazilian race relations:

> The pure Negroes will never be able, not even the most advanced representatives of the race, to be assimilated completely into white culture; their capacity for civilization—their "civilizability" so to speak, does not extend beyond merely imitating, more or less imperfectly, the habits and customs of the whites. Between the Negro's mentality and that of the Caucasian lies a substantial and irreducible difference which no social or cultural pressure, no matter how long it may be continued, can possibly overcome. (Oliveira Vianna's *Evolução do Povo Brasileiro* [1933], quoted in Degler 1986 [1971]:121)

Proper bodily comportment and the capacity for cultural refinement continue to be directly contrasted with a lack of discipline and an innate propensity for violence. This racialized chain—lack of culture, lack of discipline, lack of bodily control—explains why *cariocas* feel so comfortable reading bodies for signs of blackness that include, but are not reducible to, visual signifiers of race. Bodily conduct is seen to directly predict the capacity for crime and violence and the relative safety or vulnerability offered to others, as in the following intricate example from the *Veja* article, in which residents of Condomínio Alfa Barra predict acts of crime and violence based solely on one's choice of sandwich:

> Sob o ponto de vista deles [a classe média alta], a compra de um simples pão com mortadela transforma-se num ato quase criminoso: "Eles chegam de toda parte, compram, sentam para comer nas escadas da passerela e nos bancos, deixam copos e garrafas de plástico vazios pelo chão, sujam tudo, desrespeitam nossos filhos, que poderão ainda ser assaltados um dia. Depois, vão embora sem que nada lhes aconteça."

> From their [upper middle-class] point of view, the purchase of a simple bologna sandwich turns into an almost criminal act: "They come from all parts of town, buy food, sit to eat on the steps or the benches, leave cups and empty plastic bottles on the floor, make a mess, disrespect our children, who could even be assaulted one day. Then, they leave as if nothing had happened." (Paixão and Leite 1996:75)

In this example, the lack of financial resources and cultural refinement signified by the purchase of a bologna sandwich and the lack of manners associated with littering are directly connected to the violent act of mugging. People who cannot control what or how they eat disrespect their own bodies, just as they disrespect property, other people, and other people's rights to personal property. Various levels of rule breaking come together—nutritional ignorance and limited resources morph into robbery and assault that these youth commit without a second thought. In the beachless city of São Paulo, Caldeira also finds that symbolic distinctions are critical to linking residence in *favelas* with criminal behavior: "The list of prejudices against them is endless. . . . They are said to have broken families, to be the children of single mothers or children who were not properly brought up. Their behavior is condemned: they are said to use bad words, to be immoral, to consume drugs, and so on. In a way, anything that breaks the patterns of propriety can be associated with criminals, crime, and its spaces" (Caldeira 2000:79).

My intention here is to reveal how these "patterns of propriety" are steeped in racial ideology, even when they are not explicitly linked to whiteness or blackness. The authors of the *Veja* article lament that this type of comment is "preconceito em estado bruto" (discrimination in its purest form; Paixão and Leite 1996:75), but they have also laid the groundwork for their readers to interpret the increased presence of nonwhite male youth as a legitimate risk to their personal safety (and white flight a reasonable response) within the new context of racial contact on the beach. Through images, racially coded language, and the requisite disdain for racism, they suggest that "locals," those whiter, wealthier residents of South Zone beach neighborhoods, are within their rights to fear not only dark-skinned bodies but also the embodied cultural and linguistic practices that signify blackness.

BOA APARÊNCIA NA PRAIA: GOOD APPEARANCES ON THE BEACH

The Cruzada youth with whom I conducted fieldwork were well aware of the challenge their physical presence posed to the distribution of prime city spaces and of their own questionable right to belong in Rio's "exclusive internationally celebrated geography" (Banck 1994:50). In one group interview, two dark-skinned male youth commented that white people were moving farther and farther out of the city, to neighborhoods such as Barra da Tijuca, a wealthy coastal area associated with the "nouveau riche" located in the more distant West Zone.

EXAMPLE 4.5: A PRAIA VAI SER NOSSA (THE BEACH WILL BE OURS)

Blue:	Lá pro Arpoador [em Ipanema] tem um monte de macacos lá. [se referindo à gente negra]	Over by Arpoador [part of Ipanema beach] there are a ton of *macacos* there. [black people; literally "monkeys"]
Tiny:	Eles [os brancos] só vão ficar na Barra.	They [white people] are only going to hang out at Barra.
Blue:	A praia vai ser nossa.	The beach will be ours.

When I returned to live in Ipanema in 2014, there was indeed evidence of continued white fear and white flight, with some families moving out to the "safer" West Zone neighborhood of Barra. Yet Rio's real estate market had exploded in value, and the neighborhoods lining the beaches of the South Zone remained the province of the privileged. Geert Banck's earlier observations on the social significance of these spaces still held true: "The Rio beaches of Copacabana, Ipanema and Leblon are, nationally as well as internationally, a metaphor for a desirable way-of-life. They represent nature around the urban-corner, suggestive of health, sensuality, bodily beauty, hedonism, leisure and a sense of cosmopolitanism" (1994:50). A well-known beach sandals manufacturer named after the neighborhood and beach of Ipanema still aired advertisements for its colorful flip-flops with very light-skinned women tanning themselves on sparsely populated and scenic Rio beaches.[8]

While local residents still regularly met up at the beach with young children in tow, it was clear that the beach was no longer solely "theirs," nor was it always considered a part of their safe backyard. I was warned many times not to take my family to the beach on Sundays once summer was under way. I also received various new lessons in "beach smarts": any grouping of more than three dark-skinned males was considered suspicious, and when a large number walked together along the shore, I was supposed to ignore them and watch the sand, as this large group was likely a distraction strategy for a smaller group that would come in and steal bags, wallets, and cell phones from behind. On summer weekends, some middle-class families with children chose to leave the city to vacation in beach homes up the coast or retreated to private social clubs that had pools and playgrounds within well-guarded walls and admitted only paying members and their guests. To join these clubs, new members often had to pay a large deposit, or *luva*, as well as a monthly fee, and they generally had to be recommended by current members. One printed advertisement for an expensive social and athletic club located between São Conrado and Barra, farther into the West Zone, played on fears of dangerous social and racial contact in order to appeal to the upscale readers of the newspaper's entertainment guide:

> Imagine-se, agora, num sábado ou domingo de sol, com sua família, a caminho de qualquer praia da Zona Sul! Imaginou? Possibilidade de arrastões, areias e águas sujas, falta de espaço, de estrutura e muita, mas muita gente sem o mínimo de educação. Verdade ou exagero? Dá vontade de não sair de casa, não é verdade?

> Imagine yourself, now, on a sunny Saturday or Sunday, with your family, walking to whichever beach in the South Zone. Did you picture it? Possibility of *arrastões*, dirty sand or dirty water, lack of space, lack of infrastructure, and lots, but lots, of people without the least bit of education or manners. Truth or exaggeration? It makes you just want to stay home, doesn't it?

The ad bids readers to ask themselves, "O que eu e minha família merecemos?" (What do my family and I deserve?). The answer is no longer easy access to Rio's most famous beaches, since these beaches are now accessible to all. Privacy, security, and exclusivity are now offered only through private social and athletic clubs, such as the advertised Costa Brava Clube, which boasts that its members are "uma juventude alegre, festeira, saudável e bonita" (a group of young people who are happy, festive, healthy, and beautiful). To satisfy clients' continued desire for "nature around the urban-corner," this club's main attraction is a pool filled with ocean water amidst the jagged coastal rocks into which the pool has been built. Rio's coastline remains its crown jewel, yet it is now shared by literally hundreds of thousands of city residents who (this ad suggests) are not the desirable mix of carefree, healthy, and beautiful. Here again, racial difference and fears of racial contact are indicated only implicitly, through coded references to *arrastões* and people without manners (the new beachgoers) versus the old guard (and still-current beach condominium owners), which includes healthy, beautiful people.

What I am calling *boa aparência na praia* (good appearance on the beach) requires the cultural capital to know exactly which behaviors are appropriate, even as the rules of proper etiquette are nuanced and ever changing. The term *farofeiro* has long been used to describe poor dark-skinned youth who come from distant suburbs to enjoy a day at the beach (Farias 2006; O'Dougherty 2002). Based on the ubiquitous Brazilian side dish of *farofa*, made of manioc flour, which is commonly sprinkled on meat, chicken, beans, and rice, the term allows beach regulars to roll their eyes in disgust at both the inappropriateness of bringing elaborate homemade meals to the beach and the compulsory closeness (Veloso 2010) they now experience with uncontrolled bodies that roughhouse or even fight within these close quarters, sprinkling themselves and others with grains of sand (Freeman 2002). *Farofeiros* lack personal discipline. And yet, given rising prices and the increasing financial difficulties of the middle class, it is now far more common to see even more affluent families who live near the beach bringing coolers with drinks from home and some light snacks in what has been described as *farofa chique* (chic *farofa*).[9] Other differences in (in)appropriate bodily practices rest on distinctions of proper time and place: one middle-class friend of mine commented on the tackiness of a girl applying sun-bleaching products right next to us in public, but did admit that she uses similar hair-bleaching products in the privacy of her own home.

Beyond notions of what constitutes proper public-versus-private distinctions (Gal 2005), cultural practices recursively play out notions of distance and belonging. That is, even as beachgoers occupy the sand together, certain behaviors serve as reminders that some have traveled great distances while others live nearby. Thus much is made of the distinction between eating light snacks and hearty meals of chicken and *farofa*. Cultural practices and notions of "propriety" have long been used to restrict access to privileged city spaces. Prior to the 1940s, it was not just distance and difficult, expensive commutes that kept residents of the North Zone and suburbs, where 70 percent of people of color lived, from prestigious beaches such as Copacabana. Whereas local residents in the 1920s and 1930s walked to the beach in their bathing clothes, as they continue to do today, laws forbid passengers from riding in buses or common vans (*bondes*) dressed in bathing attire, and various proposals to set up places to change at South Zone beaches were never realized (Barickman 2009:201–3). More recently, these same rules were invoked when South Zone stations opened on the metro line in the late 1990s. As Freeman notes:

> When the first Copacabana station was opened officials sought to preserve the "civilized" and controlled atmosphere that has been the metro's trademark, and tried to discourage beach goers. The newspaper reported: "The rules for bathers who intend to use the subway are clear and not much different from those already in effect for other passengers. It is prohibited to ride without a shirt, in a bathing suit, or with wet clothes. Passengers wearing sandals, with sand on their bodies or carrying surf boards will not be admitted. Metrô Rio [the subway company] does not expect any damage to the trains with the arrival of the new passengers" (Domingo, 1998). (2008:544)

Even while the company initially enforced these rules of "civility," the metro took years to start up Sunday service, which would take nonwhite city residents to the beaches rather than taking white workers to the city center, as on weekdays. Schedule restrictions, together with restrictions regarding proper attire, show how infrastructural barriers and symbolic segregation often go hand in hand. As yet another example, South Zone neighborhood associations sought to restrict north-to-south movement by any means possible:

> Em Ipanema, o presidente da associação de moradores, David Catran, 47 anos, nascido e criado no bairro, sugere que seja feita uma triagem nos pontos da partida dos ônibus dos subúrbios. "A polícia tem de fazer uma separação e só deixar que entrem nos ônibus as pessoas de bons modos."
>
> In Ipanema, the president of the local residents' association, David Catran, forty-seven years old, born and raised in the neighborhood, suggests a triage at the bus stops back in the suburbs. "Police have to separate passengers and let only people with good manners enter the bus." (Paixão and Leite 1996:75)

The deeply racialized connotations of "good manners," the implications of surveilling those who must board buses to get to the beach in a geographically segregated city, and the implicit fears of race and class contact in public spaces all come together in this one statement, justifying exclusion and naturalizing belonging in prime (white) city spaces.

While this type of triage was not unheard of in the 1990s when the new highways opened (Francisco 2003; Penglase 2007), it touched off a nation-wide debate in 2015 when temperatures soared into the forties (well over one hundred degrees Fahrenheit) and reports of organized beach thefts and the panicked fleeing of South Zone residents and tourists again became commonplace. In addition to promising the support of one thousand police officers on patrol, police began stopping and boarding buses to search "incoming" passengers. Minors and anyone without a shirt, shoes, an ID, or enough money for return bus fare could be pulled off the buses and taken into custody. While youth activists, and the courts, agreed that it was illegal to stop and detain youth who had not been caught committing a crime, the practices continued.[10]

These recent conflicts over increased access to Rio's world-famous beaches illustrate "an entanglement of democracy," in James Holston's words, as urban citizens claim rights (and contest their exclusion) and the state struggles to curtail these rights and differentiate among its citizens: "The insurgence of urban democratic citizenships in recent decades has indeed disrupted established formulas of rule. . . . The result is an entangle-ment of democracy with its counters, in which new kinds of urban citizens arise to expand democratic citizenships and new forms of urban violence, inequality, impunity, and dispossession erode them" (Holston 2011:337). With the relative absence of public safety, and within contexts of unprecedented social mixture, *cariocas* struggle to make sense of democratic ideals suggesting that the beach should be open to all, even as it has long been the playground of the few (Carvalho 2007; Farias 2006; Francisco 2003; Freeman 2002, 2008). The resulting discussions and policies rarely mention race explicitly, even as talk about crime, violence, and rights to occupy urban spaces are replete with racial meaning. Fears of blackness intricately bind notions of disorderly conduct to phenotypical features, such that one highly presupposes the other.[11] In the following chapter, I discuss how perceptions of blackness and danger go beyond the public struggle for space represented by the *arrastão*, and beyond the widespread fear of robbery and physical vulnerability, to include situations in which privileged youth choose to socialize with poor, dark-skinned community residents, threatening the embodied whiteness they have thus far inherited and cultivated.

5. Avoiding Blackness

The Flip Side of Boa Aparência

New contestations over city spaces erupted in late 2013 and again in early 2014 when *rolezinhos* (literally "little strolls" or "get-togethers") occurred in several major Brazilian cities. Described by one blogger as "o occupy da periferia," or "the Occupy Movement of Brazil's periphery,"[1] *rolezinhos* featured poor and dark-skinned youth congregating inside shopping malls, a form of (mostly) peaceful protest coordinated through social media and designed to highlight their ongoing exclusion from these semiprivatized leisure spaces. Although very few robberies were reported in any of these events, the scenes of dozens to hundreds of youth "occupying" these privileged locales prompted panic: stores closed their doors, shoppers fled, and police were called in. (This last phase was not always peaceful.) Brazilian courts and the press debated the limits of permissible peaceful protest in these semiprivatized spaces. Public debates over the meaning of these events featured opposing perspectives on social inequality: either the protests were justifiable, due to the intentional exclusion of poor and black youth from these spaces (and the heavy surveillance they experienced once inside), or the incidents had nothing to do with discrimination and were just another example of youthful misconduct. As one political blogger posted:

> Não custa repetir o óbvio, sempre tão ignorado nesse país: não há preconceito algum quando um indivíduo, um casal, um pequeno grupo frequenta o shopping. O problema, que não tem nada a ver com cor ou renda, começa apenas quando o comportamento é inadequado para o local, especialmente com uma horda de centenas de arruaceiros.

> It doesn't hurt to repeat the obvious, which is always so readily ignored in this country: there isn't any discrimination when one individual, a couple, or a small group goes to a shopping mall. The problem, which

has nothing to do with color or income, begins when the behavior is inadequate for the space, especially in the case of a horde of hundreds of hooligans.[2]

Although this blogger explicitly denies the significance of race or class in these protests, his attention to numbers highlights the fact that the wealthiest malls rarely had more than a few dark-skinned patrons at a time. As anthropologist João Costa Vargas notes, "*Rolezinhos* test the degree to which Brazilian spaces of relative affluence are able to absorb large concentrations of Black people" (2014:10). What *rolezinhos* and the debates surrounding them made painfully clear was that high-end shopping malls sold not only consumer goods and services to primarily whiter and wealthier city residents, but also, more critically, *escape* from undesirable social and racial mixture (Caldeira 2014).

In this chapter, as in chapter 4, I wade into these fears of dangerous social and racial contact, and I propose a converse proposition to the racial imperative embedded in requests for *boa aparência* (as discussed in chapter 2): not only are Brazilians expected to demonstrate whiteness, but they are also tacitly encouraged to avoid contact with blackness. This bold assertion—that Brazilians fear that blackness tarnishes whiteness—may present an affront to some Brazilian's experiences of "cordial" race relations, and it seems to dangerously disregard the belief in, or the dream of, racial democracy (Fry 1995–96, 2000; Sheriff 2001). It also flies in the face of an even longer history of promoting racial miscegenation, both within Brazil and across Latin America (Andrews 2004; Skidmore 1974). Strict segregation and the belief that black and white people should not interact seem a very "North American thing." And yet one of the central premises of this book is that signs of blackness and whiteness circulate independently of light-skinned and dark-skinned individuals.

What I argue, based on an analysis of interactions across Rio's sharp social and racial divide, is that a fear of blackness is not the same as, or reducible to, a fear of black people. Indeed, the idea that blackness is to be avoided is much more in keeping with Brazil's long history of encouraging individuals to *melhorar a raça* (improve the race) and "whiten" future generations through assimilation and miscegenation. As I discuss further, it is also in line with long-standing insecurities over Brazilian whiteness (E. Nascimento 2007; Pinho 2009; G. Ramos 1995). Indeed, understanding the avoidance of blackness as a pillar of Brazilian racism may help us think through what sociologist Edward Telles describes as the "enigma" of the coexistence of inclusiveness and exclusiveness within Brazil (2004:6). I suggest that racial mixture can be tolerated (both within individuals and within

Brazilian society) as long as blackness is avoided. I turn here to explore how conflicts over social mixture, especially in urban spaces, are, at heart, racialized fears about a potential "descent" into blackness, illustrating what I call the flip side of *boa aparência.*

THE STIGMA OF BLACKNESS

Fears of racial mixing and concerns about distancing oneself from the presumed dangerous influence of blackness remain racial ideas more readily associated with the North American context. Peter Fry (1982) noted years ago that whereas Brazil celebrated *feijoada* (black bean stew) and *samba,* the food and dance of Afro-descended peoples, as iconic of Brazilian culture, in the United States, soul food and other black traditions were often relegated to "black culture." This comparison does not hold across the board, as the trajectories of jazz, rock 'n' roll, and other African American traditions that have "crossed over" illustrate (Roediger 2003; Smitherman 1998),[3] but a stricter separation of white and nonwhite peoples and cultures has been a long-standing cornerstone of North American racial ideology. In the United States, state and local legislation limited social interaction among whites and nonwhites through Jim Crow laws, which mandated racial segregation in public facilities from 1876 to 1965 in many southern states, and through antimiscegenation laws, which were enforced in sixteen states until as recently as 1967.[4] Although legal restrictions on racial interaction were removed in Brazil at the end of slavery in the late nineteenth century, whites in the middle to upper classes have few opportunities for significant contact with darker-skinned people outside service relationships (Cicalo 2012a, 2012b), due in large part to patterns of residential segregation (Telles 2004:214). And though interracial marriages remain more common in Brazil than in the United States, white-black marriages occur less frequently than same-race unions and white-brown marriages (which include people identifying as *pardo* on the census; see Telles 2004:187). Racial purity has never been an essential (or possible) tenet of whiteness within the history of Brazilian race relations, and yet social contact with blackness has always been considered risky.

Earlier studies of Brazilian race relations occasionally mentioned the unmentionable (and "un-Brazilian") aversion to interracial friendships or contact in public: "There are many situations in social life where white people refuse to be seen with Negroes. In such public places as high-class hotels, restaurants, or casinoes [*sic*], fashionable clubs, and dances, Negroes are not desired, and there are few whites who dare to introduce Negro friends or relatives into such places" (Willems 1949:404). Along similar lines, Roger Bastide and Florestan Fernandes reported: "O negro ainda é, para muita gente, um ser inferior, indigno de se acotovelar com o branco e de disputar na sociedade a consideração de seus semelhantes" (The Negro still is, for many people, an inferior being, unworthy of rubbing elbows with the white and of disputing with him in society as a peer; 1959:303). Even unequal service relationships showed signs of whites' fears of contact with blackness. Examining the household practices of elite Rio families in the nineteenth century, Sandra Graham (1988) reported that black wet nurses were seen as better suited to the tropical climate, but often viewed as too risky to hire due to the potential contamination of small children through the intimate practice of breastfeeding. Despite the common practice of hiring a *mãe preta* (mammy; literally "black mother"), there were widespread fears of her possible connections to disease and her ability to negatively influence her young charges (Otovo 2016:39–41). In a study of employment advertisements seeking white domestic workers in the mid-twentieth century, Oracy Nogueira (1942) found that one reason given for the explicit racial preference was to avoid contact between black maids and white children.

Within Brazilian racial ideology, the practice of *embranquecimento* (whitening) emphasizes the inferiority and undesirability of blackness as the nation, families, and individuals needed to racially "improve" through their connections with whiter people and the acquisition of "whiter" behaviors (Nogueira 1959:13; Telles 2004:158; Vargas 2011:264). As some families racially "improve," however, others necessarily lose status through their contact with blackness. As one white man from Minas Gerais explained to anthropologist Marvin Harris in the 1950s, after an interracial marriage between a black man and a white woman, "he [the husband] made himself better in the exchange. He whitened himself. The white was more stupid. She dirtied her family while cleaning his" (quoted in M. Harris 1952:54). It is still common for whiter and wealthier people to admit that while their children's friendships with specific darker-skinned individuals were fine, the choice of a black marriage partner would not be welcomed. "Eu ia ficar triste porque eu sei que os meus netos iam passar por problemas" (I would be sad because I know that my grandchildren would suffer), commented one of the light-skinned middle-class mothers I interviewed. Her husband said that while he personally would not mind his children choosing a darker-skinned partner, as he felt they had every right to do so, he had no doubt that his ears would be filled with the comments of friends and family, "Ah tua filha arrumou um negão!" (Oh, your daughter found herself a big black guy!). *Baixar o nível* (marrying down; the expression also implies a lack of culture or manners) is therefore not only a question of social class within Brazil but also a failure to "avoid the dark" (D. Davis 1999).

Marriages and the birth of children, in particular, carry the potential to jeopardize a family's racial status (Hordge-Freeman 2015). White boys used to be teased that they would marry a "Negro" when they grew up (Nogueira 1959:15), the joke emphasizing the undesirability of this possibility, and expressions such as "born on a dark night" or born from a "barriga suja" (dirty womb) can still be invoked when a baby is born darker than expected (Baran 2007:387). Sociologist Elizabeth Hordge-Freeman (2015) documents the extensive practices one pregnant woman in Bahia engaged in throughout her pregnancy, from staring attentively at pretty white people in *telenovelas* (soap operas) to avoiding looking at black people on the street, in the hopes of improving the chances that her child would be born whiter (38–39). Even within this poor, mostly nonwhite community, mothers were expected to produce lighter progeny, and they frequently examined each other's children for what they considered to be undesirable signs of blackness.

Beyond these major life events, when new members are introduced into a family, the middle-class parents I knew expressed significant concerns about their inability to control the social contacts made by their teenage children. Youth were far more likely to initiate friendships that crossed race and class divides, which also required navigating across neighborhoods and through different city spaces. Wealthier teenagers still spent most of their days in well-guarded private spaces, including private schools and extracurricular activities (such as sports and English classes) that involved significant participation fees and restricted access. They also frequently socialized either in private homes or restaurants and clubs that required money to enter. By contrast, the poor dark-skinned youth with whom I conducted research lived in what was euphemistically called a *comunidade*, or "community," and they most often hung out in public spaces, including the street in front of their housing-project buildings. Their apartments were smaller; they did not have their own bedrooms in which to entertain friends away from the gaze of parents; and they very rarely had spare cash to spend on food or drinks purchased in private, sit-down establishments. As this chapter details, the shopping mall, which did not require financial acts of consumption, was one other city space (besides public beaches) that allowed for a small amount of social contact, particularly among youth. The intentional and unintentional tendencies for whiter and wealthier families to avoid contact with blackness was thus severely compromised—and often brought into sharp focus—by teenagers' heightened mobility and independence.

RACIAL TRANSGRESSIONS

Perhaps surprisingly (or not), it was not only the "haves" who worked hard to uphold and maintain social and physical boundaries within the city. The dark-skinned male youth whom I got to know in Cruzada, a poor housing project located on incredibly expensive real estate in the upscale neighborhood of Leblon, most often discussed race and class differences through the provocative figure of the *playboy*. The *playboy*, a term I italicize since it does not have the same meaning in English, refers to a whiter, wealthier male youth commonly mentioned in the lyrics of Brazilian hip-hop in the 1990s (see chapter 6 and Pardue 2008). The term was not a positive one. It described someone who lived a life of privilege; was overly invested in his own appearance, showing off name-brand clothing and expensive commodities; and who looked down on the poor, dark-skinned youth who lived in "communities." The term was also used by Cruzada youth to describe wealthier youth from nearby condominium buildings who had formed friendships and spent significant time in their neighborhood. The negotiation of these relationships, and reactions of others toward them, brought race, class, and residential differences into sharp relief. While infrequent, this type of social interaction among youth received significant media exposure in both domestic rap songs and one popular television series, *Cidade dos Homens* (City of Men), a spin-off of the internationally acclaimed film *City of God*. Within rap songs, politically conscious rappers who lived in these stigmatized neighborhoods not only criticized these more privileged youth but also called out their peers when they tried to imitate the appearance and habits of the *playboy*. Songs such as "Pare de Babar" (Stop Sucking Up), by MV Bill (1999), foregrounded their disapproval of both the desire for whiteness and the avoidance of blackness that was frequently associated with friendships with *playboys*:

EXAMPLE 5.1: "PARE DE BABAR" (STOP SUCKING UP)

Preto se achando amarelo,	Blacks calling themselves yellow,
mulato, branco, marrom bombom	mixed, white, brown chocolate
Puxando o saco dos playboys que	Sucking up to the *playboys* that
aparecem na televisão	appear on television
Se liga preto por fora,	Pay attention black on the outside,
branco por dentro	white on the inside

Eu falo a verdade, você me ironiza,	I speak the truth, you make fun of me
eu não me arrependo	I don't regret it
Você não se informa,	You don't inform yourself,
não tem consciência,	you don't have consciousness,
não sabe de nada	you don't know anything
E fica como tapete,	And you become a doormat,
cachorrinho para a playboyzada	a lapdog to the *playboys*
Na danceteria os playboys todos	At the dance club the *playboys* are all
arrumados	dressed up
E o otário sem dinheiro,	And the idiot without money,
desarrumado, parado do lado	disheveled, standing to the side
Preto ignorante pensando que é	Ignorant black thinking that he is
moreninho	light brown
Só porque as putas falaram que	Just because the whores told him that
ele é um preto bonitinho	he is a cute black
Cada vez mais idiota ele tá ficando	He is becoming more idiotic each time
Até a prancha dos playboys ele tá	He is even carrying the *playboys'*
carregando	surfboard
Ele está sendo mais usado que a	He is being used more than an
mulher objeto	objectified woman
E só chamam de amigo quando ele	They call him a friend only when he
está por perto	is nearby
Eu fico muito puto com	I get pissed off at
os pretos como nós	blacks like us
Que ficam como papel higiênico	Who become like toilet paper
dos [play]boys	of the *[play]boys*
[Refrão] Espero que você	[Chorus] I hope you
aprenda como nós	learn like us
E pare de babar o ovo de playboy	And stop sucking up to the *playboys*

Lyrics such as these suggest that rappers engage in their own process of reading the body and that they are well aware that racialized physical features do not always predict embodied practices. This perceived mismatch is encapsulated in MV Bill's characterization of some people as "preto por fora, branco por dentro" (black on the outside, white on the inside) and includes attention to one's chosen peers, the places one frequents, and the kinds of activities (such as surfing) that one engages in.[5] In a spontaneous conversation recorded in Cruzada, presented in example 5.2, my research assistant, CW, echoes rapper MV Bill's concern that his peers were working too hard to befriend whiter, wealthier youth. Cruzada youth know that middle-class parents are often unaware of their children's forays into these stigmatized areas, and they fear that connections to their community are made primarily out of self-interest. Although structural racism affects marginalized youth on a daily basis (as described in chapter 2), these encounters brought them face-to-face with race and class difference. In example 5.2, both Cruzada youth and middle-class families work to uphold significant social boundaries, though for different reasons. They are all aware of unspoken social pressures on white people to avoid contact with black people and black spaces, even as they live in close proximity. Here Feijão (Black Bean), the Cruzada youth who nearly had his watch stolen in chapter 3, describes how, on different occasions, a *playboy* named Pedro invited several of his friends in the community to visit his home and to spend the Carnival holidays with him. According to Feijão's story, Pedro carefully chooses which youth can come, based on their physical features, and he instructs them to lie about where they live. Through this narrative, Feijão thus describes their exclusion in terms of race, class, and residence in a housing project.

EXAMPLE 5.2: *PLAYBOYS*

CW: [Os colegas da Cruzada] Tá dando muita moral pros playboy [como Pedro].

Feijão: Viu que os moleque é racista aqui. Tinha que vê. Levou Léo na casa dele, levou primo do Léo, que não tem nem intimidade. Aí levou o Guga. Falou pra Léo— que Léo— pra Léo não falar que morava na Cruzada. É mole? [. . .] Eu falei, "Léo, eu já disconfiava disso maior tempão." Caralho, o moleque já andava com ele maior tempão. Levou Gringo, primo do Léo. Parece

They're [fellow Cruzada youth] giving a lot of support to *playboys* [like Pedro]. You know that that kid is racist. You had to see. He took Léo to his house, he took Léo's cousin, who he doesn't even know. Then he took Guga. He told Léo— that Léo— told Léo not to say that he lived in Cruzada. Can you believe it? [. . .] I said, "Léo, I was already suspicious of him for a long time." Shit, the kid already hung around with him a long time. He took Gringo, Léo's cousin. He looks

	um playboyzinho, porque o moleque é branco. Levou Guga, porque é branco.	like a little *playboy*, because the kid is white. He took Guga, because he is white.
Judô:	Eu sei quem é ele.	I know who he is.
Feijão:	Levou Léo até pra passar o Carnaval. Aí, [ele falou:] "Léo, fala que tu mora numa rua ali no Leblon." [o bairro nobre da Zona Sul mais perto da comunidade da Cruzada]	He even took Léo to spend Carnival with him. Then, [he said:] "Léo, say that you live on a street there in Leblon." [the wealthy neighborhood that surrounds the housing project of Cruzada]
Bola:	Caralho.	Shit.
Feijão:	Vai se a mulher começa a investigar Léo. "Tu mora ali há muito tempo. Conhece cicrano?"	Imagine if the mother starts to question Léo. "You live there a long time. Do you know what's-his-face?"
Bola:	É.	Yeah.
Feijão:	Você ia se embolar. Léo [falou:] "É mesmo, é mesmo." Falei, "Ô rapá, amigo é o caralho, rapá."	You would be screwed. Léo [said:] "Right, right." I said, "Oh man, bullshit he is your friend, man."
Bola:	Tem que ter— tem que ter— não tem que ter vergonha de nada.	You have to— you have to— you don't have to be ashamed of anything.
Feijão:	A maioria desses playboy pega intimidade com a gente pra ficar no contesto e não ser roubado [por causa das amizades com jovens da favela]. Pedro já mete, "Eu conheço cicrano, eu conheço bertrano, não sei o quê." [. . .] Rapá, esses moleque só vem pra cá— a gente tem que tá com pé atrás. Amigo é a gente aqui, rapá. [. . .] Tu conhece quando era menor.	The majority of these *playboys* get close to us to be rebellious and not get robbed [due to their connections to poor youth from a *favela*]. Pedro already started with, "I know so-and-so, I know what's-his-name, and so on." [. . .] Man, these kids only come here— we have to be on the lookout. Friends are the people here, man. [. . .] You knew when you were younger.

According to Feijão's narrative, Pedro must hide from his mother not only his visits to the stigmatized housing project where his friends live, but also any direct connections to blackness. While Pedro's coveted social invitations seem to hinge on the physical features associated with whiteness, Feijão suggests that light skin will not ultimately be sufficient to allow his friends to fit in. Beyond their physical appearance, poor "community" youth need to act the part of entitled upper-middle-class city residents, which includes a level of familiarity and confidence that they do not possess. This kind of embodied knowledge helps determine whether they really belong in exclusive, white, and wealthy spaces. It is interesting to note that Cruzada youth's lack of sufficient cultural capital can be confirmed, in part, by the example they choose: coming from a smaller, close-knit community where all residents are known to one another because of time spent in shared public spaces, including the street in front of their buildings, they incorrectly believe that their wealthier neighbors must share similar levels of sociability. They assume that they must possess and display personal connections to mark their belonging in South Zone apartment buildings and streets. Their concern over a possible lack of recognition means that they are unlikely to display what sociologist Shamus Khan refers to as "the ease of privilege" (2011:77), which foregrounds, conversely, a casual indifference to one's surroundings (however luxurious or impressive). Rather than looking for approval from others, belonging in these spaces more often requires the display of an inner confidence. Poor community youth recounted their experiences of fear of and shame for lacking proper embodiment not only in private spaces such as individual homes and gated condominium buildings, but also in similarly exclusive and well-guarded shopping malls. In these spaces, their blackness, both in terms of physical features and (lack of) embodied knowledge, was made highly visible.

WHITE MALLS VERSUS BLACK BEACHES

Shopping malls are deeply symbolic social spaces (A. Dávila 2016), and in Rio de Janeiro at the turn of the twenty-first century, this was especially true for youth from the city's stigmatized suburbs and *favelas*. The mall was an indoor space in which they could occasionally partake in the rituals of middle-class leisure. In *Lost in Mall*, a study conducted in the equally tropical context of Indonesia, anthropologist Lizzy Van Leeuwen describes how the combination of air conditioning and the possibilities of consumption indexed not just a desirable urban space but also an exclusive lifestyle: "The Indonesian 'cooled down' upper-middle-class body now endorses its owner's role in an imagined, global middle-class community" (2011:228). In Brazil, as in Indonesia, these cosmopolitan spaces seemed to make distant connections possible through even small acts of consumption. My research assistant brought me by bus to the one South Zone mall that existed in the late 1990s in order to visit a music store that sold domestic (mostly from São Paulo) and U.S. rap. Despite the ability of poor youth to purchase things like CDs in the Rio Sul shopping mall, this space was clearly designed for whiter and wealthier patrons. The range of high-end clothing and shoe stores was impressive, duplicating those found on the commercial streets of Ipanema and Leblon. To lure these desirable customers away from the shops located just around the corner from their homes, the shopping mall offered an enclosed, guarded space where members of the middle class could shop, eat, and take in a movie all while wearing their nicer clothes and the watches and jewelry that they would not risk displaying on city streets. As such, the Rio Sul shopping mall constituted a good example of what Teresa Caldeira (2000) calls a "fortified enclave," a city space that accommodated middle-class fears of violent crime and further contributed to urban inequality.

After the turn of the millennium, the entire city of Rio began to sprout new shopping centers in neighborhoods that targeted different clientele, from upscale malls in the wealthiest areas to suburban malls meant to accommodate thousands of new members of Brazil's *"classe C"* (C class), a working class that could now afford limited consumption of home goods and name-brand items. While the pastime of shopping has become accessible to all but the poorest of Brazil's citizens (Collins 2014; Vargas 2014), the difference in these malls remains extreme. New elite malls reach ever higher to keep out shoppers of limited means. The "VillageMall," whose slogan is "O luxo é ser carioca" (True luxury is living in Rio), features Latin America's first Apple Store, amidst other stores such as Burberry, Prada, and Cartier. Another of Rio's most expensive malls opened on land that Cruzada residents once occupied, directly behind the tall government project buildings of their community. Given its location, right next to a housing project, the architecture of the mall is quite strategic: no windows are built into any of the lower floors. Looking directly out from the open-air parking lot on the roof and from the strip of windows from the sixth-floor food court, one has panoramic views of the South Zone Lagoa (lagoon), with Rio's beautiful lush-green mountains and world-famous Cristo statue in the backdrop. Looking down, however, one gazes upon urban poverty, including barefoot and shirtless children, laundry hanging from windows, and makeshift carts stacked high with beach chairs stored overnight by the

FIGURE 13. Shopping Leblon, built on land that originally belonged to Cruzada, wraps around the series of housing project buildings to maximize space in a neighborhood that has one of the highest real estate values in Latin America. Artwork by Tatiana Medeiros Veloso.

manual laborers who work at the beach nearby. While Cruzada residents believed they would receive preference for jobs at the mall, the continued whiteness and exclusivity of desirable spaces such as this one meant that Shopping Leblon was the site of one of Rio's *rolezinhos*.

Within a context of "compulsory closeness" (Veloso 2010), white middle-class *cariocas* (Rio residents) successfully avoided blackness, intentionally and unintentionally, through their time spent in these semiprivatized spaces. Even in the 1990s, Cruzada youth displayed significant concern about the segregated nature of Brazilian shopping malls. In one poignant story, Feijão (an especially talented storyteller) recounted to friends a brush with racism that he had experienced in the Rio Sul shopping mall, one of the nicer malls in Rio at the time. The incident occurred in the surfing store HB, short for "Hot Buttered," an Australian brand named after a slang term for the wax used on surfboards. While browsing through international beach fashion with Pedro, the middle-class acquaintance from example 5.2 who sometimes hung around in his community, they bumped into a friend of Pedro's named Fernando. This middle-class friend asked Pedro (in front of Feijão), "Só quer saber de Black Beach?" (Do you only hang out on Black

FIGURE 14. Shopping Leblon offers white, wealthy Leblon residents escape from Rio's compulsory social and racial mixture. Photo by Marcelo Santos Braga.

Beach now?). He spoke in Portuguese but had invented the term *Black Beach* in English (there is no such beach in Rio) to chastise Pedro for his occasional presence in the housing project of Cruzada—a crossing of unspoken race and class borders. Example 5.3 presents Feijão's narrative.

EXAMPLE 5.3: BLACK BEACH

Feijão:	Fiquei com a raiva, mané. Fui lá dentro da HB que eu não sou muito ligado em inglês. Black eu sei que é preto. E praia	I got so mad, man. I went inside HB and I'm not very good at English. Black I know means *preto*. And *praia*

	como é que é em inglês? Black Beach.	what's that in English? Black Beach.
Bola:	Black Beach.	Black Beach.
Feijão:	Aí bum. Eu tô lá com Pedro, né? "Aí Pedro. Vamos lá no Rio Sul." "Feijão vumbora." Bum. Aí ele, [Fernando:] "É né Pedro. Só quer ficar na Black Beach?"	So then *bum*. I am there with Pedro, right? "Hey there Pedro. Let's go to Rio Sul." "Feijão let's go." *Bum*. So then he [Fernando:] "Isn't that right Pedro. Now you only hang out on Black Beach?"
Bola:	Quem meteu dessa?	Who said this?
Feijão:	Tal de Fernando. Aí eu— aí— meu deus do céu.	That guy Fernando. So I— so— oh my God.
Bola:	Fernando trabalha na HB?	Fernando works at HB?
Feijão:	Não. Ele luta jiu-jítsu. Uma marra fudida. Quebro ele em dois segundos. Pode ser roxa, faixa rosa— [Risos] Aí ele falou assim, "É né, Pedro? Só quer saber de Black Beach." Falei, "Porra." Deixei sair. [Eu falei:] "Porra, Pedro. Pô. Black é preto. O que é que ele falou?" "Ah ele falou que eu só quero saber em ficar em praia de preto." [Eu falei:] "O quê? Ele falou isso?" [Risos] Caçei ele no Rio Sul . . . "Pode falar pra ele, no dia que eu ver ele—" Caralho. Fiquei dois dias caçando ele, mané. Minha raiva não tinha acabado. Falei, "Ô rapá vai tomar na bunda, rapá! Aperta a mão da gente lá e quer esculachar a gente!"	No. He fights Jiu-Jitsu. So full of himself. I could break him in two seconds. He could be purple belt, pink belt— [Laughter] So then he said, "Isn't that right, Pedro? You only want to know about Black Beach." I said, "Shit." I let him leave. [I said:] "Shit, Pedro. Damn. *Preto* means black. What else did he say?" "Ah he said that I only want to know about hanging out on the beach of the blacks." [I said:] "<u>What</u>? He said that?" [Laughter] I hunted for him throughout Rio Sul . . . "You can tell him, the day I see him—" Shit. I spent two days hunting him, man. And my anger wasn't gone. I said, "Man go take it up the ass, man! Shake our hands there and then you want to make fun of us!"

Fernando's spontaneously crafted insult "É né Pedro? Só quer saber de Black Beach?" (So, Pedro, do you only hang out on Black Beach now?) brings together local urban conflicts and global racial ideologies. To carefully unpack what it reveals about Brazilian race relations and the impetus to avoid contact with blackness, we must pay attention to ongoing struggles over city spaces and rights to the city, as well as the racial meaning embedded in embodied practices. Fernando's direct target is his friend Pedro, and yet he is clearly preoccupied with Feijão, whose presence he finds objectionable and who easily recognizes himself to be the indirect target of the insult. The first implication is that Pedro should not have brought Feijão into the mall—where he does not belong—and yet his reference to the beach, and to black people taking over sections of the beach, directly indexes what was at the time one of the most salient social struggles over urban space and belonging, as I show in chapter 4. When I played this recording for various individuals, from Cruzada residents to upper-middle-class families, everyone agreed that there was no beach called Black Beach, or *Praia de Preto* in Portuguese. But they all understood what Fernando meant, as parts of the beach directly in front of Cruzada and in front of nearby *favelas* often appear visibly darker than the rest of the famous South Zone beaches (see also Farias 2006).

Beyond the allusions to Feijão's spatial transgressions, Fernando very skillfully enacts a demonstration of Feijão's linguistic and cultural incompetence. Middle-class Brazilians have generally had years of English training (often beginning as young as age five), but they are frequently insecure about their personal skills and often loathe to speak English in public. Nevertheless, access to English and even limited English facility remain an important index of class status, and the mall is filled with stores with English names and signs, such as HB (the Australian store these three were in). Accompanying these global linguistic references are imported goods, expensive brand-name stores, and cultural tastes and practices that mark race and class distinction (Bourdieu 1984). Surfing, in particular, is readily associated with wealthy white boys, and surfing and beach fashion is abundantly available for purchase at this mall. The music store I had previously visited with my research assistant had a tiny space dedicated to hip-hop music, and it too sold the idea of imported North American style.

In this brief encounter, Fernando has administered a test of English familiarity (and surfing vocabulary), which Feijão has failed. It is a bold and risky linguistic act: if Fernando has miscalculated and Feijão *does* have suf-

FIGURE 15. Young middle-class children, with their private English school bags, wait outside the school where they take classes twice a week. A statue of a British soldier stands guard in front of the building. Photo by Marcelo Santos Braga.

ficient English to understand the insult, Feijão is likely to react. But Fernando has not miscalculated, and Feijão is left in a subordinate role, uncomfortably located between ratified and unratified participant (Goffman 1981); he has effectively been "cut out" of the conversation (Levinson 1988:190). Like a small child standing within a group of adults, he can listen, but it is assumed that he does not understand and is unable to directly participate. Feijão plays out his assigned role, understanding that he is being discussed, because the term *black* is available to him, but shamed into silence since he cannot understand the rest of the phrase. He must stand by and wait for Fernando to leave before he can admit to his (already obvious) lack of sufficient English resources. Fernando thus channels larger urban struggles over resources and belonging into a pointed, individual attack: exhibit A is Feijão's lack of embodied linguistic and cultural knowledge. Patrons in a surfing-inspired clothing store filled with images of Australian (and global) whiteness do not all know how to surf, of course, but they do need to demonstrate the proper linguistic knowledge and bodily comportment to legitimately occupy such spaces.[6]

Brazilian anthropologist Leticia Veloso (2011) has studied the rise of Brazil's "new lower middle class," which began in the early 2000s, and the

FIGURE 16. The surfing store HB (Hot Buttered) is an Australian chain that sells popular expensive beach attire. Photo by Marcelo Santos Braga.

reactions to the increased resources now possessed by millions of previously poor Brazilians. While academics, including Veloso, prefer to describe this group as a new working class (with still-meager resources), this rapid and sizable class mobility has produced noticeable changes and increased social contact, especially in Brazilian cities such as Rio. Veloso finds that upper-middle-class Brazilians object, in particular, to patterns of increased consumption, suggesting that money should be invested in education and health care for one's family instead of being spent on tangible and expensive commodities such as plasma screen TVs. And yet, beyond larger moral debates, her informants were quite often preoccupied with issues of bodily comportment that seemed to justify their right to consume:

> People "do not know how to behave in a mall," they will say, because "they are loud, and they scream, and they push their way around other people, and they are not dressed properly," so "it bothers other patrons." Or, as a young white and very athletic man commented as we were both

waiting in line at a sporting goods store in a shopping center: "It is outrageous what these people are doing to our mall. This is an expensive store. I should not have to wait in line for all those people to buy these shoes that they don't even have a place to wear. Where are they going to jog? In the *favela*?" (Veloso 2011)

The "Black Beach" example is unusual and, I would argue, critical, because it ignores a cultural imperative to talk about Brazil's social divide as one between socioeconomic classes that display radically different tastes, expectations, and values. The imperative to remain racially "cordial" thus entails a polite failure to discuss these cultural differences in terms of race. Unlike the middle-class consumers whom Veloso studied, Fernando explicitly reveals the push to avoid contact with blackness. Indeed, it is perhaps unsurprising to find that it is youth who are the most willing to engage in racial transgressions, and then the most willing to talk about them, even as this talk further violates social taboos. This may be another reason that Fernando turns to English for his blatantly racial remark.

The term *black*, as Feijão points out, is well known in Brazil, mostly through U.S. popular culture and music, such as soul, that traveled globally during the U.S. Civil Rights Movement (see chapter 6 and also Alberto 2009; Covin 2006; McCann 2002). Decades later, its use still contrasts strongly with the terms available in Portuguese to describe blackness, most commonly *preto* and *negro*. The phrase "Black Beach" also alludes to the English phrase "Black Power," which signifies active opposition to the racial ideology of whitening and Brazilian beliefs in the benefits of racial mixture. As historian Paulina Alberto notes, "By this logic, blackness, as a radically oppositional cultural and political identity, was the unfortunate consequence of racism and racial segregation in the United States, but was wholly out of place in the tolerant and *mestiço* nation of Brazil" (2009: 5). Through the phrase "Black Beach," Fernando thus accuses Pedro of engaging in the un-Brazilian and racially *intolerant* act of preferring blackness. As Cruzada youth discussed in the previous conversation, it is assumed that whiter and wealthier youth choose to hang out in their community in order to "ficar no contesto" (be rebellious), which includes garnering the limited advantages of connections to the city's most dangerous areas, flouting their parents' rules and imposed limitations, and defying societal expectations. It is thus possible to interpret these relationships as small racial rebellions that violate not only unspoken imperatives to avoid contact with blackness but also the national imperative to practice racial tolerance. Racial tolerance, it must be emphasized, does not allow for racial preferences of any kind.

Through his multilayered insult, Fernando suggests that there is something deeply disturbing (and possibly even racist) about Pedro's choice to intentionally seek out friendships with poor dark-skinned community residents.[7] As I show in the following sections, public displays of a preference for blackness often provoke strong feelings of racial anxiety among the whiter middle class, as they violate the unspoken norms of Brazilian race relations and threaten their connections to whiteness.

THE INSECURITY OF WHITENESS

The *Playboys* and Black Beach stories narrated by Cruzada youth were readily understood to be examples of racism on the part of the middle-class Brazilians I interviewed: These incidents included direct racial references intended to exclude people based on race. What was not as readily acknowledged was that these situations also hinted at a deep preoccupation with the instability of whiteness. Sociologist Erving Goffman's (1963) notion of the "courtesy stigma" helps explain the situations I have thus far related in this chapter, in which contact with stigmatized others threatens to transfer stigma to friends or acquaintances. And yet the risks posed by blackness run deeper in Brazil than mere external association; they bring to the surface internalized fears of a long history of race mixing. While whiter and wealthier Brazilians comfortably discuss and even joke about their family's nonwhite ancestry (as in Gabriela's story discussed in chapter 3; see also Pinho 2009; Rosa-Ribeiro 2000), there are clearly times when this racial heritage can be the source of grave shame or insult. Within a larger global context, Brazilians have historically understood themselves to be a "mongrel" nation, and the expression "o complexo de vira-lata" (the complex of the mixed-breed) is frequently invoked to explain Brazil's concerns about its inferior status, particularly in relation to its relative lack of culture, civilization, and modernity (A. Silva 2014; see also Schwarcz 1998). Brazilians continue to collectively bristle at their experiences being treated as nonwhite (and even black) when they visit or move to the United States (Joseph 2015; Ramos-Zayas 2007; Sheriff 2001). Across Latin America and the Caribbean, individuals, families, and nation-states have long struggled to acquire and display sufficient whiteness, as I discuss in chapter 3, harboring implicit and explicit fears that they will never shed their associations with nonwhiteness, which include both African and indigenous heredity (see, for example, Godreau 2002, 2015; Hale 2006; Roland 2013; Wirtz 2014).

In addition to this national "inferiority complex," light-skinned Brazilians can be called out as "white but not quite white" (Pinho 2009:40), based not only on the hint of black physical features but also on the display of behaviors associated with blackness. For example, when a Brazilian makes a mistake or fails to demonstrate proper restraint or grace, a friend or family member may jokingly comment, "Coisa de preto" (That's a black thing), or "Ele tem um pé na África" or "pé na senzala" (He must have a foot in Africa, or a foot in the slave quarters). These "jokes" hinge on the idea that all Brazilians have some black ancestry and that one's racial heritage can "slip out" and negatively influence one's behavior at any time. These expressions are rarely used toward or about mere acquaintances, who might take them as an affront instead of as a friendly jest, and they are most frequently uttered in reference to a third party who is not present to defend themselves. Only as a more blatant and face-threatening joke or insult could one say to a dark-skinned person that he or she just did a "black thing" or remark, "Só podia ser preto mesmo" (Only a black person would do that).

Beneath these expressions lies a clear racial hierarchy that stigmatizes nonwhiteness and feeds the fears of white people that the presence of even some blackness can inadvertently reveal itself. Whiteness suggests decorum, respectability, and civilized control. But the presumed lack of racial purity in Brazil—what has been called "virtual whiteness" (E. Nascimento 2007:64) or the implication that one is *branco por procuração* (white by proxy; see Pierson 1942:139)—means that one's whiteness is always vulnerable and subject to attack. Across Spanish-speaking Latin America and the Caribbean, where *mestizaje* (race mixture) is also national lore and a common experience, we find the expressions "se le salió lo de negro" (the black in you came out) in Puerto Rico (Godreau 2002:295; 2015:201) and "te salió el indio" (the Indian in you just came out) in the Andes (Postero 2006:11). Both of these sayings are employed to chide mixed-race adults and children for a lapse in good manners or judgment. As Elisa Larkin Nascimento notes of Brazil, "The mestizo [is] never completely secure in the enjoyment of social privilege" (2007:64).

Given these deep-seated racial concerns over whiteness, characterized by sociologist Guerreiro Ramos as a "traço paranóico," or a trace of paranoia, throughout Brazil (1994:227), signs of nonwhiteness and middle-class youth's voluntary associations with blackness provoked significant anxiety, especially for parents. It was feared not only that blackness might "rub off" given sufficient contact with darker-skinned peers and time spent in the *favela*, but also that brown-skinned individuals could be read as black given their *potential* blackness. Here we have the opposite of historian Carl Degler's proposed "mulatto escape hatch," as described in his 1971 book, *Neither Black nor White*. According to Degler's theory, light-skinned Brazilians of African descent could achieve social mobility through their associations with whiteness. In contrast, contact with black people, black spaces, and black practices all threaten to move one in the "wrong" direction. The so-called mulatto escape hatch becomes instead a trap door that mixed-race individuals might unwittingly fall through. I turn now to explore the specific case of one brown-skinned middle-class youth, nicknamed Bola (Ball), who lived simultaneously in two seemingly opposed worlds, studying for college entrance exams in the homes of whiter and wealthier school peers while also spending significant time in Cruzada hanging out on the street with poor dark-skinned friends. Language, and slang in particular, was critical to Bola's movement in and out of these different spaces. Reactions to his language make audible wider middle-class fears about the possibility of downward mobility, a "fall" associated not only with poverty and connections to "dangerous" city spaces, but also with "excessive" contact with blackness. Bola's choice to seek out blackness and to disavow his achieved whiteness, to the dismay of those around him, helps reveal the unspoken flip side of *boa aparência.*[8]

THE *PLAYBOY* BANDIT

I met Bola through his close friendship with my main research assistant, CW. The two had met two years prior, on a basketball team at a private social club (where CW had been recruited). In soccer-obsessed Brazil, basketball is not a common sport, and it is readily associated with North American blackness, hip-hop culture, and the U.S. "ghetto" (Roth-Gordon 2009a). CW and Bola often walked part of the way home together after practice, as Bola lived in the wealthy neighborhood that surrounded Cruzada. One day CW said that he would walk Bola through his neighborhood to the other side, and after that, Bola wound up hanging out more often and meeting CW's friends. He was well regarded by many of the youth I spoke to, who described him as *humilde* (humble) and had given him such tongue-in-cheek nicknames as "playboy revoltado" (the rebel *playboy*) and "playboy bandido" (the *playboy* bandit). These monikers were meant to tone down the implied insult of calling out his race and class privilege through the slang term *playboy* (Roth-Gordon 2007a), suggesting that he was also (positively) linked to blackness and criminality and thus could also lay claim to masculinity and toughness (see also Bucholtz 2011). Bola appreciated these nicknames, and he described himself as a "playboy bandido dentro da lei" (a *playboy* bandit who stays within the law). Indeed, neither Bola nor the friends he hung out with in Cruzada were heavily invested in drinking, drugs, or criminal activity while I knew them.

Though considered trustworthy and respectful, Bola did conform to some of the local expectations of *playboys* and their reasons for voluntarily choosing to enter poor communities—namely, to be associated with toughness and to protect themselves against theft. A friend of mine who taught at the private school that Bola attended told me that Bola had once shown off a purportedly stolen watch that he had purchased in Cruzada. He had also claimed residence in Cruzada to avoid being robbed on a public bus. He clearly felt a strong connection to the neighborhood, and on one written survey that I gave him, he checked off both Leblon *and* Cruzada as the neighborhoods where he lived. While his mother, who was a widow, placed their income in the "10–20 minimum salaries" bracket, Bola checked off the box for the highest household income of "over 20 minimum salaries." (The minimum salary at the time was approximately R$120 (US$100) per month.) During this phase of my research, Bola was also dating a girl from a nearby *favela*.

Racially, Bola had marked *pardo* (brown, mixed race) on the written survey that I gave him, but when I asked his friends from Cruzada, they disagreed about whether they would racially classify him as *branco* (white), *amarelo* (yellow, the racial category intended for Brazilians of Asian descent), or *preto* (black). They knew that he preferred to think of himself as black. Example 5.4 comes from an interview that I conducted with Bola and CW's cousin Tiny. In this exchange, Bola describes in detail his various experiences growing up darker than middle-class friends but now being lighter than his new friends in Cruzada:

EXAMPLE 5.4: NÃO ME CONSIDERO BRANCO (I DON'T THINK OF MYSELF AS WHITE)

Bola:	Esse negócio, tá ligado? Eu fico muito chateado com neguim que me considera branco. Fico puto. Na moral.	This business, you know what I'm saying? I get very annoyed when people think of me as white. I get pissed. Seriously.
Jennifer:	Porquê?	Why?
Bola:	Ah, porque eu— eu não sou branco.	Ah, because I— I'm not white.
Tiny:	Agora, se a sua mãe fosse branca, eu considerava você branco. A mãe dele é— é mais escura que ele.	Now, if your mother were white, I would consider you white. His mother is— is darker than he is.
Bola:	Entendeu? Eu não me considero branco. Não—	Understand? I don't consider myself white. No—

nem— nem fisicamente.
Nem— nem aqui dentro,
tá entendendo? Eu
não considero branco de
nenhum jeito. Aí, quando falam
[que eu sou branco],
tá ligado,
fico chateado com essa parada
à vera. Quando— é tipo assim,
negócio de brincadeira. Aí é
difícil, brincadeira
comigo. Se você— ainda mais
na minha família, que meu irmão
é branco. Meu outro irmão
assim de— de raça, vamos
dizer de cor de pele, um irmão
é branco e o outro é um pouco
mais— mais moreno. Ele—
eles— desde pequeno,
"Ah neguinho." Tudo
era "neguinho." Mas,
sabe, já te
expliquei.
De um tom, sabe?
Positivo assim, porque eu era
mais escurinho. O meu cabelo,
bum. Maior blackão. [Risos]
Assim enroladinho. Aí "neguim
não sei o quê, não sei o quê,"
entendeu? Sempre
deu na minha família.
Sempre minha tia, minha Dina
[falava:] "Oi neguim"
não sei o quê, assim zoando.
"Ô neguim! Ô pivete!
Aí, não sei o quê."
Tá entendendo? [Risos do Tiny]
Sempre— sempre—

not even— not even physically.
Not— not even here inside,
are you understanding me? I
don't consider [myself] white at
all. So, when they say
[that I'm white],
you know what I'm saying,
I get annoyed by this
a lot. When— it's like,
a way of joking. But it's
difficult, to joke about this
with me. If you— especially since
in my family, my brother
is white. My other brother
like in— in terms of race, let's
say color of skin, one brother
is white and the other is a little
more— a little browner. He—
they— since I was young,
"Oh little black kid." Everything
was "little black kid." But,
you know, I already
explained this to you.
In a tone, you know?
Positive like, because I was
darker. My hair,
bum. Big Afro. [Laughter]
Like all tight curls. So "little kid
and so on, and so on,"
understand? That always
happened in my family.
My aunt would always, my aunt
[would say:] "Hi little black kid"
and whatever, like to tease me.
"Hey black kid! Hey street kid!
And so on."
Understand? [Tiny laughs]
Always— always—

	tipo assim, me ligaram—
Jennifer:	Mas de uma forma carinhosa?
Bola:	É. Mas sempre me ligando

assim, a— a— aos
negros, tá entendendo? E eu
nunca, tá ligado?
[. . .]
A medida que eu— depois
que eu fui crescendo essa
conciência, eu nunca
me considerei branco.
Nenhum— nenhum
momento, tá entendendo?
Eu nunca me considerei branco
e sem— aí, se também, a
maioria dos meus amigos,
eram brancos. E eu, sou mais
escuro que a maioria. Então
sempre falam,
"Qual é, negão?"
Não sei o quê. Sempre eu era—
tá entendendo? Como se fosse
um— um negro no
meio da— dos
brancos. Aí num— mas eu não
ligava, sabe? Ainda mais
que a maioria falava tudo
na moral, sabe?
Assim, sem querer—
sentido negativo. E eu
sempre me acostumava porque
eu me achava— tipo
minha consciência é que eu sou
negro, tá entendendo? Aí o que
que aconteceu? Aí cheguei lá
na Cruzada. Aí a maioria
mais escuro que eu. Aí
tem uns que falaram

like, connecting me—
But in a caring way?
Yeah. But always connecting
me like, to— to— to
black people, understand? And I
never, know what I'm saying?
[. . .]
As I was— after
I developed this
consciousness, I never
considered myself white.
Not even— not even one
moment, understand?
I never considered myself white
and without— and also, the
majority of my friends,
they were white. And I, I am
darker than the majority. So
they always would say,
"What's up, big black guy?"
And so on. I was always—
you know? It was as if I were
one— one black person in
the middle of— of all these
white people. But not— I never
cared, you know? Especially
since the majority would say it
totally normally, you know?
Like, without meaning—
negative meaning. And I
always got used to it because
I would think of myself— like
my consciousness is that I am
black, understand? And then
what happened? I arrived there
in Cruzada. And the majority
were darker than I was. So
there were some that would say

não sei o quê, não sei o quê,
tipo quando falaram que eu sou
branco, eu me bolo. Aí eu fico
puto. "Não branco. Eu sou
branco o caralho! Não sei o
quê, bababá. Não tem
branco aqui não, não sei o quê."
Aí já, aí tá entendendo?
Eu, porra, não gosto, cara.
Porra minha— minha mãe
mais escura que eu. Meu pai,
meu pai era brancão,
brancão, tá entendendo? Meu
pai era português.
Aí, a ma— meu avô era
nordestino, mas ele não era
escuro. Minha avó era
filha de— de— de—
de negro legal. Escurão. Mas
só que minha avó
nasceu, nasceu, nasceu
da mesma cor que eu,
tá entendendo? Nasceu—
nasceu mais clara, mas os
pais da minha avó
eram negros, tá entendendo?
Acho até a minha— minha—
da minha avó não. Os pais.
É. Os pais da minha avó,
minha bisavó,
acho que a mãe dela chegou a
ser, sabe, tipo escravo,
tá entendendo? E— e eu me
liguei muito nesses negócio.
Minha raiz parece ser— minha
raiz é— pra mim, é—
eu puxei esse lado, mais o lado
da minha mãe. Meus outros

blah blah blah, blah blah blah,
like when they say that I am
white, I go crazy. Then I get
pissed off. "I am not
white. Bullshit! Blah blah
blah, ba ba ba. There aren't any
whites here, and so on."
Like, so do you understand?
I, damn, I don't like it, man.
Damn my— my mother
is darker than me. My father,
my father was really white,
really white, understand? My
father was Portuguese.
So, my— my grandfather was a
northeasterner, but he wasn't
dark. My grandmother was the
child of— of— of—
of a real black. Really dark. But
then when my grandmother
was born, she was born, she was
born the same color as me,
understand? She was born—
she was born lighter, but the
parents of my grandmother
were blacks, understand?
I think that even my— my—
my grandmother no. Her parents.
Right. My grandmother's
parents, my great-grandmother,
I think that her mother was
even, you know, like a slave,
understand? And— and I always
paid attention to these things.
My roots seem to be— my
roots are— for me, it's—
I take after that side, more
my mother's side. My other

irmãos não. Puxaram—	brothers don't. They were— they
são brancos. Puxaram o lado	are white. They take after my
do meu pai. E eu nunca tive	father's side. And I never was
vergonha de— de— de	ashamed to— to— to
falar que eu sou negro. Essas	say that I am black. Things
parada assim não, tá	like this, do you
entendendo?	understand?

Bola's racial narrative is interesting on multiple levels. He seems to recite the comfortable white Brazilian tale about having *um pé na cozinha* (a foot in the kitchen, a reference to slavery and having a distant black relative). This expression was once (in)famously uttered by former Brazilian president Fernando Henrique Cardoso. Such casual references to slavery are often viewed by the Brazilian Black Movement as little more than a reiteration of the idea that all Brazilians are racially mixed, thus minimizing the existence of racial difference and structural racism. In sharp contrast, however, Bola is clearly striving to make those connections real and specific in order to make a more solid claim to blackness. It is hard to tell from this narrative whether Bola always appreciated being viewed as darker than his friends and family while growing up; many Brazilians do have racialized nicknames lovingly conferred on them in their childhood and never taken by the individual to be insulting or offensive. What is clear is that Bola is working hard to be viewed as anything but white, and the time he has spent in Cruzada over the past few years has enhanced that desire.

Bola's language in example 5.4 is typical of the language he uses in Cruzada—chock-full of the pragmatic markers discussed in chapter 3 that are actively disdained by members of the middle class. Expressions like *não sei o quê* (literally "I don't know what"; similar to the expression "and/or whatever" in English) and the frequent use of tag questions like *tá ligado?* (you know what I'm saying?) seem like filler to middle-class listeners and give the impression of inarticulateness and lack of education. His speech style was thus meant to back up the message he is trying to convey. He sounds more like a dark-skinned community member who has grown up with his friends on the street than a "white" middle-class kid who has been trained in proper grammar and essay writing since the first grade. I now turn to literature on passing and also "crossing," the practice of taking up a language and identity (of a racially stigmatized group) that is not one's "own" (Rampton 1995), to examine how Bola does the opposite of what is expected of him: he works hard to give up the personal whiteness that he has acquired (see chapter 3) and to project clear signs of blackness instead.

LINGUISTIC AND RACIAL CROSSING

In a study of narratives of white-to-black racial passing entitled *Near Black,* Baz Dreisinger discusses the postbellum North American fear that "whites could 'become' black by way of association with blacks, or by acting in a manner that was identified with blacks" (2008:22). The vulnerability of whiteness, especially for those poor whites who shared close proximity with newly freed black slaves, revealed "cultural anxieties about a potentially disappearing white essence" (2008:16). I draw on this rare study of "reverse" passing here not to assert that Bola really is "white" and pretends to be "black." Dreisinger's discussion of "white" people who act or are mistaken for "black" encourages us to think through the indeterminacy of the phenotypical features associated with race. Bola is viewed as dark by the people he grew up with (and by members of his family) and perceived as light by most Cruzada residents. The concept of passing suggests that one is living in a situation and embracing a racial experience and identity that are not the expected ones (Rottenberg 2003; Wald 2000). This is true of Bola's situation, as the life that he has been born into affords him the trappings and label of whiteness, despite his medium-brown skin. As Bola alters his cultural and linguistic practices, the people he associates with, and the spaces he occupies, he attempts to change both how he thinks about himself and the racial designation that he receives from others (a topic discussed further in chapter 6). Not all individuals (even within Brazil) share this same degree of phenotypic flexibility, but the ability to shape the racial reading of one's body is not Bola's alone.

The directionality implied by passing is generally one of improvement and uplift; one attempts to pass into a more privileged group. In contrast, researchers have used the term *crossing* to talk about individuals who have chosen to affiliate with a stigmatized group, often through their linguistic and stylistic choices. In this sense, Bola is also "crossing," in that his movement across well-established race and class borders is a choice, one that allows him to straddle these different lifestyles simultaneously. Sociolinguistic studies of crossing (and what has been called *stylization*) pay careful attention to the ways that speakers use language to play with (seemingly fixed) associations between specific linguistic features and racial affiliation (Bucholtz 2011; Cutler 2014; Hewitt 1986; Rampton 1995). In my own research, I was interested in the speech style Bola used, as well as the reactions of listeners who heard him speak.

To assess how Bola was perceived, I played recordings of Bola's interactions with other Cruzada youth in metalinguistic interviews with both "insiders" (those who lived in the community and knew him) and "outsiders" (those who did not personally know him or have any contacts within Cruzada). I included two conversational recordings that Bola participated in, and I did not initially provide any background information about the speakers. In the first example, Bola talked with his Cruzada friends about what it meant to trust other people. In the second, taken from the same conversation, Bola, Tiny, and a friend named Negão (literally "big black guy"; a common Brazilian nickname and term of address) talked about Bola's weekly allowance from his mother. The amount they discuss, R$20 per week (about US$17), at a time when the average monthly salary of many Cruzada residents was only R$120 (US$100), should have alerted listeners to the possibility that Bola was not, in fact, a community resident. But few picked up on this fact, influenced instead by his linguistic performance. Example 5.5 offers a snippet of a larger section of Bola's conversation that was played during the interviews. Of particular interest is his frequent use of slang, especially the repetition of the pragmatic markers highlighted in bold:

EXAMPLE 5.5: DÁ VINTE SUADO (SHE SWEATS TO GIVE ME TWENTY)

Bola: Minha mãe— minha mãe **tipo assim** ela tem que me dar— vamos dizer ela me dá vinte reais todo fim de semana. Tem vezes que ela não pode me dar vinte não, **tá ligado?** Tem vezes que **bum**. "Não dá pra te dar vinte." Dá dez. "Qual é, mãe? **Não sei o quê**." Ela dá vinte, mas dá vinte suado.

My mother— my mother **like** she has to give me— let's say she gives me R$20 [US$17] every weekend. There are times when she can't give me twenty, **you know what I'm saying?** There are times when **bum**. "I can't give you twenty." She gives me ten. "What's up with that, mom? **And whatever**." She gives [me] twenty, but she sweats to give [me] twenty.

Tiny: Ela te dá vinte por semana?

She gives you twenty a week?

Bola: É. Dá vinte suado, **tá ligado?** Dá isso, dá aquilo, dá a merenda, **não sei o quê**. "Tô cheia de coisa [contas] **não sei o quê**. Não dá pra te dar hoje."

Yeah. But she sweats to give [me] twenty, **you know what I'm saying?** She has to give this, give that, give money for snack, **and so on**. "I've got a ton of things [bills] **and whatever**. I can't give it to you today."

Listeners across various group interviews agreed that Bola spoke the most slang in both conversations. When asked about the speakers (who they could not see), interviewees who did not know them agreed that they were lacking education, poor, from the hills (a reference to *favelas*), and likely dark-skinned. I played the same recordings for the speakers themselves, a few of their parents, and some of their friends from the community and asked what they thought the middle class would say about their speech. They all responded similarly, suggesting that middle-class listeners would react strongly and negatively to the amount of slang and the nonstandard parts of their language. Bola himself was very aware that whiteness was linked to proper speech and grammar—and that his (perceived) lack of linguistic skill would be linked to nonwhiteness. He summarized this relationship succinctly: "Já está tudo ligado. Negro. Pobre. E . . . fala errado. . . . Estas três coisas." (It's all connected. Black. Poor. And . . . speaks incorrectly. . . . These three things.)

When asked, he also guessed that his mother would think that his speech was "feio, sem educação" (ugly, without education or manners). When I revealed to middle-class respondents that Bola lived in a nearby wealthy neighborhood, that he currently attended a private high school with a good reputation, and that he had recently passed the college entrance exam to attend a public (and therefore prestigious) university, their shock was palpable. They spent a long time theorizing *why* he would spend time in a housing project if he did not live there (drugs? attraction to danger or crime? lack of parental attention?). They were amazed by the naturalness of what they considered completely impoverished, uneducated, and often nonsensical speech. "Bola tem uma vida dupla!" (Bola has a double life!), exclaimed one middle-class mother. Another announced: "Vai ganhar o Oscar! Não é nem o Jack Nicholson esse ano! É Bola! Porque— Deus do céu!" (He is going to win an Oscar! It's not even going to be Jack Nicholson this year! It will be Bola! Because— oh my God!).

Brazilian anthropologist Teresa Caldeira has noted that "people from all social classes believe that a strong mind originates within a strong family, one that properly disciplines children and protects them from bad companions" (2000:95). Along similar lines, Ann Stoler notes that, within colonial contexts, "a direct line [was] drawn from language acquisition to motherhood to morality" (2002:121). It was thus unsurprising to find that interviewees were quick to blame Bola's mother. Despite their suspicions that Bola must have little contact with his mother and no parental guidance, Bola's mother was well aware of his friendships in Cruzada and had visited CW's mother at one point to check up on her son and his activities in the community. She was comfortable with the people whom her son had met, and she did not worry about him spending time in their community as long as she knew what he was up to. And yet she reacted to the recordings of her son's language just as the other middle-class families had: "É uma tristeza isso aqui! Meu Deus do céu! Que diálogo horroroso isso! [Eu rio] Não, eu acho! Não vou dar crédito a isso aqui . . . Que bando de marginal!" (How sad this is! Oh my God! What a horrible dialogue! [I laugh] No, I think so! I won't give credit to this . . . It sounds like a group of marginals [criminals]!) She said she would not believe based on the recording that one of the speakers (her son) was on his way to college, as it sounded as if none of them had passed junior high. As she reflected on the conversation in a private interview with me, she voiced the anxieties of other middle-class parents:

> Eu achei o papo como se tivessem falado numa linguagem completamente diferente da minha. . . . Eu fico assustada até! [Jennifer: Assustada porque?] Fico. Fico assustada. Porque falaram falaram e não disseram nada. Porque você investe— estou falando em termos de mãe, né, você faz um investimento— na hora tu ver o teu filho com uma linguagem nessa, entrando com uma faculdade . . . meu Deus do céu! . . . Tem que se policiar!

> I thought this conversation was spoken in a language completely different from mine. . . . I am even frightened! [Jennifer: Why frightened?] I am. I am frightened. Because they are talking and talking, and they aren't saying anything. Because you make an investment— I am speaking as a mother, right, you make an investment— and the minute you see your son speaking like this, about to go to college . . . my God! . . . One has to control oneself!

As I illustrate in chapter 3, the linguistic discipline associated with standard Portuguese is readily linked to class status through the acquisition of certain knowledge, skills, and dispositions (Bagno 1999, 2003). In her book *Fear of Falling: The Inner Life of the Middle Class*, Barbara Ehrenreich discusses similar fears among middle-class North Americans:

> In this class no one escapes the requirements of self-discipline and self-directed labor; they are visited, in each generation, upon the young as they were upon the parents. . . . If this is an elite, then, it is an insecure and deeply anxious one. It is afraid, like any class below the most securely wealthy, of misfortunes that might lead to a downward slide. But in the middle class there is another anxiety: a fear of inner weakness, of growing soft, of failing to strive, of losing discipline and will. (1989:15)

As we spoke, Bola's mother made a point of saying that she was not too old to remember the enjoyment of speaking slang in her day, but what she heard in the recording was *demais* (too much). She worried that her son would be so *viciado* (addicted) to slang that when he needed to use his Portuguese to impress someone on a job interview, he would be unable to do so. Yet these fears of potential loss—of class standing and linguistic training thrown out the window—cannot be understood outside a deeply racialized context. Bola's social status depends not only on the educational opportunities his mother has provided (the "investment" she has made in him) but also on a racial positioning that requires avoiding unnecessary contact with blackness and presenting oneself as white. Despite the fact that Bola phenotypically displays signs of racial mixture, his class status should give him access to the embodied practices associated with whiteness. And yet this is precisely what Bola has chosen to eschew and what his mother cannot force him to continuously perform. Articulating this racialized dilemma (that one can offer "proper" training but not force a child to embody it), the São Paulo–based hip-hop group Racionais MC's (The Rationals) mischievously rap about a lack of parental control and the disturbing lure of blackness in their song "Negro Drama" (The Drama of Black People):[9]

EXAMPLE 5.6: "NEGRO DRAMA" (THE DRAMA OF BLACK PEOPLE)

Mil fita	A thousand problems
Inacreditável, mas seu filho	Unbelievable, but your son
me imita	imitates me
No meio de vocês	Amongst you
Ele é o mais esperto	He's the smart one
Ginga	He knows how to swagger
e fala gíria	and how to speak slang
Gíria não. Dialeto	Not slang. It's a dialect
Esse não é mais seu	This one's no longer yours
Hó	Ho!
Subiu	He went up
Entrei pelo seu rádio	I entered through your radio
Tomei	and took him
Cê nem viu	You didn't even see
Nós é isso ou aquilo	We are this or that
O quê?	What?
Cê não dizia	Didn't you always say
Seu filho quer ser preto	Your son wants to be black?
Rhá	Ha! Hee!
Que ironia	What irony!

Weismantel and Eisenman have suggested that wealth and well-being "accrue" in white bodies (1998:137), and other research (e.g., Bashkow 2006; Weismantel 2001) has emphasized the ways that bodies become physically changed due to a lifetime of racialized experiences. And yet, here, Racionais MC's mock the long-term investment that middle-class parents have made in their children's whiteness. Neo-Lamarckian ideas about the power of environment are wielded to reinforce feelings of racial vulnerability and the inability to guarantee personal whiteness for one's children. It is not only Bola's language that his mother no longer controls; his very racial status can change through the simple act of turning on the radio! The racialized embodied practices into which parents have carefully disciplined their children can be disregarded and disappear. The threat of racial loss is made palpable ("You didn't even see!"), and it clearly has extended beyond Bola's specific situation to become the topic of a Brazilian rap song.

Writing about intimate experiences within the domestic sphere in the context of colonial racism, Stoler similarly uses the fear of "theft" to describe situations in which Europeans from the metropole worried about local influences on their children in a dangerous tropical climate where daily contact with nonwhite natives was unavoidable: "Servants could steal more than the sexual innocence of European children. They could redirect their cultural longings, the smells they preferred, the tastes they craved, and their sexual desires" (2002:156). She notes that "what sustained racial membership was a middle-class morality, nationalist sentiments, bourgeois sensibilities . . . and a carefully circumscribed 'milieu'" (Stoler 1995:105). As young children become more independent teenagers, Brazilian parents can no longer secure their prodigy's "milieu," nor can they easily stifle their rejection of national racial imperatives which suggest that they must demonstrate whiteness and avoid blackness. Parental anxiety over their children's language and their bodies exemplify some of the main concerns of this book. Whiteness cannot be secured through phenotypical features alone, and signs of blackness circulate and can stick to lighter-skinned bodies. While this is a connection that middle-class people are often comfortable making regarding youth on the beach, it is a far more troubling situation to find it in their own homes, on the well-groomed bodies of their own children.

Bola's mother struck me as laid-back, open, and comfortable with the challenge her son made to some of Rio's most entrenched patterns of social, racial, and residential segregation. At least one of the other mothers expressed a strong desire to meet her, describing her as "*corajosa*" (courageous) for letting her son occupy spaces that were seen as dark (literally) and dangerous. She claimed that in Bola's mother's place, she would "morrer de medo" (die of fear). And yet Bola's desire to play with blackness did ultimately provoke his mother's more deeply entrenched—and racialized—fears. She would allow her son to associate closely with dark-skinned people, and he could frequent black spaces—both activities that required his movement across the well-established social borders that middle-class parents and youth alike continue to uphold (as in the *Playboys* and Black Beach examples). But to bring blackness back home with him, to literally carry it on his body and in his language and to have his racial "sensibilities" altered: this frightened even her. She felt as though she could keep watch over the companions he chose (though mostly from afar) and regulate his activities and whereabouts (if and when she chose to), but she could not ultimately control how others would read his body. It was not people who were visibly black but rather others' ability to read the signs of blackness that worried her.

Bola and his mother bring us to an unfortunate but revealing truth about Brazilian racism: lighter-skinned people can tolerate dark-skinned people, preferably in small numbers (the "problem" of the *rolezinhos* with which I opened this chapter), often in positions of subordination, and most commonly balanced out by "whiter" others. But too much blackness remains dangerous. Bodies that bear physical signs of blackness should be "improved" by whiter, more civilized behaviors and light-skinned companions (Nogueira 1959:13; Telles 2004:158; Vargas 2011:264). Lighter-skinned bodies that intentionally take on blackness, without seeking to mitigate or lessen its effects, go against the grain of *boa aparência* (good appearance) and the unspoken imperative to avoid blackness. This anxiety-provoking refusal to avoid blackness is the subject of the following chapter, in which I discuss the acts of "intentional communication" (Hebdige 1979) embedded in the bodily practices of politically conscious Brazilian rappers and rap fans, such as Bola, who actively wish to be identified as black.

6. Making the *Mano*

The Uncomfortable Visibility of Blackness in Politically Conscious Brazilian Hip-Hop

At the Brazilian MTV Video Music Awards in 1998, Mano Brown, lead singer for the politically conscious rap group Racionais MC's (The Rationals) made one of his first (and rare) public appearances in front of mainstream media. Accepting one of two awards for their CD *Sobrevivendo no Inferno* (Surviving in Hell; Racionais MC's 1998), Mano Brown thanked his mother, who, he said, "lavou muita roupa pra playboy pra eu tá aqui" (washed a lot of clothes for *playboys* for me to be here today). Mano Brown is the quintessential "brown brother" of Brazilian rap (the literal translation of his name, also a reference to James Brown), and his public criticism of the white middle-class and elite male youth whom he refers to as *playboys* was completely in keeping with the lyrics that he had just won awards for. But in this more mainstream setting, his remarks provoked public ire as they explicitly referenced and critiqued well-established race and class boundaries. Responding in early 2015 to a YouTube clip of this award ceremony that was uploaded in 2010, one commenter wrote:[1]

> Sorte tua mesmo mano brow [*sic*] que existiu uma família descente onde o pai é trabalhador a mãe guerreira e o filho teve boas condições e roupas boas do qual gerou o emprego para tua mãe. Podia ter agradecido a esta família também e estes seres humanos que não prejudicam ninguém. Humildade não é só não sair da favela [quando ficou famoso].

> It was also lucky for you mano brow [*sic*] that there existed a decent family where the father works and the mother is also a fighter and the son lives in good conditions and has nice clothes which helped generate that job for your mother. You could have thanked that family too and those human beings who don't hurt anyone. Humility isn't just not leaving a shantytown [after he turned famous].

161

Perhaps what is most interesting about this strong response (beyond the fact that it was posted seventeen years after the actual event) is the way that the commenter attempts to reframe Brazilian inequality. According to "Kleber Poeta," some people work hard to maintain their very fortunate circumstances, and other people, who are not so lucky, benefit from what these hard workers can offer (honest, if low-paying, manual labor positions). Beyond the subtle references to old, "benevolent" master-slave relationships, it is significant that Kleber Poeta refrains from mentioning anything about race or racial inequality, even though this was implied in Mano Brown's choice of the term *playboy*. His message to Mano Brown is thus not only an admonishment to "be humble" in accepting the position that he was born into and that he has now risen above through his musical success, but also an implicit request to be racially "cordial" and downplay the significance of racial difference.

As I discuss in this chapter, Racionais MC's and politically conscious Brazilian hip-hop reached the peak of their popularity at a time when Brazil was struggling with what I have called the country's "comfortable racial contradiction." International pressure had helped end Brazil's slave trade and later outlaw slavery. International pressure was back, more than one hundred years later, in the leadup to the 2001 World Conference Against Racism, Racial Discrimination, Xenophobia and Intolerance, held in Durban, South Africa (Htun 2004). Internal pressure from black activist groups and Brazilian scholars was also mounting. Race-based NGOs, some of them internationally funded, were forcefully encouraging the Brazilian government to recognize racism and to pass legislation that would (1) mandate affirmative action policies at the nation's prestigious (and free) public universities; (2) turn over land to descendants of former runaway-slave colonies; (3) require the teaching of Afro-Brazilian history and culture in schools; (4) change the date of the national black Brazilian holiday from honoring Princesa Isabel (for "freeing the slaves") on May 13, to November 20, in remembrance of a rediscovered Afro-Brazilian hero, Zumbi dos Palmares, leader of the largest *quilombo* (escaped-slave colony), who died in 1695; and (5) classify all Brazilians with African ancestry as "black" under the census category of *negro*. The first four of these racial reforms did eventually pass (at least in some states), and the use of the racial term *negro* gained popular acceptance within a few years of Mano Brown's provocative critique. These legislative changes were an unprecedented (and heavily contested) acknowledgment of blackness by the Brazilian state (Htun 2004).

Within a nation that continues to pride itself on its racial mixture, and in a country that enjoyed the flattering, if outdated, international acclaim of its status as a racial democracy, hip-hop's call to recognize racial difference was not well received. As I have explained in the previous chapters, implicit racial imperatives continue to encourage Brazilians to seek out whiteness and to avoid blackness. To these, I add a third: the social and racial imperative to be cordial. Despite these unspoken guidelines and this carefully constructed code of daily conduct, rappers at the turn of the twenty-first century fought to make blackness visible. I do not focus here on how politically conscious youth "assume" their blackness, nor do I examine how they take up black identities or achieve what they call "race consciousness" (A. Silva 2014), though this is often how they describe their political goals. Instead, I am more interested in examining the work that they engage in to make blackness visible on their bodies and the discomfort that this has provoked within Brazilian society. Amid strong protest, Brazil does now (for the first time in its history) legally recognize racial difference. But the country remains deeply divided and ambivalent about how to deal with this challenge to the firm belief in racial cordiality and racial tolerance.

BLACK POWER HAIR AND THE EXAMPLE OF SOUL

The rising popularity of domestic (Brazilian) and imported North American hip-hop in the 1980s and 1990s was not the first time a preference for black culture and the "hypervisibility" of blackness inspired strong reactions. Anthropologist Peter Fry (1982) notes that Brazil has historically embraced many African traditions (from the national dish of *feijoada* to the celebrated music of *samba*), incorporating them into national culture as signs of Brazil's pride in its racial mixture. However, beyond these emblems of *brasilidade* (the "harmonious" mixing of African, European, and Native heritage), overt associations with blackness have often been carefully avoided. Affiliation with African religions (such as Umbanda and Candomblé) and music and dance (including, most notably, *capoeira*) was once risky and inspired everything from acts of state violence and oppression to general disdain, even by Brazilian academics (see, for example, Landes 1986 [1971], 1994). It is thus useful to compare the moment in which politically conscious hip-hop was received to the controversy that ensued during Brazil's relatively recent embrace of "soul" in the 1970s. Academics and black organizations have described the importation of soul as a historic moment that was critical to the start of current-day Brazilian racial empowerment groups such as black nongovernmental organizations (black NGOs; see Alberto 2011; Dunn 2001). And yet, at the time, the Brazilian press, as well as famous musicians and intellectuals, lambasted soul fans for taking up "a racist, foreign, commercial fad" (McCann 2002:52). For our purposes here, two aspects of this cultural and political moment are worth noting: First, fans of soul took up cultural and linguistic practices to increase the visibility of blackness on their bodies (as hip-hop fans do also). Second, the strong reaction that described these bodily practices as "imported" and even "racist" sheds light on how connections to blackness were especially risky, given a larger sociopolitical context in which the Brazilian military dictatorship was enforcing racial tolerance and prohibiting discussions of racial difference (Alberto 2009; Covin 2006; J. Dávila 2013; Hanchard 1998; Nobles 2000).

In the 1970s, the most visible sign of an affiliation with soul was the large iconic Afro that Brazilians labeled, in a mix of English and Portuguese, *cabelo black-power* (black power hair; see also Hordge-Freeman 2015). As I discuss further in this chapter, hair is a critical part of making a *mano* or a *playboy* in politically conscious hip-hop, and it serves as a powerful reminder that phenotype is impossible to interpret outside cultural practice. Large Afros are cultivated and not, of course, the natural state of curly hair (Pinho 2010:144). Connecting fans both visually and audibly to North American racial ideology and the "black is beautiful" movement, English phrases similarly played a part in changing how bodies looked and sounded. In one of the first accounts of soul in the Brazilian media, notably entitled "Black Rio: O orgulho (importado) de ser negro no Brasil" (Black Rio: The (imported) pride of being black in Brazil), journalist Lena Frias in 1976 described how Brazilian youth watched films such as *Wattstax* in large group screenings with fists raised in the air, chanting along with Jesse Jackson, "I am somebody." To further embody these sentiments and these experiences in everyday life, phrases from the film were then "memorized, repeated, embroidered onto clothing, sung, hummed, danced, [and] whistled" (Frias, quoted in Alberto 2009:16).

In an academic article entitled "When Rio was Black," historian Paulina Alberto (2009) describes how the consumption of soul by disenfranchised youth provoked the shock and anger of many middle-class Brazilians at the time. Similarly, accounts by journalists reveal the hidden racialized divide through which white Brazilian rockers who consumed and styled their bodies after foreign music posed no inherent threat to themselves or others, but poor black youth who relied on "imported" style were deemed imitative, inauthentic, and dangerously un-Brazilian. For example:

> For [Brazilian journalist] Tarlis Batista, soul was an "adhesion to musical formulas produced in an assembly line, abroad," and "could hardly suggest anything beyond the mere conformity of a simple

people, unprepared perhaps to resist being bombarded with fads by the media." Batista concluded this after a conversation with a young *black*, who reportedly "barely knew the meaning of some of the English expressions he repeats to everyone: *'I'm somebody.' 'White Power.' 'The Beautiful Black'*"—which Batista called "mere repetition of foreign words, with an incorrect pronunciation." (Alberto 2009:27)

This statement from the 1970s draws heavily on racial ideas of the inferiority of blackness, with its assumptions about the gullibility and lack of sophistication of black youth. It calls to mind many of the critiques made of North American and Brazilian hip-hop (see, for example, Rose 2008). But it should also prompt the question: what is at stake here? Why were Afros and stock phrases in English so aggravating to members of the Brazilian middle class? Even the term "black soul," spoken in English, was seen as offensive: "It was an obscenity flaunting itself in the cultural capital of Brazil" (Covin 2006:51). Elsewhere I have described how these practices indicated poor black youth's participation in forms of global consumption, which, in turn, challenged the exclusive claims to modernity made by the Brazilian white middle class and elite (Roth-Gordon 2013; see also McCann 2002). But for the moment, I am most interested in how these bodily practices not so subtly suggested that the tables had turned. Brazilian youth of African descent were demonstrating their awareness that their bodies were constantly being "read," and were intentionally, and provocatively, giving their audiences plenty of new reading material.

As the strong public scorn for soul made clear, these new messages of black pride could easily be reinterpreted as signs of nonwhite inferiority and a lack of true cultural (and linguistic) capital (Bourdieu 1994). More dangerously for the people so affiliated, they were also read as signs of disobedience and political rebellion,[2] leading one sixteen-year-old girl to be expelled from her Copacabana high school in 1977 when she refused to cut her Afro (see McCann 2002:52). To further emphasize how much these embodied practices mattered—not only to individuals but also to the Brazilian state—Alberto (2009:10) reminds us that the "fad" surrounding soul music attracted the attention of Rio's secret police, who documented it as "a potential threat to public order and safety" (see also Hanchard 1998:113). Decades later, the controversy surrounding soul's iconic hairstyle continues: both a female Bahian journalist and a *carioca* (Rio) actress were denied passports in 2014 when they presented photos of themselves with "black power" Afros. The Federal Police issued them passports only when new photos were taken, with their hair tied back.[3] It is interesting to note that Brazilian passport applications do not include racial categories as part of the personal identifying information that is collected. And yet reactions to this 1970s-inspired hairstyle show how the state continues to be on the lookout for (and fear) bodies that show signs of "excessive" and "hypervisible" blackness.

RACE TRAFFICKING

While I was conducting fieldwork in the late 1990s in Rio's South Zone *comunidade* of Cruzada (*comunidade* serving as a euphemism for a poor, and poorly maintained, community or housing project), I saw signs of the popularity of both domestic and imported hip-hop all around me. Large murals and graffiti depicted album covers and song lyrics; U.S. sports team logos and references to New York (the legendary birthplace of hip-hop) adorned the most coveted clothing items; and fans took on nicknames of popular rappers (such as KLJ and Mano Brown). Youth I met traded, borrowed, and sometimes bought rap CDs to listen to with individual headphones and personal music players as well as on boom boxes at impromptu nightly gatherings on the public street in front of their buildings. A truly devoted fan listened to the most popular rap songs over and over, to memorize the lines of the sometimes eight-minute songs by heart, as lyrics were not printed on album covers and could not yet be easily acquired by searching the Internet. The groups these youth listened to included the São Paulo–based rap group Racionais MC's (The Rationals), which would go on to sell 1.5 million copies of its award-winning album *Sobrevivendo no Inferno*, and local rapper MV Bill, who was about to release his first album. Unlike other, more commercially driven artists, these groups could be described as "politically conscious." Taking inspiration from African American legends such as Public Enemy and KRS-One, politically conscious Brazilian rap focuses on recounting the stark realities of Brazil's social and geographic periphery, including the dramatic situations of social inequality, the oppressive environment of crime and violence, the dangers of drug use and gang involvement, and daily experiences with police brutality and racism.

The rappers' and their fans' understanding of race and racial inequality is heavily influenced by the U.S. Civil Rights Movement.[4] This includes an embrace of the confrontational stance Brazilians readily associate with North American race relations, a stance that directly contradicts the Brazilian preference for *racismo cordial*, or cordial racism (Fry 1995–96; Sansone 2003). Under the logic of *racismo cordial*, individuals downplay racial differences that might lead to conflict or disagreement, politely "tolerating" blackness but not discussing it directly. Rappers and rap fans also loudly reject the Brazilian social imperative to work toward racial "improvement" through strategies of *boa aparência* (good appearance, or looking and acting white; see chapter 2). Through their attitude, their comportment, and their bodily practices, they openly rebuke the figure of the *negro comportado* (well-behaved black person) and his assigned place in Brazil's racial hierarchy.

When I met Rio rappers MV Bill and DJTR, before they had recorded and released their first CD, they eagerly described their chosen album title: *Traficando Informação* (Trafficking Information; released under this title in 1999). As they explained to me, "If you tell the truth around here, it is like you are a drug dealer." At the time, I understood that their critique of Brazilian structural racism, their revalorization of blackness, and their insistence on a black-white racial binary (which ignored Brazil's pride in its racial mixture) seemed dangerous and illicit "truths" that had to be illegally imported into Brazil. The term *traficando informação* also seemed to encapsulate the rather chilly reaction they often received from broader Brazilian society, which did not see them as legitimate Brazilian musical artists. This is one reason why winning the Brazilian MTV awards was a big deal and why Mano Brown's speech received so much attention.

Situating the rise of politically conscious Brazilian hip-hop within its historical context, however, I have come to believe that their participation in what I have often called *race trafficking*, drawing on MV Bill and DJTR's term, commits the more serious "crime" of making blackness visible. Noticing blackness in Brazil, as I show in this book's opening with the case of the Brazilian journalist sued for racism, has a long history of being seen as "un-Brazilian," improper, and impolite (Guimarães 1995). Forcing others to notice your blackness, as rappers and rap fans work so hard to do, seems especially aggressive and offensive. While black NGOs are also publicly chastised for their "importation" of North American racial beliefs, in addition to the cultural practices that these organizations take from the Caribbean or Africa to inspire Brazilian black pride (Pinho 2010; Sansone 2003), rappers have been especially efficient at wearing a defiant form of blackness on their bodies as signs of intentional racial confrontation (cf. Sansone 2003). Whereas the military dictatorship sent a recent and quite explicit message to not think about divisive racial differences in Brazil, politically conscious rappers, who picked up steam as the country slowly returned to democracy in the 1980s, have been adamant in their response: they are thinking about it.

FIGURE 17. A fan listens to MV Bill's album *Traficando Informação* (Trafficking Information), which rejects *racismo cordial* (cordial racism) and a climate of racial tolerance. Photo by Marcelo Santos Braga.

BLACK BROTHERS AND WHITE *PLAYBOYS*

Rappers worldwide often take up tough, irreverent, and hard-core stances that link them to the somber album covers, hard-hitting lyrics, and aggressive musical sounds first popularized by African American rappers (see, for example, Alim 2006; Rose 1994). As Derek Pardue notes of Brazilian rap, "Hip hop masculinity is about fashioning and displaying hard bodies and hardened faces" (2008:146; see also Mendoza-Denton 2011). In the photo which graces the cover of his debut album, MV Bill (1999) stands unsmiling with no shirt on, displaying his dark muscular chest and a large tattoo. As with the cold, distancing stares Mano Brown is famous for, MV Bill's physical posture is uncompromising and even threatening in order to foreground the challenge he poses to *o sistema*, or "the system" (see also A. Costa 2014). This is not the face of cordial racism, and MV Bill wants his audience to know that he is not interested in being racially "tolerated."

I turn here to describe not only the bodily practices that male rappers engaged in to manage their image but also their clear awareness of how they are being racially interpreted by others. In example 6.1, Rio rappers MV Bill and DJTR explain their chosen hairstyle, which is meant to connect them to African American role models:

EXAMPLE 6.1: PRETO É LADRÃO (THE BLACK GUY IS A THIEF)

MV Bill:	Então quando você raspa a cabeça, corta careca igual 2Pac, entendeu? Você já está agredindo. [a sociedade brasileira] Que esse não é o visual que eles querem. Eles querem o visual do— do negro comportado [o invés de negro assumido], entendeu? Agora o branco, não. O branco pode fazer o cabelo asa delta. Pode cortar aqui, fazer rabo de cavalo. Tá bonito.	So when you shave your head, shave it just like 2Pac, you understand? You are already harassing them. [Brazilian society] Because this isn't the visual that they want. They want the visual of— of the *negro comportado* [the well-behaved black person], understand? Now for white people, this isn't the case. The white guy can wear his hair in a high-top fade. He can cut it here, grow a pony tail. It looks good.
DJTR:	Pode até raspar. [. . .]	He can even shave his head. [. . .]
MV Bill:	Pode raspar. Pode fazer, que tá bonito. [. . .] O branco quando raspa a cabeça, aqui é universitário. O preto é ladrão, tá entendendo?	He can shave it. He can, since it will look good. [. . .] Here when the white guy shaves his head, he's a university student. The black guy is a thief, understand?

Throughout this conversation, MV Bill and DJTR attempt to teach me various lessons about racial meaning and racial hierarchy in Brazil. First and foremost, they want me to understand the ways that bodies are racialized differently due to the combination of phenotype and cultural practices. For them, the most significant contrast is the freedom offered to bodies read as white, while signs of blackness continue to link their bodies and bodily practices to danger and criminality. They simultaneously provide a second, more subtle lesson in reading bodies. If blackness required only the typical suite of phenotypical features (dark skin, tightly curled hair, broader facial features, etc.), then it would not matter *how* one chose to wear one's hair. And yet, as with soul fans who opted for *cabelo black-power*, this has never been the case: the cultural and sociopolitical contexts in which one styles one's hair are deeply implicated in the production of racial meaning. Both DJTR and MV Bill shave their heads because it links them to the toughness of other black rappers whom they admire, even as they are aware that society can ignore these intentions and choose to read them solely in terms of black criminality.

As a final point, MV Bill suggests through his choice of words that these hairstyles enact a kind of *symbolic violence* (Bourdieu 1994). As with the bologna sandwiches mentioned as a sign of poor beach behavior and a lack of bodily control that could easily lead to physical violence (see chapter 4), signs of nonwhiteness (from food choices to hairstyles) are linked to racialized and innate predispositions toward criminality and disorder. In his explanation, MV Bill suggests that a hairstyle does not merely predict violence; the practice is *itself* violent. A shaved head on a body read as black has disrupted the peace—a peace that reigns when black people quietly accept their place in Brazilian society and humbly wear their signs of acquiescence. Bodies with sufficient signs of whiteness do not suffer the same consequences when they engage in similar cultural practices; their excess whiteness offers them some protection from these racializing assumptions (see also Roth-Gordon 2011). Part of white privilege, then, consists of this stylistic freedom, whereas bodies read as black have more limited options. They can seek to "manage" the signs of their blackness, using established strategies of *boa aparência* (including hair straightening), or they can seek to show their *consciência* (consciousness) and *assumir sua negritude* (assume their blackness) through hairstyles that simultaneously link them to criminality and danger.

Aware that they could not opt out of these racial readings, but still hoping to revalorize black practices and the meanings of blackness (see also Pinho 2010), rappers and rap fans spoke quite explicitly about their bodily practices. At one rap concert that I attended in April 1998, Mano Brown addressed his *carioca* audience—predominantly other poor male *favela* (shantytown) youth—in order to transition into one of their older and better-known songs, "Hey [Play]Boy" (Racionais MC's 1990). In example 6.2, he offers a straightforward guide to making the *mano* (black brother) through attention paid to the body:

EXAMPLE 6.2: NÓS SOMOS TODO UMA REVOLUÇÃO (WE ARE ALL A REVOLUTION)

Nós somos todo uma revolução, só, falou mano? A revolução da atitude, tá ligado?	We are all a revolution, that's it, right brother? The revolution of attitude, know what I'm sayin'?
Eu tenho um maior orgulho,	I take a lot of pride,

morô? De usar minha bombeta,
de usar minha jaqueta, morô,
mano? De cortar o cabelo
assim, porque essa é minha vida,
tá ligado? Eu não
preciso usar topete
para imitar playboy,
[gritos, aplausos] morô, mano?
Tá ligado? [ovação]
Minha vida é essa, morô?

okay? In wearing my cap,
in wearing my jacket, okay,
brother? In cutting my hair like
this, because this is my life,
you know what I'm sayin'? I don't
need to have a wavy forelock of
hair to imitate a *playboy,*
[shouts, applause] okay, brother?
Know what I'm sayin'? [applause]
This is my life, okay?

"The revolution" that politically conscious rappers seek is a racial revolution in which poor black-identified youth change their stance toward whiteness and work to visibly display blackness on their bodies. Fans are asked to demonstrate this stance through their aesthetics and through patterns of consumption associated with the imagery of urban African Americans. For poor male youth who are hip-hop's primary audience, this includes short or braided hair, baseball or ski caps, and oversized baggy clothing. The Yankees logo is especially valued, not for its references to baseball (a sport that is poorly understood and poorly regarded in Brazil), but because it is a common marker of hip-hop fashion and blackness worldwide. These North American signifiers identify a Brazilian youth as a *negro assumido* (a black person who has "assumed" his or her blackness), instead of the disparaged *negro acomodado* (a black person who accommodates others). In example 6.3, Mano Brown continues to address his audience at the show and sets his bodily aesthetics and patterns of consumption in explicit contrast to the cultural practices he associates with "black people who sell out" through an embrace of whiteness. He warns his audience about what he views as a lamentable recent shift toward assimilation or whitening among poor community youth:

EXAMPLE 6.3: PAZ ENTRÉ NÓS (PEACE AMONG US)

De lá pra cá mano? De lá pra cá,
vários preto se vendeu. Vários
preto alisou o cabelo,
morô, mano? Vários
preto curtia New
Wave. Vários preto virou
roqueiro. Vários mano traiu

Since then brother? Since then,
a lot of blacks sold out. A lot of
blacks straightened their hair,
okay, brother? A lot of
blacks started listening to New
Wave. A lot of blacks turned into
rock fans. A lot of brothers betrayed

nação, morô mano? Mas
então é o seguinte, porque
o rap é a minha vida, morô? É
minha gíria, minha bombeta, meu
estilo de vida. É o que eu sei fazer.
É o que me deu força para tá
aqui até hoje, morô?
**Paz entre nós. Foda-se os
playboys!** [começo da música:
"Hey [Play]Boy"]

the nation, okay brother? But
the thing is, because
rap is my life, okay? It's
my slang, my cap, my
lifestyle. It's what I know how to do.
It's what gives me the strength to be
here today, okay?
**Peace amongst us. Fuck the
*playboys!*** [start of song:
"Hey [*Play*]*Boy*"]

Speaking directly to his fans, Mano Brown downplays the importance of the phenotypical features of the body. Bodies can appear "black," but their participation in "white" practices is deeply significant and of racial importance. Indeed, his concern, which was the "silver lining" for elite Brazilian intellectuals for the better part of a century, is that dark-skinned bodies can be successfully "whitened" (J. Dávila 2003; D. Davis 1999; Skidmore 1974). In his pitch to take up an anti-assimilationist stance, Mano Brown calls out hair choices that are associated with *boa aparência*, including straightening one's hair to achieve what is commonly called *cabelo bom* (good hair), in contrast to *cabelo ruim* (bad or kinky hair; see Jacobs-Huey 2006; Pinho 2010). Research with black Brazilian women who identify as *negras assumidas* similarly finds that they demonstrate their racial pride by refusing to participate in the common practice of straightening their hair (Caldwell 2007; Hordge-Freeman 2015). Mano Brown is equally concerned about the racial implications of the music one listens to. In the rap song "Pare de Babar (o ovo de Playboy)" (Stop Sucking Up [to *Playboys*]), presented in example 5.1, Rio rapper MV Bill (1999) sharply criticizes youth who "look" black but act white ("preto por fora, branco por dentro") as reflected in their participation in sports such as surfing and their preference for such spaces as expensive dance clubs. The *playboy-mano* opposition that is so central to politically conscious Brazilian hip-hop thus often downplays the physical features associated with race and instead draws heavily on *ideas* about blackness and whiteness and the ways that these can be displayed through cultural and linguistic practices.

This difference between racial displays is artistically portrayed in a cartoon by André Mello that accompanied an article in the national newspaper *O Globo* entitled "Racionais MC's são os 'manos' contra os 'playboys'" (Racionais MC's are the "brothers" against the "*playboys*"). Mello draws two male figures, one with light-brown skin and the other a paler white; they both grimace and menacingly hold up fists to each other. Despite the fact that their skin color is not made to look dramatically different, the two male youth are contrasted through the "predictable set of accessories" that accompany their racialized bodies (Weismantel 2001:184). Thus the rapper wears a ski cap, labeled "MC," and he sports heavy-metal jewelry around his neck, around his wrist, and on every finger. By contrast, the *playboy* is drawn with a prominent *topete*, that controversial wavy forelock of hair that Mano Brown mocks in example 6.2, as a strong marker of his whiteness. His tools of whiteness include a cell phone clipped to his waist (an expensive novelty in the late 1990s), an earring, and a big watch.

It is also of interest that the accompanying article, by Arnaldo Jabor (1998), praises the nationally renowned rap group for its painfully honest portrayal of "esta brutal divisão de rendas" (this brutal income division) and denounces the Brazilian middle class when we "falamos de nariz tapado: 'Que horror!' E é só." (speak with our noses covered, "The horror!" And do nothing.). Yet for all his praise, he mentions nothing of Racionais MC's loud denunciation of racism, repeatedly pointing to poverty as the source of their misery, anger, and exclusion. He is not the only one to actively ignore the racial critique that rappers advertise on their bodies and through their language. The binary opposition that rappers and rap fans seek to solidify between *manos* (black brothers) and *playboys* (wealthy, privileged white boys) often loses its racial meaning for middle-class Brazilians who prefer to discuss social inequality solely in terms of class. In my conversations with middle-class families, most were adamant that *playboys* were rich, overprivileged kids, not middle-class ones. Unsurprisingly, and despite the work that rappers and rap fans perform to make these racial differences more pronounced and visible (including their calling out of whiteness), members of the middle class whom I interviewed said nothing about race in their description of a *playboy* (Roth-Gordon 2007a).

DISPLAYING BLACKNESS

Apart from well-known rappers, rap fans took up the challenge of constantly displaying blackness and demanding the same from their peers. In previous publications, I have analyzed how rap fans not only wore blackness on their bodies (through their choice of hairstyles, clothes, and accessories) but also how they actively sought to publicly affirm their connection to the

Racionais MC's são os 'manos' contra os 'playboys'

Finalmente um fato político novo aparece na paisagem pop

FIGURE 18. Politically conscious Brazilian hip-hop pits *manos* (black brothers) against *playboys* (white wealthy male youth) in an attempt to make race and class differences more visible. Image by André Mello. Used with permission granted by Agência O Globo.

blackness of hip-hop through their daily speech. I offer here a few examples of what I call *conversational sampling* (Roth-Gordon 2009a, 2012), a linguistic practice in which youth quoted from popular politically conscious rap songs in their daily speech. (This is why memorizing eight-minute songs was so essential to my research assistant CW and his friends.) While lyrics were occasionally sung, or led to the singing of the rest of a song, they were just as easily spoken within regular conversational speech, offering knowledgeable listeners the opportunity to demonstrate their recognition of the source by repeating the lyrics or adding others in response. In example 6.4, two Cruzada youth, CW and Smoke, ask to listen to a friend's personal music player, but the friend, nicknamed Dog, refuses to hand it over, because

he is embarrassed by what he has been listening to. A verbal racial struggle
ensues:

EXAMPLE 6.4: PERIFERIA É PERIFERIA (PERIPHERY IS PERIPHERY)

CW:	Deixa eu ver [o aparelho]. Deixa eu mariar. Deixa eu mariar. Não. Deixa eu mariar. Só pra me criticar. [. . .]	Let me listen [to the player]. Let me check it out. Let me check it out. No. Let me check it out. Just so I can make fun. [. . .]
Dog:	Não, tem nada pra tocar aí.	No, there's nothing good playing.
Smoke:	Cho ver, cho ver, cho ver.	Lemme see, lemme see, lemme see.
CW:	Porra, tá com uma marra de playboy fudida, heim. [. . .]	Shit, you have the attitude of a fucking *playboy*, huh. [. . .]
Dog:	Tá me confundindo com quê?	You are confusing me with what?
Smoke:	Playboy.	*Playboy*.
CW:	Daqui a pouco tu tá usando topetinho aí.	Soon you'll be wearing your hair with a little forelock.
Smoke:	É.	Yeah.
Dog:	Sou é **"periferia é periferia,"** rapá. [. . .] **"Periferia é periferia, Racionais no ar, filho da puta, plá plá plá."**	What I am is **"periphery is periphery,"** man. [. . .] **"Periphery is periphery, Racionais on the air, son of a bitch, *pla, pla, pla.*"**

In this conversation, the negotiation of what or who Dog "is" fuses the
consumption of music and hairstyle with a stance toward or away from
whiteness. The wrong song can suggest one's participation in acts of assimilation and imply whitening or "selling out." In order to defend himself
from this racialized attack, Dog linguistically equates himself with a
Racionais MC's title and then continues on to sing lyrics from two different
songs, ending with a verbally aggressive profanity term and the onomato-
poetic *plá plá plá* (meant to represent gunshots; see also Roth-Gordon
2007b). The use of sound words to represent gunfire is discussed by Mano
Brown in lyrics to the song "Capítulo 4, Versículo 3" (Chapter 4, Verse 3;
Racionais MC's 1998). "Minha palavra vale um tiro e eu tenho muita
munição" (My word is like a bullet and I have lots of ammunition). Later in

the song he raps, "A fúria negra ressuscita outra vez" (The black fury rises again). Rappers and rap fans thus draw on and reinforce connections between blackness and violence to demonstrate their strong contempt for racial cordiality and the push to whiteness.

In this face-threatening exchange between friends, Dog's retort hinges on demonstrating sufficient signs of blackness. To counteract the fact that the wrong kind of music could make him look like a *playboy*, Dog must quickly display the comportment, sensibilities, and consumption practices of a *mano*. To index toughness and a rejection of whiteness, Dog takes up the aggressive stance of rappers, using linguistic features such as profanity, sound words, and references to rap songs. Compare Mano Brown's parting shot in example 6.3, "Paz entre nós. Foda-se os playboys!" (Peace amongst us. Fuck the *playboys*!), with rap fan Dog's linguistic defense "Periferia é periferia, Racionais no ar, filho da puta, plá plá plá" (Periphery is periphery. Racionais on the air, son of a bitch, *plá plá plá*).[5] Such a strong linguistic response is needed because this racial challenge cannot go unanswered. Just as his friend Mano did when stopped and interrogated by the military police (in example 2.2), Dog leans heavily on the racial meanings embedded in specific spaces and practices, and it is language that helps solidify these connections.

Bola, the *playboy bandido* (playboy bandit) described in chapter 5, provides his own illustration of this defiant display of blackness as he works through how he was racially read by others. As I have previously mentioned, Bola is from a solidly middle-class background. He lives in a wealthy neighborhood; he has studied at a well-known private school in the South Zone; and he has followed the common trajectory of middle-class youth, as the education his mother has provided for him has earned him high enough scores on college entrance exams to enter a prestigious public university in Rio. His interest in basketball, instead of the national sport of soccer, led to a friendship with CW, my research assistant who lived in a neighboring housing project. When I met him, Bola was spending significant amounts of time hanging around in Cruzada, where he constantly had to negotiate his partly "outsider" status. Not only was he significantly wealthier than other community residents, and on a different career path, but he was lighter-skinned than many of them, though darker-skinned than his wealthy schoolmates. Affiliation with politically conscious hip-hop was an easy way to take on blackness. Because the *mano-playboy* opposition relied so heavily on racial positioning, rather than just phenotype, one's attitude was everything. Of course, outside the world of hip-hop and hip-hop fandom, one could not guarantee a similar racial reading.

In example 6.5, Bola tells me and his friend Tiny, who is CW's cousin, about the anxiety he experienced upon receiving his forms back from the Brazilian army:

EXAMPLE 6.5: PRETO TIPO "B+" (A TYPE "B+" BLACK GUY)

Tiny:	Aí, o teu veio "negro"? [o formulário do exército]	So, yours came with "*negro*"? [his form for the army]
Bola:	Ah?	Huh?
Tiny:	O teu veio que cor?	Yours came with what color?
Bola:	Aí tá. [. . .] Aí o meu cuti— cor da pele. Aí veio moreno, moreno não sei o quê. Eu: "Ah, que beleza!" Fiquei felizão, tá entendendo?	Oh okay. [. . .] So my complex— skin color. So it came out *moreno* [brown], *moreno* something. I [was like]: "Ah, sweet!" I was super happy, understand?
Jennifer:	Que eles não botaram branco para você?	That they didn't put down white for you?
Bola:	É lógico! Se me desse branco, eu ia reclamar. Eu ia falar: "Onde tem branco aqui, minha filha? Meu cabelo, meu cabelo é aqui. Minha cor. Não tem branco aqui não." Aqui. Botei o papel aqui. Tem branco aqui? [Risos] Fode. Ia me revoltar, já. Sou preto. Preto tipo— tipo— //assim—	Of course! If they had given me white, I would have complained. I would have said: "Where is there a white guy around here, my daughter? [term of address] My hair, this is my hair. My color. There aren't any white people here no." I [would have] put the paper in front of her. Is there a white person here? [Laughter] Shit. I would have gone crazy. I am black. Black like— like— //a—
Tiny:	//Um "B+"	//A "B+"
Bola:	Mentalmente, mentalmente eu sou "A," tá entendendo? //Mas fisicamente assim, um	Mentally, mentally I am an "A," understand? //But physically like, a
Tiny:	//"B" um— um "B–" um "B+" um "B+" um "B+" Tá bom. [Risos]	//"B" a— a "B–" a "B+" a "B+" a "B+" That's good. [Laughter]

Bola:	Tá entendendo? Porra,	Do you understand me? Shit,
	na moral, quando vi moreno,	seriously, when I saw *moreno*,
	eu fiquei— meu sorriso veio	I was— my smile went from
	aqui a aqui. Eu: "Ah,	here to here. I [was like]: "Ah
	que beleza!" Porra, sei lá.	sweet!" Shit, I don't know.
	Era— se botasse branco	It was— if they had put white
	ali, a pessoa era como se	there, it would be like the
	tivesse me—	person was hum—
	me humilhando, sabe?	humiliating me, you know?

Bola's relief at being labeled *moreno*, instead of placed into the category of "white" (which he obviously feared was a strong possibility), is worth exploring for several reasons. To begin with, his reaction evokes his mother's, described at the end of chapter 5. When Bola begins to spend more time in the housing project of Cruzada, his mother is not worried about him having contact with the poor, darker-skinned people who live there. She grows increasingly concerned, however, when their linguistic behavior influences his own and when slang-filled utterances that index blackness threaten to erase the linguistic grooming she has carefully engaged in (and paid for) over the course of many years. She ultimately fears that he could be read as an uneducated black kid from a shantytown—and treated as one. Bola, too, is concerned that bodies can be misread. Despite his mental attitude and the many racial signs he intentionally displays on and through his body, from his clothing, to his posture, his language, and his hip-hop affiliation, the Brazilian army could still decide to categorize him as white. Their opposing fears that the same body could be treated as "black" or, alternatively, categorized as "white" stem not only from his brown skin and "mixed" racial features but, more important, from the fact that bodies are always read within specific contexts.

In recounting this story, Bola has a new audience that he hopes to influence. He tells this story precisely because the army form has not resolved his racial status, his racial identity, or the racially fraught environment that he lives in. He wants to prove to his friend Tiny and to me, the North American researcher, that he is definitely not white, that he is more *mano* than *playboy*. But being a *mano*, just like identifying as nonwhite, requires constant acts of racial positioning and work on the body. He draws on his knowledge of hip-hop for some fancy linguistic footing (Goffman 1981) and racial stance work (McIntosh 2009). Not only have groups such as Racionais MC's popularized particular speech styles, including a lot of profanity and slang to associate themselves with the black space of *a periferia* (the periphery), but they have also coined expressions meant to evoke North American themes of racial empowerment. This generation's versions of "black is beautiful" and "Black Power" included *4P: poder para o povo preto* (4P: power for the black people) and *preto tipo A* (literally "a class A black person"). *Preto tipo A* is commonly defined as a black person who is racially conscious, places value in being black, and who fights for his rights and deserves respect. In the song Bola "samples" from, "Capítulo 4, Versículo 3" (Chapter 4, Verse 3), Racionais MC's criticize a *preto tipo A* who eventually "sells out" and aspires after white culture: "Mas começou colar com os branquinhos do shopping; Ai já era. Ih mano, outra vida, outro pique" (But he began to hang out with the little white guys of the shopping mall. So that was it. Brother, another life, another pace). Bola's negotiation of his racial "grade" (ultimately, his friend awards him a B+) is thus a claim to blackness backed up with insider hip-hop knowledge. His quoting of a phrase made popular through Brazilian rap lyrics allows him to affiliate himself with black culture and distance himself from accusations of whitening and whiteness and the attendant "humiliation."

Displaying pride in being "black" was another way of making blackness visible, particularly through the choice of terms used to describe one's body. In example 6.5, my assistant CW and his friend KLJ (nicknamed after the rapper) discuss the growing preference in the 1990s for the racial term *negro* (black), instead of the color term *preto* (also black), which was still more commonly used on the census and in daily life. The distinction between these two terms exemplifies one particular debate over Brazilian "exceptionalism," which relies on the idea that Brazil has avoided racial conflict because Brazilians notice color but do not see or identify with racial groups (Fry 1995–96, 2000). CW and KLJ show how understandings of these two terms were changing, due in part to the popularity of hip-hop and in part to the work of black activists and NGOs (see also Garcia 2006).[6]

EXAMPLE 6.6: PRETO É CHÃO (BLACK IS THE COLOR OF THE FLOOR)

CW:	Tu é preto, ou é branco? Heim? A pergunta que ela tá te fazendo.	Are you *preto* [black], or are you white? Huh? The question she's asking you.
KLJ:	Se eu sou o quê?	If I'm what?
CW:	Preto ou é branco?	*Preto* or are you white?
KLJ:	Eu sou negro. Preto é o asfalto.	I'm *negro* [black]. Asphalt is *preto*.

CW:	Lápis de cor.	Colored pencils.
Jennifer:	Preto é o quê?	What is *preto*?
KLJ:	Preto é— é— é cor, lápis de cor. É asfalto. É pneu. A minha cor é negra. Cor— cor . . . negra. Preto é chão, chinelo, pneu.	*Preto* is— is— is a color, colored pencils. It's asphalt. It's a tire. My color is *negra*. Color— color . . . *negra*. *Preto* is the floor, sandals, a tire.
CW:	Isso aqui. Marcelo sempre falava isso, "Preto? Eu é negro." Ele arrumou uma confusão no hospital. Porque era "preto— preto, pardo, e branco." [se referindo ao formulário que Marcelo teve que preencher no hospital]	That's right. Marcelo always said that, "*Preto*? What I am is *negro*." He created a scene in the hospital. Because it said "*preto*— black, brown, and white." [referring to a form Marcelo had to fill out in the hospital]
KLJ:	É negro, rapaz.	It's *negro*, man.
CW:	"Preto? Eu sou é negro. Pode ir tirando essa porra daí. Eu sou é negro."	"*Preto*? What I am is *negro*. You can get rid of this crap here. What I am is *negro*."

Here Cruzada youth participate in what was one of the more salient racial struggles at the time—trying to change the linguistic terms that have been employed to describe Brazilians of African descent. Racial classification figured strongly in the debates over affirmative action at the start of the twenty-first century (as I am about to discuss), yet the struggle over racial categories can be traced back at least eighty years, as black activists worked at, and eventually succeeded in, semantically shifting the term *negro* from a negative term, used by slave masters to describe their less docile and more "rebellious" slaves, to a positive term that signified black pride (Garcia 2006). *Negro* thus became the term of choice for black activists. Influenced by these messages of racial empowerment, CW and KLJ dismiss *preto* as merely a color that applies only to objects, and they agree that the more respectful term for people of African descent is *negro*. These defiant acts of black pride, such as crossing out given color options to write in their preferred racial term, challenged Brazil's own pride in its racial tolerance, which hinges on the downplaying of racial difference. Racial tolerance was about to endure an even greater challenge, however, as black activists convinced the Brazilian government to implement racial quotas at the nation's most prestigious public universities (Tavolaro 2008).

CHALLENGING RACIAL TOLERANCE

As Brazilian state and federal universities began to enact affirmative action policies at the turn of the millennium, they each made different decisions about how to confirm racial difference in order to distribute quota spots. Could the applicant self-identify? Or did one's blackness have to be visible to others? What would prevent racial fraud? Was it even possible to tell who is black in Brazil (Santos 2006)? Among the most controversial policies was the formation of a committee that would judge photos taken of applicants on the day they submitted their college applications at the Universidade de Brasília. In 2007, a picture-perfect case landed in the hands of those who disagreed with the quota policy in the first place. Identical twins, identified as children of a black father and a white mother, both took photos and submitted their applications on the same day, but the judges' decisions were not the same. On its cover, the news magazine *Veja* highlighted the medium-brown-skinned twins (who have no other "black" phenotypical features) and the situation of their dramatically split vote. For the staged cover photo, one twin was photographed in a white shirt against a white background; the other, in a black shirt against a black background. The caption read: "Eles são gêmeos idênticos, mas . . . segundo a UnB, um é branco e o outro é negro," (They are identical twins, but . . . according to the University of Brasília, one is white and the other is black; see Zakabi and Camargo 2007). The fact that *Veja* freely identified one parent as "white" and the other as "black" did not seem to contradict the point that the magazine sought to make by publicizing this unusual case: race, and blackness, could not be read off of bodies, and claiming otherwise was a risky, potentially embarrassing enterprise. While the country was proud of its history of criminalizing racism (as early as 1951), it remained divided about legally acknowledging the existence of racial difference and structural racism.

Veja is a fairly conservative news magazine, and it was therefore not surprising to find that it did not support the policy of racial quotas and that it would use the debacle of the identical twins to reassert its belief that Brazil is not a racist country:

> As políticas raciais que se pretende implantar no país por força da lei têm potencial explosivo porque se assentam numa assertiva equivocada: a de que a sociedade brasileira é, em essência, racista. Nada mais falso.

> The racial policies that they are planning to institute throughout the
> country by force of law have the potential to explode because they base
> themselves on a false assertion: that Brazilian society is, at its heart, racist.
> Nothing could be further from the truth. (Zakabi and Camargo 2007)

Subtle and not-so-subtle allusions to the perils of recognizing racial difference pervade the article. Classifying people by the color of their skin is
something engaged in by the Nazis and South Africa's apartheid regime.
The United States, a favorite racial anxiety–provoking comparison (Rosa-
Ribeiro 2000), gets a brief mention at the beginning of the article through
an allusion to Martin Luther King Jr.:

> Um absurdo ocorrido em Brasília veio em boa hora. Ele é o sinal de que
> o Brasil está enveredando pelo perigoso caminho de tentar avaliar as
> pessoas não pelo conteúdo de seu caráter, mas pela cor de sua pele.
>
> An absurd occurrence in Brasília has come just in time. It is the sign
> that Brazil is headed on the dangerous path of trying to judge people
> not by the content of their character, but by the color of their skin.
> (Zakabi and Camargo 2007)

Just in case the reader is not clear that officially noticing racial difference is
the harbinger of racial conflict, the authors conclude: "O Brasil, que tinha o
privilégio de ser oficialmente cego em relação à cor da pele de seus habi-
tantes, infelizmente corre o risco de ser mergulhado no ódio racial" (Brazil,
which had the privilege of being officially blind in relation to the skin color
of its inhabitants, unfortunately runs the risk of being thrown headfirst
into racial hatred; Zakabi and Camargo 2007).

I draw on these statements, akin to what is argued by journalists like *O
Globo*'s Ali Kamel (2006) in his book *Não Somos Racistas* (We Are Not
Racist), to explain the importance of the belief in racial tolerance that rappers were seen to (and chose to) violate. Racial tolerance is the opposite of
the racial hatred so clearly on display in the Holocaust, during South Africa's
apartheid regime, and throughout the history of U.S. race relations, and it
suggests (however falsely) that the Brazilian state has successfully protected
its residents from those experiences of brutal racial violence and conflict.
Racial tolerance is also far easier to defend and to continue to believe in than
racial democracy, which suggests that people are not treated differently
because of the color of their skin. (Many Brazilians now agree that they are.)

The note of panic in the *Veja* article stems from the belief that noticing
racial difference (and blackness, in particular) necessarily leads to racial tur-
moil and hatred. This, in and of itself, is nothing new to those familiar with
Brazilian race relations. The nation has long compared its generally peaceful

state of racial coexistence to the state of near-constant racial conflict seen in the United States. Points of transnational contrast include the United States's incredibly bloody war to end slavery; the dozens of laws that enacted racial barriers and segregation based on complicated formulas that determined amounts of blackness; the decades of graphic scenes of lynching; the equally graphic (and well-publicized) scenes of civil rights protests met with brutal acts of police violence; and the even more recent rioting after police incidents involving Rodney King, Trayvon Martin, and Michael Brown (to name just a few). To Brazilian eyes, such scenes of savage violence and racial hatred seem not only ugly but also downright uncivilized.

Race has long been the one area in which Brazil understood itself to be superior to the United States. The idea of importing "lessons" (in the form of affirmative action laws) from their inferior in race relations thus seems, to some Brazilians, both backwards and insulting (Fry et al. 2007). But I think even those who study comparative race relations have not emphasized strongly enough the way that a North American history of racial violence has led Brazil to enforce ideas of racial tolerance, justifying unspoken rules that Brazilians should peacefully stay "in their place." It is racial tolerance, not racial democracy, that allows the YouTube commenter "Kleber Poeta" in this chapter's opening vignette to suggest that Mano Brown should show his humility by thanking the family that paid his mother to wash their son's expensive clothes. Mano Brown's mother was not being treated as an equal by the family, nor did she have the same rights and resources, but she was not being actively mistreated, nor are there visible acts of violence and hatred in the typical *patroa-empregada* (homeowner–domestic worker) relationship (Goldstein 2003). It is his own display of a "civilized" racial tolerance that also dictates that Kleber Poeta need not mention the whiteness of this family or the blackness of Mano Brown's mother, just as he also politely ignores the racial critique and cries of racism for which Mano Brown has just received national acclaim.

Although many people (including some Brazilian race scholars) are still unhappy with Brazil's new policies that rely on the recognition of racial difference, affirmative action has survived multiple court challenges. Black activists and antiracist scholars seem to have won this particular battle. In 2015, protests were organized in several Brazilian cities under the banner "Marcha Nacional Contra o Genocídio do Povo Negro" (National March Against the Genocide of Black People), but few Brazilians would agree that they are living through an era of black genocide, nor would they agree that the Brazilian nation-state has acted violently against black people since the end of slavery (see also Hanchard 1998:56; C. Smith 2016:83–84). A protest against the genocide of black people is the Brazilian equivalent of the Black Lives Matter campaign, which swept across social media in the United States in response to the police killings of unarmed black men in cities across the country. Although there are many differences between the two national contexts and the issues that prompted the protests, the concern over disproportionate levels of state violence toward poor black men is shared, as is the "antiprotest" sentiment that seeks to defend law and order and dismiss the claims of structural racism.

Racial tolerance suggests that although Brazil maintains a racial hierarchy, it has managed to keep the peace over centuries, which (proponents of this argument imply) is ultimately beneficial for all Brazilians. The mainstream success of politically conscious hip-hop in the 1990s, debates over federal affirmative action quotas at the turn of the millennium, and recent national protests against the genocide of black people all challenge this belief that racial tolerance "saved" Brazil from the terrible racism and racial conflicts experienced by other nations, and these developments make visible the presence of Brazilians who no longer want to accept their part in the racial "deal" of tolerance.[7] Rappers and rap fans respond to the polite ignoring of racial difference by dialing up their embrace of cultural and linguistic practices linked to blackness. In so doing, they turn the tables on when and how Brazilians must pay attention to race. "Reading" bodies for racial signs is a discreet and seemingly noninvasive act that, I argue in this book, Rio residents perform constantly and without much explicit discussion. Being forced to "see" and recognize blackness on the bodies of others seems, to many, unnecessarily coercive, divisive, and even "unpatriotic."

While politically conscious Brazilian hip-hop revels in the display of a hypervisible blackness, Brazilians on the whole still struggle with their long legacy of treating blackness as a stigma that should be hidden, "managed," or politely ignored. Racial cordiality suggests that Brazilians can avoid distasteful and dangerous racial conflict by emphasizing social relations and "conviviality" (R. Anderson 2012:63; A. Costa 2016).[8] And yet, shortly after the peak of attention that politically conscious hip-hop received in mainstream media, the political challenges of affirmative action, which require Brazilians to declare a race and embrace their blackness, have forced the issue of racial difference further into the public consciousness. Brazil's "comfortable racial contradiction" continues, as many Brazilians (including some who do, or could, identify as black; see S. Mitchell 2016) prefer quotas based on socioeconomic class that do not force them to acknowledge and emphasize racial difference. I take up this larger question of what it means to "see" race in the conclusion.

Conclusion

"Seeing" Race

Nearly twenty years after my first visit to Brazil, I returned to Rio de Janeiro with my whole family to live in Ipanema while I conducted new research on race, parenting, and privilege. My white biological son and my adopted middle son and adopted daughter (both African American and dark-skinned) all attended a well-known, large Brazilian private school in the neighborhood, where we were well received. One day, after I had attended a parent meeting at the school, I stopped by my six-year-old daughter's after-school swimming lesson in the school's indoor pool. I had planned to watch her swim a lap, mark my presence, and then run home to work on this book while she finished her group lesson. She swam across the pool, and I gave her a big wave. She came over and, before I could tell her that I was leaving, she asked (in English): "Is my skin black?" I realized that book writing was going to have to wait. "What do you mean?" I responded while trying to figure out what had prompted this inquiry. Apparently, while the students were waiting to swim their laps, a girl from her class, Giovanna, had told her (in Portuguese) that her skin was black, and my daughter had disagreed.

My daughter, Sophie, had been in Brazil long enough to understand what Giovanna meant, but, in that moment, her nonnative fluency was compounded by the tricky relationship between color and race. "My skin is not black," she told me (not for the first time). "It is brown." Another girl, Raíssa, whom Sophie didn't know, had jumped in to take Giovanna's side. "Your skin is black," she told my daughter confidently. A fairly innocent observation of racial difference had now turned into a two-on-one disagreement. I reminded Sophie that people sometimes describe race differently than color. "My skin is not this color," I said I as pointed to something white, "but people call me white." Brazilians and Brazilianists who study

185

race relations for a living will appreciate the irony of the Brazilian calling my daughter *negra* (using a racial term), while my daughter, the North American, relied on a color term to argue that she was "brown." I tried to explain that she could be both brown and black.

I called over the swim instructor and explained the situation. She assured me that she would talk to the girls, as an older woman nearby (most likely a waiting grandmother), clucked disapprovingly at the girls' comments. "As it is commonly understood," Elisa Larkin Nascimento observes, "a racist is someone who speaks of racism or mentions that someone else is black; silence is considered the nonracist attitude" (2007:5). I talked to several parents, including Giovanna's mother, whom I knew. "Giovanna has been talking about Sophie's color," she immediately acknowledged. "And I told her that we call her *negra*, not *preta*," she said, distinguishing between two Portuguese terms for the color black. She mentioned that other classmates had been talking about Sophie's visible difference, and this too was confirmed by their parents. They were dismayed by the current situation, which violated their preference not to notice racial difference, and at least one father rushed to tell me and Sophie that she was beautiful: "Ela é linda! Sophie, você é linda!" As anthropologist Denise Ferreira da Silva has noted, "To name someone black, without the qualification that this person does not share negative meanings associated with blackness, is highly offensive" (1998:228).

The swim instructor explained to the girls that there was nothing seriously different about them: "How many eyes do you have? How many does Sophie have? How many noses? You are the same!" The next day, Sophie's classroom teacher got defensive when I suggested that maybe she had heard the kids discussing this already (she said she had not). She decided to address the situation by explaining to the class that they should always defend their friend, and she reiterated what Giovanna's mother had told Giovanna prior to the "incident." The more respectful term for someone with skin like Sophie was *negra*, not *preta*, as the hip-hop–affiliated youth in my study had argued back in the late 1990s (see chapter 6). Afterward, Giovanna drew Sophie a card, with one dark-brown hand next to a peach-colored one that represented her own very light skin, and wrote: "Você é a minha amiga" (You are my friend).

I share this story not because it is unique to (or even representative of) my daughter's experience in Rio. Only a few months after we returned from Brazil to our home in Tucson, Arizona, Sophie received another lesson in the visibility of her blackness, from Mia, a girl who was adopted from Guatemala (and was thus brown-skinned but not as dark as Sophie). Mia was so upset that my daughter chose to draw her skin brown at art camp that she reached over and colored black on my daughter's self-portrait. More conversations ensued, and they were friends by the end of the week.

Despite the seemingly happy endings, these tales of color and race "confusion" belie more pressing social imperatives to (not) notice racial difference and to process the meanings of blackness (Fazzi 2004). Although Sophie's friends both in Rio de Janeiro, Brazil, and Tucson, Arizona, are having similar conversations, it should go without saying that there is nothing "natural" about these children's observations. The developmental milestone they have hit is a burgeoning ability to process the real-world situations of inequality that they have been born (or moved) into. In both the private Brazilian swim lessons and the private North American art camp, Sophie is often the only dark-skinned child present. The teachers are almost always lighter-skinned, and darker-skinned adults occupy only low-level service jobs, when they are even present in these spaces. To begin to understand how and why skin color is unequally distributed across the hierarchically structured environments that they move through, Brazilian and North American children have to draw on racial ideas that are centuries old and yet have been inflected with local, national, cultural, and historical nuances. They must learn, in short, to "see" race.

This day at Sophie's swimming lessons helpfully encapsulates how what I have called Brazil's comfortable racial contradiction persists, even as the world of Brazilian race relations keeps changing. The readiness of middle-class observers to discuss the situation, with their children, with teachers, and with other parents, and how they discuss it, provides useful examples of what is "new." What has been described as "cultural censorship" (Sheriff 2001), the "hypernegation of race" (Vargas 2004), and "the ideology of racial exceptionalism" (Hanchard 1998) still influences people's (un)willingness to acknowledge racial difference, social etiquette that Giovanna and her friend Raíssa had violated. But metadiscussions about how to properly talk about race were now possible, including discussions of preferred terminology, which had also changed. The term *negra* was no longer primarily associated with slavery and insult. Anthropologist Robin Sheriff asked dark-skinned *favela* (shantytown) residents of Rio in the early 1990s why they did not like being called *negro*. In her book *Dreaming Equality*, she recounts the most memorable response: "With considerable invective, [one woman] leaned over me and replied, 'How would you like it if someone called you a worthless, ugly thing, shit, dirt, less than a dog?'" (2003:95; see also M. Harris 1952:61). Some of the Brazilian parents and the clucking grandmother clearly objected to the children's "noticing" my daughter's racial difference, and some rushed to combat the negative associations that blackness still carries ("She's beautiful!"), but using the term *negro* to sound more respectful when discussing blackness was now widespread.

The similarities to the Paulo Henrique Amorim conviction with which I open this book are also instructive. Talk about racial difference, if not avoided entirely, must be polite and respectful, and critiques of underlying structural racism are still silenced. As I stood around discussing the situation with parents, teachers, and grandparents, all *moreno* (light brown) or light-skinned, the only dark-skinned people in the room were never consulted. These women (and there were several) were the nannies and the poorly paid school assistants whose job was to peel little bodies out of wet bathing suits, take them to the bathroom, shower them, and get them ready for parent pick-up. Not only did these women have intimate physical contact with the very children whom we were discussing, but at least one of them (an assistant whom I had interviewed) had personal experience dealing with situations of racism that her own daughter had encountered at a public school. The blatant racial hierarchy in the room was not addressed while we discussed this racial incident, nor was it disturbed (see also Windsor 2007).

On a different day, I took my family to a new museum in downtown Rio. At a hands-on exhibit where one used alphabet soup letters to write messages in the sand, a young girl who looked to be around ten spelled out "*não racismo.*" She was light-skinned, as were the vast majority of other museum patrons that day. Perhaps she was responding to new laws that require schools to teach about Afro-Brazilian culture and history. Or maybe she was sharing her version of the well-publicized slogans of that year's World Cup (after several high-profile expressions of fan racism). In the current climate, the antiracist ideas that she spelled out made her seem mature, well educated, and "civilized" (Guimarães 1995). But few Brazilians of African descent would visit this museum and see her message.

Together, these examples illustrate the three racial "facts" of Brazil that I emphasize in chapter 1 of this book: (1) structural racism continues to be deeply embedded; (2) positive views of whiteness and negative ideas of blackness persist; and (3) racial tolerance is preferred, while noticing racial difference is to be avoided. My objective here, based on a detailed analysis of cultural and linguistic practices, has been to better understand how this racial contradiction encourages Rio residents to "read" bodies for signs of race and racial capacity, even as the racial implications of these readings are not fully acknowledged, rarely explicitly discussed, and even actively downplayed.

DINHEIRO EMBRANQUECE (MONEY WHITENS)

This book has explored both the comfortable daily conversations that occurred within established race and class boundaries, as well as the more complicated interactions that stretched dangerously across them. As a counter to the analysis that I have just provided of reactions to my daughter's experience as her peers began discussing racial difference in Brazil, some may rightfully point out that among the nannies, the domestic housemaids who were there to pick up children, and the poorly paid janitors and school assistants, there were also several lighter-skinned women who, like their darker-skinned colleagues, would not have been invited by educated middle-class parents to join in our conversation about how to talk about racial difference and racism. This is, and has long been, the sticking point to recognizing racism and racial hierarchy within Brazil: how can one single out for blame the stigma of blackness, or the pervasiveness of racism, if lighter-skinned people are also subject to discrimination, are made invisible to the middle class through their relegation to service work, and are struggling to achieve social mobility? This is precisely why Rio's state university (UERJ) has affirmative action policies that currently allow 20 percent of students to enter under racial quotas reserved for those who willingly self-identify as black (in addition to demonstrating financial need), while another 20 percent of spaces are reserved for the highest-scoring public school students (who are assumed to be poor but do not necessarily identify themselves as black).[1] Individuals, and the state, continue to grapple with how to make sense of and address the multiple factors of inequality in Brazil. The intersections of race and class are complicated: Rio residents never "see" race without also seeing class, and one's class status influences how one "sees" (and can discuss) race.

It is, in part, class that leads lighter-skinned middle-class parents to dismiss the darker-skinned assistants who clearly have experience with how to describe their own blackness and how to respond to others when they notice it. We might also describe it as an example of racial tolerance, or "racial cordiality," not to consult them and, in the process, remind them of their (stigmatized) blackness. The phenotypical similarities that these women share with my daughter that are there for the "seeing" are intentionally not operationalized. On the other hand, lighter-skinned nannies and poorly paid assistants demonstrate no embodied and racialized signs of cultural refinement or sophistication. I would argue that they are read by middle-class parents as "near black" (Dreisinger 2008) or as "blackened whites" (D. Silva 2001), tainted by their associations with their many co-workers who are dark-skinned and seen as projecting the same linguistic and cultural lack associated with nonwhiteness (see also chapter 3). As they watch predominantly light-skinned children in their expensive swimming classes at a private pool, two nannies may chat with each other, but not (unless invited) with the middle-class family members (mostly mothers and grandmothers) who sit right next to them. They are socially and symbolically segregated because of where they live, because of their lack of financial and cultural resources, and because of their distance from the refinement and sophistication associated with whiteness. Despite their phenotype, they are further read as nonwhite given their positions as manual laborers who deal with their young charges' "dirt," from their clothes, to their dishes, to their bodily waste and their unclean bodies (Boddy 2005; McClintock 1995; Stoler 2002; see also Douglas 2002 [1966]). They may have "lightness" (*brancura*), but they do not project "whiteness" (*branquitude*; Schucman 2014:169; see also Sovik 2009:50).

Reactions to my daughter demonstrate the importance of this distinction from the other side. She has dark skin and tightly bound curls, which refused to stretch themselves into the bouncy ponytails that I was supposed to put in her hair for her class performance in the Festa Junina (June Festival, where children are dressed up to look like country bumpkins). The big black freckles a friend drew on her face with black eyeliner pencil didn't show up so well either. But where her physical body refused to conform to the bodies of her lighter-skinned peers, she exuded whiteness in every other way possible. She had a white mother and a white father, both of whom showed up at every single school event, jostling the other parents for a prime spot in the audience with their fancy imported cell phones and cameras (tools of whiteness, appropriately purchased abroad). She wore neat, clean, and currently "in fashion" clothing that displayed logos with the right kinds of global connections. When she opened her mouth, her ungrammatical and halting Portuguese belied a fluent English that radiated worldliness and intellectual capacity, especially coming from such a young child. She also carried herself with an air of entitlement, stubbornly ignoring the fact that she and her brother stuck out in the otherwise all-white and exclusive spaces that we frequented.[2] Despite her black phenotype, Sophie successfully displayed what Ann Stoler (1995, 2002) describes as the "bourgeois sensibilities" associated with whiteness.

White and wealthy people did not have trouble treating Sophie well in Ipanema, which many Brazilians would take as a sign of their civility, Brazil's racial tolerance, and their own personal lack of racism. And yet their open acceptance of her presence in these predominantly white spaces revealed their careful training to *not* react to her physical blackness, even when she was one dark-skinned face in a sea of light-brown and whiter ones. Back in the 1950s, Brazilian sociologist Oracy Nogueira commented on the "tact" that white people were expected to display around nonwhites in not mentioning race, behavior that followed the dictum, "Never speak of rope in a hanged man's house" (1959:xxiii; see also Damasceno 2000). This cultivated practice of "not noticing" by the whiter middle class contrasted sharply with the reactions of the poor dark-skinned service workers who cleaned up at social clubs and entertained children at *casas de festas* (private birthday party spaces), people who often looked at my daughter with a sense of pleasant, but palpable, surprise. It was not that members of the middle class did not notice her phenotypical blackness or that this did not carry meaning. The assistant I interviewed by the pool said that she had heard several mothers wondering aloud (when I was not there) whether Sophie was a *bolsista* (student on financial aid), an assumption they made based primarily on her phenotypical features as they watched her swim. While lightness and whiteness often overlap, they are *not* the same thing, and *cariocas* of all social positions have been trained to recognize the differences.

Sophie was viewed as an obvious racial "exception" by all, an assessment that no one could articulate out loud, especially in my presence. Indeed, Brazil's comfortable racial contradiction embraces racial exceptions like Sophie, as they deny larger patterns of structural racism, ignore the implicit negative messages attached to blackness, and allow Brazilians to demonstrate racial tolerance and cordiality (E. Costa 1985). But, as Sophie's story also demonstrates, the simple mathematical equation that the familiar Brazilian expression *dinheiro embranquece* implies (blackness + money = whiteness) belies a far more complicated racial "calculus" (M. Harris 1970), one that academics have long struggled to understand.[3] As I have illustrated through the analysis of everyday interactions throughout this book, Rio residents continue to "read" bodies (including Sophie's) for signs of blackness and whiteness, even though they are much more inclined to talk about what they "see" in terms of class differences. What the six-year-olds did that day was force everyone in their vicinity to acknowledge the inescapable fact of their collective ability to "see" race on Sophie's body, despite her "white" sensibilities. They were also forced to reckon with their familiarity with centuries of racial thinking and their ubiquitous experiences with racial hierarchy, both of which they reinforced through their reassurances of her beauty and their dismissal of the other visibly "black" people in the room.

Because there have probably always been rules about what Brazilians should and should not say, this book has not focused exclusively on what educated and polite members of the middle class were willing to say about race or even on experiences that dark-skinned poor Brazilians would overtly link to racism. My goal instead is to reveal how ideas about race and racial capacity continually influence daily interactions across race and class lines. For example, the dark-skinned and poor male youth discussed in chapter 2 increased their chances of being granted respect and citizenship rights by suspicious and notoriously brutal military policemen when they took care to speak politely, use standard Portuguese, and drop references to white spaces and white practices. Given the insecurities surrounding Brazilian whiteness, even lighter-skinned members of the middle class sought to justify and solidify their own class privilege through the demonstration of cultural and linguistic practices that associated them with the racialized traits of discipline, civility, and refinement (as discussed in chapter 3). Defying the social and racial imperative to display whiteness, brown-skinned male youth diligently added slang associated with the *favela* to their daily speech in order to identify themselves with a proud black stance taken up by politically conscious hip-hop (see chapter 6). And yet, despite the strategic embrace of cultural and linguistic practices, racial readings remain open to interpretation, unintentionally attracting additional police surveillance and the scorn of wealthy South Zone residents for male suburban youth when they come, in large numbers, to take their place on Rio's most internationally acclaimed beaches (see chapter 4). Along similar lines, as I show in chapter 5, the well-groomed bodies of brown-skinned members of the middle class can be "misread" as black when adolescent children dangerously take on embodied practices associated with blackness. Rio residents play endlessly with these different racial permutations; they cannot escape them or think their way out of them, regardless of how well they learn to censor their speech and practice racial tolerance.

LIMITING RACE TO WHAT WE CAN SEE

Astronomers, my older son tells me excitedly, do not just study what they can see. They must make assumptions and predictions based on what cannot be seen, either because an object's existence was fleeting (in grand universe time) or because we do not (yet) have the technology to register it. This does not, however, mean that astronomers just "make things up." Their predictions of what must be there, somewhere, are based on complicated calculations involving reactions, patterns, and the things that they can see around it. These last few sentences exhaust my knowledge of astronomy, but they do help explain why I have dedicated my academic career to "seeing" race, even in places where others do not see it, with the goal of treating race as "a powerful force even if only intermittently apparent" (Collins 2007a:1006). In part, this book draws on my training as a linguistic anthropologist to suggest that race is not just "seen" but also "heard." Brazilians, on the whole, readily recognize the existence of regional accents and distinguish between the "correct" speech of the middle class and the "incorrect" and "uneducated" speech of the poor (see Bagno 1999, 2003). As racial ideology draws on notions of rationality, discipline, and refinement to posit the superiority of whiteness, it is of no surprise to linguistic anthropologists to find that language plays an important role in the construction of racial difference, even as that role may differ across national and regional contexts.

In Brazil, and in Rio more specifically, I have not found a "dialect" or a linguistic variety that links to a specific racial "group." Nor has this study set out to identify distinct racial groups. And yet, in Rio, *gíria* (slang) is readily linked to *favelas*, poverty, and blackness, while standard Portuguese conversely calls to mind the educated, the white, and the wealthy. The mistake has been to suggest, as some have, that we can find linguistic differences that contribute to the construction of racial meaning in Brazil only if "black" people speak differently than "white" people. This is sometimes the case in the United States, with its very different racial history and where residential segregation is also more extreme (Telles 2004). But, in this book, I have chosen to approach racial and linguistic difference from a different angle. I do not hold phenotype or racial identity as a constant (as I discuss in chapter 2), nor do I suggest that race and language necessarily form a series of one-to-one relationships (Ochs 1992). Rather what I find is that race, class, and residential stigma overlap and that this set of imagined differences can be heard. As Bola, the middle-class youth who chose to hang out in the housing project of Cruzada spelled out for me: "Já está tudo ligado. Negro. Pobre. E . . . fala errado. . . . Estas três coisas." (It's all connected. Black. Poor. And . . . speaks incorrectly. These three things.) Thus it is not that dark-skinned and light-skinned poor shantytown residents speak differently because of their inherent racial difference, nor that they speak differently because they choose to identify with opposing racial groups. When they speak similarly to each other, and they are all heard and understood to be speaking "like black people," particularly by members of the whiter middle class, this is how we "see" language create racial difference, even as it does not entirely align with phenotype.[4] Within the Brazilian context, and within the fraught and dangerous city of Rio de Janeiro, evidence of blackness and whiteness must be found through an examination of the individual body and its practices (D. Silva 1998), and listening to the way that someone speaks is critical to this process.

I have mentioned that Rio residents are not the only ones to read race through careful attention paid to linguistic and cultural practices, and it is this understanding of how race works and of how it can be separated from phenotype that I have sought to develop here. With its comfortable racial contradiction, Brazil offers a unique context in which to watch racial ideas of whiteness and blackness as they tenaciously uphold everyday interactions, even as the act of noticing racial difference is supposed to be kept *embaixo do pano* (under the tablecloth), as Brazilians like to say. Strong social and racial imperatives encourage Brazilians (1) to display whiteness (through the embodiment of white practices, what has been called *boa aparência*, or a "good appearance"), (2) to avoid blackness (through the avoidance of social mixture, particularly in public spaces), and (3) to be "cordial" (through an intentional "not noticing" of racial difference). My interest in how race works, however, is not mere academic curiosity. As people go about their lives, making decisions and reacting to the world around them, they draw on ideas that dangerously establish levels of humanity, assigning differential values to different bodies and lives (Alves 2014; Alves and Vargas 2015; C. Smith 2015, 2016; Vargas 2011; Vargas and Alves 2010).

Poverty and residence in a shantytown are powerful sources of stigma in Rio de Janeiro, as they have been for more than one hundred years. But I have suggested that we will never understand Rio's staggering inequality or how race has survived for centuries in countries both temperate and tropical, both hostile and cordial, both racially segregated and racially mixed, until we recognize the ways that racial ideas continue to inform people's everyday lives. To do this, we must look beyond where people think they "see" race and follow racial ideas as they link whiteness to rationality, discipline, and refinement and as they associate blackness with a perpetual lack of these traits. Even as Brazilians now bring about legal proceedings for racial insult (Guimarães 2003; Racusen 2004) and as they vigorously debate their government's role in creating or ameliorating conditions of racial disparity, these racial ideas continue to circulate and inform daily interactions in ways that remain underexamined and unacknowledged. These ideas have allowed people, over hundreds of years, to actively engage in unthinkable violence, and they continue to allow people to tolerate equally brutal but far more quiet situations of neglect. These are the ideas that we cannot afford to ignore simply because they are hard to see.

Notes

CHAPTER 1. BRAZIL'S "COMFORTABLE RACIAL CONTRADICTION"

1. This is the highest appellate court in Brazil for nonconstitutional matters of federal law. For the latest ruling on this case, which has been appealed multiple times, see "STJ envia a juiz do DF condenação de Paulo Henrique Amorim por injúria racial," Consultor Jurídico, June 24, 2016, http://www.conjur.com .br/2016-jun-24/stj-manda-paulo-henrique-amorim-cumprir-pena-injuria-racial (accessed July 24, 2016).

2. See "Paulo Henrique Amorim responde ação por racismo," Consultor Jurídico, July 28, 2011, http://www.conjur.com.br/2011-jul-28/paulo-henrique-amorim-responde-acao-penal-racismo (accessed July 24, 2016).

3. Paulo Henrique Amorim is not the first to use this term to critique structural racism. Nearly forty years ago, black activist Abdias do Nascimento criticized the fact that an African descendent could achieve social mobility only when he "já não é mais um negro: trate-se de um assimilado que deu as costas às origens, ou seja, um 'negro de alma branca,'" (was no longer a black person, once he had assimilated and turned his back on his origins and become "a black with a white soul"; see Nascimento 1978:97).

4. Racusen notes that up until the late 1990s, charges of racism were easily dismissed as *injúria*, or "interpersonal disputes between colourless individuals," in order to "prioritize the appearance of harmony" (2004:795).

5. See "Casal sofre racismo após publicar foto no Facebook," Pragmatismo Politico, August 25, 2014, http://www.pragmatismopolitico.com.br/2014/08 /casal-sofre-racismo-apos-publicar-foto-facebook.html (accessed July 25, 2016).

6. See "'Não sou racista,' diz Patrícia Moreira, que pede 'perdão' a goleiro Aranha," Globo, September 5, 2014, http://g1.globo.com/rs/rio-grande-do-sul /noticia/2014/09/patricia-moreira-quebra-silencio-e-da-entrevista-sobre-caso-de-racismo.html (accessed July 25, 2016).

7. It is not uncommon today to have "antiracists," or those who support state action to combat racism, accused of racism by "antiracialists," who think that the state should not be reifying racial difference, in particular by drawing on North American racial definitions and policies. See Bailey 2009:22–35 for a useful summary and history of these various positions.

8. Another common cultural practice, the *jeitinho* (literally "little way," which includes granting favors or bypassing rules or laws) illustrates this Brazilian preference for avoiding conflict (Barbosa 1992).

9. These statistics come from 2010 census data collected by Instituto Brasileiro de Geografia e Estatística, the Brazilian Institute of Geography and Statistics (IBGE).

10. See also discussions of "covert racializing discourses" (Dick and Wirtz 2011) and "covert racist discourse" (Hill 2008).

11. See "Dia da consciência negra, by Angeli—parte 2" Blog da Kikacastro, November 20, 2013, http://kikacastro.com.br/2013/11/20/dia-da-consciencia-negra-by-angeli-parte-2/ (accessed July 28, 2016).

12. For more on what are likely planned destructions of inconveniently located *favelas*, see Alves and Vargas 2015 and also the forthcoming documentary film *Limpam com Fogo* (Cleaning with Fire), which investigates a suspicious series of fires in *favelas* on prime real estate in São Paulo.

13. To understand the incredible overlap of race and class in Rio de Janeiro, see "A estreita relação entre raça, renda e local de moradia," Desigualdades Espaciais, June 22, 2016, https://desigualdadesespaciais.wordpress.com/2016/06/22/a-estreita-relacao-entre-raca-renda-e-local-de-moradia/ (accessed July 28, 2016).

14. For similarities to what Jane Hill (2008) calls "the folk theory of racism" in the United States, see the introduction to her book *The Everyday Language of White Racism*. See Bailey (2004) for evidence that most residents of the state of Rio de Janeiro do recognize the existence of racism in Brazil, though this quantitative study does not explain how Brazilians most commonly define and understand racism.

15. The United States has its own legacy of "whitening," in which various ethnic groups changed status over time to be viewed as racially white, thus expanding the "white" population and leaving other groups, including African Americans, Native Americans, and (often) Latinos and Asian Americans, as the contrasting nonwhite racial Others (Brodkin 1998; Haney-López 2006; Jacobson 2001; Roediger 1991). Groups can also lose their whiteness as has been the experience of Arab, Muslim, or Middle Eastern Americans (Gualtieri 2009).

16. This concern over the relative "blackness" of Brazil continues today. Anthropologist Robin Sheriff recounts her surprise when she was accosted by one middle-class Brazilian during her initial fieldwork in the mid-1980s: "People in your country think that all Brazilians are *negros*, right?" (2001:151; see also Pinho 2010:220; Seigel 2009).

17. This is not the only Brazilian fairy tale (translated into English) to include as its moral the possibility of an individual turning from black to white

(as a result of good deeds). See also the tale "How Black Became White" (Eells 1917).

18. Indeed, when I asked North Americans to try to invent a racist fairy tale, complete with princess, prince, castle, and happy ending (but complicated by race), they could come up only with a Romeo and Juliet–West Side Story version in which the prince and princess came from different racial backgrounds— to which families and kingdoms could object.

19. Light-skinned people were not and are not always considered racially white in the U.S. context either. This includes poor white southerners (Hartigan 2005; Wray 2006); Asian, Middle Eastern, Arab, and some European immigrants (Gualtieri 2009; Haney-López 2006; Jacobson 2001; Roediger 1991); and religious minorities such as Jewish people (Brodkin 1998).

20. This celebration of Brazil's shared heritage did not go as planned. After releasing the doves, the Guarani boy pulled out a red banner demanding recognition of indigenous land rights. His protest was not aired, as the live broadcast cut away from the scene. See "Indigenous Boy Protests on Pitch during World Cup Opening Ceremony," Survival, June 16, 2014, http://www.survivalinternational .org/news/10292 (accessed August 28, 2016).

21. For a discussion of how African Americans participated in promoting the idea of Brazil as a racial democracy, see Hellwig 1992 and Hanchard 1998.

22. See "Justiça condena jornalista Paulo Henrique Amorim a prisão," *Tribuna da Bahia,* February 1, 2016, http://www.tribunadabahia.com .br/2016/02/01/justica-condena-jornalista-paulo-henrique-amorim-prisao (accessed July 31, 2016).

23. See also Matthew Pratt Guterl's description of the ways North Americans can also "see race in every detail but vehemently reject racism" (2013:91).

24. Linguistic anthropologist Kristina Wirtz describes her own work as a study of the "ideologies and practices of embodiment that implicate the racialization of those bodies" (2014:92).

25. For a helpful discussion of racial performativity, see Wirtz 2014:13–16, 88–89 and also Inda 2000. In a short piece, critical legal scholar Ian Haney-López (1998) similarly adds "racial choices" to his definition of race.

26. The recent spread of images of the *favela* includes exhibitions in such unlikely places as a Paris metro stop (Jaguaribe 2014), illustrating a new global brand of Brazilian poverty that anthropologist Erika Robb Larkins (2015) calls "Favela, Inc."

27. I thank Jim Fox and Karin Van den Dool for bringing this expression to my attention.

CHAPTER 2. "GOOD" APPEARANCES

1. African Americans are also encouraged to "act white" to prove their "racial respectability" (Carbado and Gulati 2013; see also Fordham 2008 and Rottenberg 2003). For a discussion of how indigenous Brazilians must also

negotiate their relationship to whiteness and white or "Brazilian" practices, as well as how Brazilians and the Brazilian nation-state continue to negotiate their relationship to indigeneity, see Conklin 1997; Devine Guzmán 2013; A. Ramos 1998; and Warren 2001.

2. The "one drop rule," fears over interracial contact and miscegenation, and legalized racial segregation and exclusion in the United States illustrate how blackness needed to be "managed" in the North American context as well, due to the risks it posed to white racial purity (F. Davis 1991).

3. According to one blog, a São Paulo agency was going to be sued for this practice. See "Empresa Paulista Seleciona a Partir da Cor da 'Cútis,'" Correio Nagô, May 18, 2011, http://correionago.ning.com/profiles/blog/show?id=4512 587:BlogPost:125602&xgs=1&xg_source=msg_share_post (accessed August 19, 2016).

4. For a useful discussion of the complicated relationship between feelings and identity construction, see chapter 4, "Creating Identities," in Woronov 2015.

5. There are obvious parallels to the Black Lives Matter campaign and highly publicized police killings of unarmed black people in the United States.

6. For the effects of this violence on women, particularly mothers and grandmothers, see Alves 2014; Perry 2013; C. Smith 2016.

7. See "Congresso Nacional tem redução no número de representantes negros," Correio Nagô, n.d., http://correionago.com.br/portal/congresso-nacional-tem-reducao-no-numero-de-representantes-negros/ (accessed August 6, 2016).

8. Transcription conventions are as follows:

(?)	Transcription not possible
(word)	Uncertain transcription
[laughter]	Researcher's note (includes conversation details as well as clarifications for the reader)
. . .	Noticeable pause (untimed)
[. . .]	Speech omitted
<u>underline</u>	Emphasis or increased amplitude
::	Vowel elongation
—	Self-interruption; false start, break in the word, or sound abruptly cut off
//	Simultaneous speech (noted before speech of both participants)
.	Sentence-final falling intonation
,	Phrase-final intonation
?	Question rising intonation
bold	Lexical items or example discussed in the text

9. The list of those eligible for special treatment shows how much respect was conferred on those with a college degree: "ministros de Estado e do Tribunal de Contas, governadores, prefeitos, chefes de polícia, integrantes do Parlamento e de assembleias legislativas, oficiais das Forças Armadas e militares, magistra-

dos, e 'diplomados por qualquer das faculdades superiores da República'" (ministers of the state and of the Federal Court of Accounts, governors, mayors, police chiefs, members of Congress and legislative assemblies, officials from the armed forces and the military, judges, and "graduates of whatever university in the Republic"). See Mariana Oliveira, "Cela especial para quem tem diploma não afronta Constituição, diz AGU," *Globo.com*, April 20, 2015, http://g1.globo.com/politica/noticia/2015/04/cela-especial-para-quem-tem-diploma-nao-afronta-constituicao-diz-agu.html (accessed August 6, 2016).

10. Relevant, too, is Lívia Barbosa's discussion of the *jeitinho*, which she describes in her title as "a arte de ser mais igual do que os outros" (the art of being more equal than others; see Barbosa 1992).

11. The status of *trabalhador* does not necessarily imply whiteness, but it does suggest a distance from racialized criminality.

12. This phrase is also found in the lyrics of "Capítulo 4, Versículo 3," by Racionais MC's (1998).

13. Linguistic anthropologist Jillian Cavanaugh similarly illustrates how a linguistic style "embodies the values of the particular place in which it is anchored" (2012:78).

CHAPTER 3. INVESTING IN WHITENESS

1. As an interesting corollary to the North American belief in one's ability to possess whiteness, the Rachel Dolozal case or "scandal" in 2015 suggests that white people can't easily *dispossess* themselves of whiteness, even if they want to (cf. Ignatiev and Garvey 1996).

2. In a similar relational vein, though with a different outcome, historian Melissa Nobles found that in families in which one spouse was white, the family often assumed the racial identity of the white member for purposes of the census (2000:100).

3. For related work on racialized bodies that can and cannot properly discipline themselves, see W. Anderson 2006; Briggs 2003; Burke 1996; Chin 2001; Hale 2006; Irving 2000; Jacobs 2009; Kosek 2006; McClintock 1995; Roth-Gordon 2011; Stoler 1995, 2002; Urciuoli 1996.

4. Linking these concepts, linguist Deborah Cameron includes language standards as examples of "elaborate, institutionalized forms of verbal hygiene" (1995:2).

5. See also Laura Graham's study (2011) of how textual manipulations of an indigenous leader's speech by newspapers allowed them to withdraw their support for his politics and present him as less coherent and "civilized."

CHAPTER 4. FEARS OF RACIAL CONTACT

1. These statistics come from 2010 census data collected by Instituto Brasileiro de Geografia e Estatística, the Brazilian Institute of Geography and Statistics (IBGE). Not all Brazilians, in São Paulo or Rio de Janeiro, who are of

African descent choose to classify themselves under the census category of *preto* (black).

2. I thank Kristina Wirtz for this helpful observation.

3. See also Auyero (2012) for a discussion of what Brazilians would recognize as a familiar "politics of waiting" in Argentina.

4. Middle-class disdain for the police is also apparent in this narrative. As anthropologist Jan Hoffman French notes, "The military police . . . [are] coded as a black space, which is occupied mostly by black men who are seen as marginal, corrupt, and uneducated individuals and considered no better than the criminals and bandits they are charged with controlling" (2013:171).

5. The lyrics and video can be found at http://letras.mus.br/ultraje-a-rigor/41271/ (accessed August 19, 2016).

6. See, for example, "Tumulto assusta banhistas na praia de Ipanema no Rio de Janeiro," Globo.com, September 14, 2014, https://globoplay.globo.com/v/3629578/ (accessed August 12, 2016).

7. See Patrícia Silveira de Farias, "Pegando uma cor na praia: Relações raciais e classificação de cor na Cidade do Rio de Janeiro," Programa de Pós-graduação em Sociologia e Antropologia, July 21, 1999, http://www.ppgsa.ifcs.ufrj.br /teses-e-dissertacoes/pegando-uma-cor-na-praia-relacoes-raciais-e-classifica-cao-de-cor-na-cidade-do-rio-de-janeiro/ (accessed August 12, 2016).

8. See "'Sempre Nova Sempre Ipanema' é a nova campanha da Grendene," Blog da Propaganda, January 14, 2014, http://www.propaganda.blog.br/sempre-nova-sempre-ipanema-e-nova-campanha-da-grendene/#axzz3VedCMJ7g (accessed August 12, 2016).

9. See, for example, Natália Cancian, "'Farofa chique' vira opção aos preços altos em Maresias (SP)," *Folha de S.Paulo*, January 5, 2014, http://www1.folha .uol.com.br/cotidiano/2014/01/1393470-farofa-chique-vira-opcao-aos-precos-altos-em-maresias-sp.shtml (accessed August 12, 2016).

10. See Carolina Heringer and Rafaella Barros, "PM aborda ônibus e recolhe adolescentes a caminho das praias da Zona Sul do Rio," *Globo.com Extra*, August 24, 2015, http://m.extra.globo.com/noticias/rio/pm-aborda-onibus-recolhe-adolescentes-caminho-das-praias-da-zona-sul-do-rio-17279753. html#ixzz3jjssBBn1 (accessed August 12, 2016).

11. I thank Kristina Wirtz for making this point.

CHAPTER 5. AVOIDING BLACKNESS

1. See Rudá Ricci, "O fenômeno do rolezinho, o occupy da periferia," De Esquerda em Esquerda, January 12, 2014, http://rudaricci.blogspot.com /2014/01/o-fenomeno-do-rolezinho-o-occupy-da.html (accessed August 13, 2016).

2. See "Os rolezinhos socialistas," Rodrigo Constantino (blog), January 30, 2014, http://rodrigoconstantino.com/artigos/os-rolezinhos-socialistas/ (accessed August 13, 2016).

3. As linguist Geneva Smitherman has noted of the problematic political economy of the "crossover" of African American English and hip-hop in the U.S. context: "Whites pay no dues, but reap the psychological, social, and economic benefits of a language and culture born out of struggle and hard times" (1998:218).

4. Even more recently in U.S. history, at the turn of the twenty-first century, the states of South Carolina and Alabama finally removed from official record their (unenforceable) antimiscegenation laws, with 20 percent (South Carolina) and 40 percent (Alabama) of state residents voting against their removal (see also Sollors 2000).

5. Note that MV Bill's insult *"preto por fora, branco por dentro"* (black on the outside, white on the inside) is similar to the racialized description *negro de alma branca* (black with a white soul), for which journalist Paulo Henrique Amorim was convicted of *injúria racial* (racial injury), as I discuss in this book's introduction.

6. On the construction of Australian masculinity and whiteness through connections to surfing and beach culture, see Moreton-Robinson (2011). Bank (2015) also shows how whiteness and blackness are constructed through the space of South Africa's beaches.

7. As I show in chapter 4, the term *praia* (beach) has a double meaning in Brazilian Portuguese, not only referencing struggles over the actual urban space of the beach but also suggesting that Pedro wanted to know only about "black things."

8. For a comparison to the U.S., and a discussion of white youth's attempts to "cross over" and take on African American culture and language, often through hip-hop, see Bucholtz 2011; Cutler 2014; and Roediger 1998, 2003.

9. For the full lyrics and rap video, see Vagalume, http://www.vagalume.com.br/racionais-mcs/negro-drama.html#ixzz3COalX7pt (accessed August 13, 2016).

CHAPTER 6. MAKING THE *MANO*

1. See Racionais Mc's Melhor clip de Rap (MTV BRASIL), https://www.youtube.com/watch?v=ED7reoeXNPU (accessed February 9, 2015).

2. This is also true of Brazilians who wear their hair in dreadlocks (see, for example, Hordge-Freeman 2015:225).

3. See "PF volta a rejeitar 'black power' em foto de passaporte," *A Tarde.com.br*, August 9, 2014, http://atarde.uol.com.br/bahia/salvador/noticias/pf-volta-a-rejeitar-black-power-em-foto-de-passaporte-1612943 (accessed August 14, 2016).

4. Politically conscious Brazilian hip-hop does draw also on a history of black activism within Brazil (Jones–de Oliveira 2003), even as these connections are not as clearly articulated.

5. Here Dog mixes the title of the Racionais MC's song "Periferia é Periferia" (Periphery Is Periphery) with a refrain from the popular song "Capítulo 4, Versículo 3" (Chapter 4, Verse 3).

6. The term *negro* was used in the early to mid-twentieth century by groups such as the Frente Negra Brasileira (Black Brazilian Front) and Teatro Experimental do Negro (Black Experimental Theater; Alberto 2011; Davis 1999).

7. Decades ago, black activist Abdias do Nascimento (1978) lodged similar protests, suggesting that racial tolerance, and specifically the push to "whiten," constituted a form of "cultural genocide" against black people.

8. Robert N. Anderson (2012) also points out that there are forms of racial cordiality at play in the U.S. South.

CONCLUSION

1. Schwartzman (2009) indicates that self-identification practices among students, including applicants of African descent who do not identify themselves as black, may not always match what policy makers expected when they passed these laws.

2. On the perceptible confidence of middle-class African Americans when they visit Brazil, see Vargas 2004:466.

3. Back in 1942, Donald Pierson documented another related expression, "Negro rico é branco, e branco pobre é negro" (A rich black person is white, while a poor white person is black; 1942:152), which was commonly used to show that class, rather than race, was the more important social factor, as I discuss further in chapter 2.

4. This is true in the U.S. context as well, where middle-class African Americans are often told that they "talk white" (Fordham 2008), and whites can sometimes acquire African American English if they live among black people (Sweetland 2002), to say nothing of other race and language combinations that a multiracial context opens up.

References

Agha, Asif. 2007. *Language and Social Relations*. New York: Cambridge University Press.

Alberto, Paulina L. 2009. "When Rio Was Black: Soul Music, National Culture, and the Politics of Racial Comparison in 1970s Brazil." *Hispanic American Historical Review* 89(1): 3–39.

———. 2011. *Terms of Inclusion: Black Intellectuals in Twentieth-Century Brazil*. Chapel Hill: University of North Carolina Press.

Alim, H. Samy. 2006. *Roc the Mic Right: The Language of Hip Hop Culture*. New York: Routledge.

Almeida, Ana Carolina Canegal de. 2010. "Fronteiras Urbanas: Interpretações Sobre a Relação entre Cruzada São Sebastião e Leblon." Master's thesis, PUC-Rio.

Alves, Jaime Amparo. 2014. "Neither Humans nor Rights: Some Notes on the Double Negation of Black Life in Brazil." *Journal of Black Studies* 45(2): 143–62.

Alves, Jaime Amparo, and João Costa Vargas. 2015. "On Deaf Ears: Antiblack Police Terror, Multiracial Protest and White Loyalty to the State." *Identities: Global Studies in Culture and Power Online*, 1–21.

Anderson, Robert N., III. 2012. "The End of Cordiality and the Invention of Racism? Evidence from Recent Cultural Production." *The Latin Americanist* 56(4): 57–78.

Anderson, Warwick. 2003. *The Cultivation of Whiteness: Science, Health, and Racial Destiny in Australia*. New York: Basic Books.

———. 2006. *Colonial Pathologies: American Tropical Medicine, Race, and Hygiene in the Philippines*. Durham, NC: Duke University Press.

Andrews, George Reid. 1991. *Blacks and Whites in São Paulo, Brazil, 1888–1988*. Madison: University of Wisconsin Press.

———. 2004. *Afro-Latin America, 1800–2000*. New York: Oxford University Press.

Arias, Enrique Desmond. 2006. *Drugs and Democracy in Rio de Janeiro: Trafficking, Social Networks, and Public Security.* Chapel Hill: University of North Carolina Press.

Auyero, Javier. 2012. *Patients of the State: The Politics of Waiting in Argentina.* Durham, NC: Duke University Press.

Azevedo, Thales. 1975. *Democracia Racial: Ideologia e Realidade.* Petrópolis, Brasil: Vozes.

Bagno, Marcos. 1999. *Preconceito Lingüístico: O Que É, Como se Faz.* São Paulo: Edições Loyola.

———. 2003. *A Norma Oculta: Língua & Poder na Sociedade Brasileira.* São Paulo: Parábola Editorial.

Bailey, Stanley R. 2004. "Group Dominance and the Myth of Racial Democracy: Antiracism Attitudes in Brazil." *American Sociological Review* 69(5): 728–47.

———. 2009. *Legacies of Race: Identities, Attitudes, and Politics in Brazil.* Stanford, CA: Stanford University Press.

Banck, Geert A. 1994. "Mass Consumption and Urban Contest in Brazil: Some Reflections on Lifestyle and Class." *Bulletin of Latin American Research* 13(1): 45–60.

Bank, Leslie. 2015. "Frontiers of Freedom: Race, Landscape, and Nationalism in the Coastal Cultures of South Africa." *Anthropology Southern Africa* 38(3–4): 248–68.

Baran, Michael D. 2007. "'Girl, you are not Morena. We are Negras!': Questioning the Concept of 'Race' in Southern Bahia Brazil." *Ethos* 35(3): 383–409.

Barbosa, Lívia. 1992. *Jeitinho: A Arte de Ser Mais Igual do que os Outros.* Rio de Janeiro: Editora Campus.

Barickman, B.J. 2009. "'Passarão por Mestiços': O Bronzeamento nas Praias Cariocas, Noções de Cor e Raça e Ideologia Racial, 1920–1950." *Afro-Ásia* 40: 173–221.

Bashkow, Ira. 2006. *The Meaning of Whitemen: Race and Modernity in the Orokaiva Cultural World.* Chicago: University of Chicago Press.

Bastide, Roger, and Florestan Fernandes. 1959. *Brancos e Negros em São Paulo.* São Paulo: Companhia Editora Nacional.

Beaton, Mary Elizabeth, and Hannah B. Washington. 2015. "Slurs and the Indexical Field: The Pejoration and Reclaiming of Favelado 'Slum-Dweller.'" *Language Sciences* 52: 12–21.

Bento, Maria Aparecida Silva. 1995. "A Mulher Negra no Mercado de Trabalho." *Estudos Feministas* 3(2): 479–88.

Boddy, Janice. 2005. "Purity and Conquest in the Anglo-Egyptian Sudan." In *Dirt, Undress, and Difference: Critical Perspectives on the Body's Surface.* Adeline Masquelier, ed. Pp. 168–89. Bloomington: Indiana University Press.

Bonilla-Silva, Eduardo. 2014. *Racism without Racists: Color-Blind Racism and the Persistence of Racial Inequality in the United States.* Lanham, MD: Rowman and Littlefield.

Borges, Dain. 1993. "'Puffy, Ugly, Slothful and Inert': Degeneration in Brazilian Social Thought, 1880–1940." *Journal of Latin American Studies* 25(2): 235–56.

Borges, Doriam, Eduardo Ribeiro, and Ignacio Cano. 2012. *Os Donos do Morro: Uma Avaliação Exploratória do Impacto das Unidades de Polícia Pacificadora (UPPs) no Rio de Janeiro.* Rio de Janeiro: Fórum Brasileiro de Segurança Pública, LAV/UERJ.

Bourdieu, Pierre. 1984. *Distinction: A Social Critique of the Judgement of Taste.* Richard Nice, trans. Cambridge, MA: Harvard University Press.

———. 1994. *Language and Symbolic Power.* John B. Thompson, ed. Cambridge, MA: Harvard University Press.

Bourdieu, Pierre, and Loïc Wacquant. 1992. *An Invitation to Reflexive Sociology.* Chicago: University of Chicago Press.

Briggs, Charles L., with Clara Mantini-Briggs. 2003. *Stories in the Time of Cholera: Racial Profiling during a Medical Nightmare.* Berkeley: University of California Press.

Brodkin, Karen. 1998. *How Jews Became White Folks: And What That Says about Race in America.* New Brunswick, NJ: Rutgers University Press.

Brown, Kathleen. 2006. "Body Work in the Antebellum United States." In *Haunted by Empire: Geographies of Intimacy in North American History.* Ann Laura Stoler, ed. Pp. 213–39. Durham, NC: Duke University Press.

Bucholtz, Mary. 2011. *White Kids: Language, Race, and Styles of Youth Identity.* Cambridge: Cambridge University Press.

Burdick, John. 1998. *Blessed Anastacia: Women, Race, and Popular Christianity in Brazil.* New York: Routledge.

———. 2013. *The Color of Sound: Race, Religion, and Music in Brazil.* New York: New York University Press.

Burke, Timothy. 1996. *Lifebuoy Men, Lux Women: Commodification, Consumption, and Cleanliness in Modern Zimbabwe.* Durham, NC: Duke University Press.

Butler, Judith. 1990. *Gender Trouble: Feminism and the Subversion of Identity.* New York: Routledge.

———. 1993. *Bodies That Matter: On the Discursive Limits of "Sex."* New York: Routledge.

Cahill, Cathleen D. 2011. *Federal Fathers and Mothers: A Social History of the United States Indian Service, 1869–1933.* Chapel Hill: University of North Carolina Press.

Caldeira, Teresa P.R. 2000. *City of Walls: Crime, Segregation, and Citizenship in São Paulo.* Berkeley: University of California Press.

———. 2014. "Qual a Novidade dos Rolezinhos?" *Novos Estudos* 98: 13–20.

Caldwell, Kia Lilly. 2007. *Negras in Brazil: Re-envisioning Black Women, Citizenship, and the Politics of Identity.* New Brunswick, NJ: Rutgers University Press.

Cameron, Deborah. 1995. *Verbal Hygiene.* New York: Routledge.

Cano, Ignácio. 1997. *Letalidade da Ação Policial no Rio de Janeiro.* Rio de Janeiro: ISER.

———. 2010. "Racial Bias in Police Use of Lethal Force in Brazil." *Police Practice and Research* 11(1): 31–43.

Carbado, Devon W., and Mitu Gulati. 2013. *Acting White? Rethinking Race in "Post-racial" America*. New York: Oxford University Press.

Carneiro, Sueli. 2011. *Racismo, Sexismo e Desigualdade no Brasil*. São Paulo: Selo Negro.

Carr, E. Summerson. 2011. *Scripting Addiction: The Politics of Therapeutic Talk and American Sobriety*. Princeton, NJ: Princeton University Press.

Carvalho, Bruno. 2007. "Mapping the Urbanized Beaches of Rio de Janeiro: Modernization, Modernity and Everyday Life." *Journal of Latin American Cultural Studies* 16(3): 325–39.

Cavanaugh, Jillian R. 2012. "Entering into Politics: Interdiscursivity, Register, Stance, and Vernacular in Northern Italy." *Language in Society* 41(1): 73–95.

Chevigny, Paul. 1995. *Edge of the Knife: Police Violence in the Americas*. New York: The New Press.

Chin, Elizabeth. 2001. *Purchasing Power: Black Kids and American Consumer Culture*. Minneapolis: University of Minnesota Press.

Cicalo, André. 2012a. "Nerds and Barbarians: Race and Class Encounters through Affirmative Action in a Brazilian University." *Journal of Latin American Studies* 44(2): 235–60.

———. 2012b. *Urban Encounters: Affirmative Action and Black Identities in Brazil*. New York: Palgrave Macmillan.

Coates, Ta-Nehisi. 2012. "Fear of a Black President." *Atlantic*, September. http://www.theatlantic.com/magazine/print/2012/09/fear-of-a-black-president/309064/. Accessed August 7, 2016.

Cogdell, Christina. 2004. *Eugenic Design: Streamlining America in the 1930s*. Philadelphia: University of Pennsylvania Press.

Collins, John F. 2007a. "Recent Approaches in English to Brazilian Racial Ideologies: Ambiguity, Research Methods, and Semiotic Ideologies; A Review Essay." *Comparative Studies in Society and History* 49(4): 997–1009.

———. 2007b. "The Sounds of Tradition: Arbitrariness and Agency in a Brazilian Cultural Heritage Center." *Ethnos* 72(3): 383–407.

———. 2014. "An Ethnography of the Week(s) before the Flood: Cash Money, Progressive Politics, and Revolt in Millennial Brazil." *Anthropological Quarterly* 87(3): 919–24.

———. 2015. *Revolt of the Saints: Memory and Redemption in the Twilight of Brazilian Racial Democracy*. Durham, NC: Duke University Press.

Conklin, Beth A. 1997. "Body Paint, Feathers, and VCRs: Aesthetics and Authenticity in Amazonian Activism." *American Ethnologist* 24(4): 711–37.

Corrêa, Sílvia Borges. 2009. "Lazer, Trabalho e Sociabilidade na Praia de Copacabana." In *Consumo: Cosmologias e Sociabilidades*. Lívia Barbosa, Fátima Portilho, and Letícia Veloso, eds. Pp. 135–56. Rio de Janeiro: Mauad Editora.

Costa, Alexandre Emboaba da. 2014. *Reimagining Black Difference and Politics in Brazil: From Racial Democracy to Multiculturalism.* New York: Palgrave Macmillan.

———. 2016. "The (Un)Happy Objects of Affective Community: Mixture, Conviviality and Racial Democracy in Brazil." *Cultural Studies* 30(1): 24–46.

Costa, Célia. 2015. "Cruzada Faz 60 Anos com Altos Aluguéis e Promessa do Governo: Conjunto Habitacional Foi Criado para Abrigar as Famílias Removidas de Favela na Lagoa." *O Globo,* September 27. http://oglobo .globo.com/rio/cruzada-faz-60-anos-com-altos-alugueis-promessa-do-governo-17617871. Accessed August 17, 2016.

Costa, Emília Viotti da. 1985. *The Brazilian Empire: Myths and Histories.* Chicago: University of Chicago Press.

Covin, David. 2006. *The Unified Black Movement in Brazil, 1978–2002.* Jefferson, NC: McFarland.

Cutler, Cecilia A. 2014. *White Hip-Hoppers, Language, and Identity in Postmodern America.* New York: Routledge.

Damasceno, Caetana Maria. 1999. "Women Workers of Rio: Laborious Interpretations of the Racial Condition." In *Race in Contemporary Brazil: From Indifference to Inequality.* Rebecca Reichmann, ed. Pp. 229–49. University Park: Pennsylvania State University Press.

———. 2000. "'Em Casa de Enforcado não se Fala em Corda': Notas sobre a Construção Social da 'Boa' Aparência no Brasil." In *Tirando a Máscara: Ensaios sobre o Racismo no Brasil.* Antônio Sérgio Alfredo Guimarães and Lynn Huntley, eds. Pp. 165–99. São Paulo: Paz e Terra.

DaMatta, Roberto. 1981. "Digressão: A Fábula das Três Raças, ou O Problema do Racismo à Brasileira." In *Relativizando: Uma Introdução à Antropologia Social.* Pp. 58–87. Petrópolis: Editora Vozes.

———. 1991. "'Do You Know Who You're Talking To?' The Distinction between Individual and Person in Brazil." In *Carnivals, Rogues, and Heroes: An Interpretation of the Brazilian Dilemma.* Pp. 137–97. Notre Dame, IN: University of Notre Dame Press.

———. 1995. *On the Brazilian Urban Poor: An Anthropological Report.* Democracy and Social Policy Series, Working Paper 10. Notre Dame, IN: University of Notre Dame, Helen Kellogg Institute for International Studies.

Daniel, G. Reginald. 2006. *Race and Multiraciality in Brazil and the United States: Converging Paths?* University Park: Pennsylvania State University Press.

Dávila, Arlene M. 2016. *El Mall: The Spatial and Class Politics of Shopping Malls in Latin America.* Oakland: University of California Press.

Dávila, Jerry. 2003. *Diploma of Whiteness: Race and Social Policy in Brazil, 1917–1945.* Durham, NC: Duke University Press.

———. 2012. "Brazilian Race Relations: A Changing Context." *The Latin Americanist* 56(4): 1–10.

———. 2013. *Dictatorship in South America.* Malden, MA: Wiley-Blackwell.

Davis, Darién J. 1999. *Avoiding the Dark: Race and the Forging of National Culture in Modern Brazil.* Aldershot, UK: Ashgate.

Davis, F. James. 1991. *Who Is Black? One Nation's Definition.* University Park: Pennsylvania State University Press.

Degler, Carl. 1986 [1971]. *Neither Black nor White: Slavery and Race Relations in Brazil and the United States.* Madison: University of Wisconsin Press.

Dick, Hilary Parsons, and Kristina Wirtz. 2011. "Racializing Discourses." *Journal of Linguistic Anthropology* 21(S1): E2–E10.

Devine Guzmán, Tracy. 2013. *Native and National in Brazil: Indigeneity after Independence.* Chapel Hill: University of North Carolina Press.

Dorey, Annette K. Vance. 1999. *Better Baby Contests: The Scientific Quest for Perfect Childhood Health in the Early Twentieth Century.* Jefferson, NC: McFarland.

Douglas, Mary. 2002 [1966]. *Purity and Danger: An Analysis of the Concepts of Pollution and Taboo.* New York: Routledge.

Dreisinger, Baz. 2008. *Near Black: White-to-Black Passing in American Culture.* Amherst: University of Massachusetts Press.

Du Bois, William Edward Burghardt. 1920. *Darkwater.* New York: Harcourt, Brace and Howe.

Dunn, Christopher. 2001. *Brutality Garden: Tropicália and the Emergence of a Brazilian Counterculture.* Chapel Hill: University of North Carolina Press.

Dzidzienyo, Anani. 1971. *The Position of Blacks in Brazilian Society.* London: Minority Rights Group.

Eckert, Penelope. 2000. *Linguistic Variation as Social Practice: The Linguistic Construction of Identity in Belten High.* Malden, MA: Wiley-Blackwell.

Edmonds, Alexander. 2010. *Pretty Modern: Beauty, Sex, and Plastic Surgery in Brazil.* Durham, NC: Duke University Press.

Eells, Elsie Spicer. 1917. *Fairy Tales from Brazil: How and Why Tales from Brazilian Folk-lore.* New York: Dodd, Mead.

Ehrenreich, Barbara. 1989. *Fear of Falling: The Inner Life of the Middle Class.* New York: Pantheon Books.

Fanon, Frantz. 1967. *Black Skin, White Masks: The Experiences of a Black Man in a White World.* New York: Grove Press.

Farias, Patrícia Silveira de. 2006. *Pegando uma Cor na Praia: Relações Raciais e Classificação de Cor na Cidade do Rio de Janeiro.* Rio de Janeiro: Prefeitura da Cidade do Rio de Janeiro, Secretaria Municipal das Culturas.

Fazzi, Rita de Cássia. 2004. *O Drama Racial de Crianças Brasileiras: Socialização entre Pares e Preconceito.* Belo Horizonte, Minas Gerais: Autêntica.

Fender, Stephen. 2006. "Poor Whites and the Federal Writers' Project: The Rhetoric of Eugenics in the Southern Life Histories." In *Popular Eugenics: National Efficiency and American Mass Culture in the 1930s.* Susan Currell and Christina Cogdell, eds. Pp. 140–63. Athens: Ohio University Press.

Fernandes, Florestan. 1969. *The Negro in Brazilian Society.* New York: Columbia University Press.

Ferraz, Gabriel. 2013. "Heitor Villa-Lobos e Getúlio Vargas: Doutrinando Crianças por Meio da Educação Musical." *Latin American Music Review* 34(2): 162–95.

Figueiredo, Angela. 1994. "O Mercado da Boa Aparência: As Cabeleireiras Negras." *Bahia Anályse & Dados* 3(4): 33–36.

———. 2002. *Novas Elites de Cor: Estudo sobre os Profissionais Liberais Negros de Salvador.* São Paulo: Annablume.

Fischer, Brodwyn. 2004. "Quase Pretos de Tão Pobres? Race and Social Discrimination in Rio de Janeiro's Twentieth-Century Criminal Courts." *Latin American Research Review* 39(1): 31–59.

———. 2008. *A Poverty of Rights: Citizenship and Inequality in Twentieth-Century Rio de Janeiro.* Stanford, CA: Stanford University Press.

———. 2014. "A Century in the Present Tense: Crisis, Politics, and the Intellectual History of Brazil's Informal Cities." In *Cities from Scratch: Poverty and Informality in Urban Latin America.* Brodwyn Fischer, Bryan McCann, and Javier Auyero, eds. Pp. 9–67. Durham, NC: Duke University Press.

Fordham, Signithia. 2008. "Beyond Capital High: On Dual Citizenship and the Strange Career of 'Acting White.'" *Anthropology and Education Quarterly* 39(3): 227–46.

Francisco, Dilmar. 2003. *Arrastão Mediático e Racismo no Rio de Janeiro.* XXVI Congresso Brasileiro de Ciências da Comunicação. Belo Horizonte, Minas Gerais, Brasil.

Frankenberg, Ruth. 1993. *White Women, Race Matters: The Social Construction of Whiteness.* Minneapolis: University of Minnesota Press.

Freeman, James. 2002. "Democracy and Danger on the Beach." *Space and Culture* 5(1): 9–28.

———. 2008. "Great, Good, and Divided: The Politics of Public Space in Rio de Janeiro." *Journal of Urban Affairs* 30(5): 529–56.

French, Jan Hoffman. 2013. "Rethinking Police Violence in Brazil: Unmasking the Public Secret of Race." *Latin American Politics and Society* 55(4): 161–81.

———. 2015. "From Honor to Dignity: Criminal Libel, Press Freedom, and Racist Speech in Brazil." *Vanderbilt E-journal of Luso-Hispanic Studies* 10.

Freyre, Gilberto. 1978 [1933]. *Casa Grande & Senzala.* Rio de Janeiro: José Olimpio.

Fry, Peter. 1982. *Para Inglês Ver: Identidade e Política na Cultura Brasileira.* Rio de Janeiro: Zahar Editores.

———. 1995–96. "O Que a Cinderela Negra Tem a Dizer sobre a 'Política Racial' no Brasil." *Revista da USP* 28: 122–35.

———. 2000. "Politics, Nationality, and the Meanings of 'Race' in Brazil." *Daedulus* 129(2): 83–118.

Fry, Peter, Yvonne Maggie, Marcos Chor Maio, Simone Monteiro, and Ricardo Ventura Santos. 2007. *Divisões Perigosas: Políticas Raciais no Brasil Contemporâneo.* Rio de Janeiro: Civilização Brasileira.

Gal, Susan. 2005. "Language Ideologies Compared: Metaphors of Public/ Private." *Journal of Linguistic Anthropology* 15(1): 23–37.

Garcia, Januário. 2006. *25 Anos 1980–2005: Movimento Negro no Brasil.* Brasilia: Fundação Cultural Palmares.

Godreau, Isar P. 2002. "Changing Space, Making Race: Distance, Nostalgia, and the Folklorization of Blackness in Puerto Rico." *Identities: Global Studies in Culture and Power* 9(3): 281–304.

———. 2015. *Scripts of Blackness: Race, Cultural Nationalism, and U.S. Colonialism in Puerto Rico.* Urbana: University of Illinois Press.

Goffman, Erving. 1963. *Stigma: Notes on the Management of Spoiled Identity.* Englewood Cliffs, NJ: Prentice-Hall.

———. 1981. *Forms of Talk.* Philadelphia: University of Pennsylvania Press.

Goldstein, Donna M. 2003. *Laughter Out of Place: Race, Class, Violence, and Sexuality in a Rio Shantytown.* Berkeley: University of California Press.

Gomes, Laurentino. 2007. *1808: The Flight of the Emperor: How a Weak Prince, a Mad Queen, and the British Navy Tricked Napoleon and Changed the New World.* Guilford, CT: Lyons Press.

González Stephan, Beatriz. 2001. "The Teaching Machine for the Wild Citizen." In *The Latin American Subaltern Studies Reader.* Ileana Rodríguez, ed. Pp. 313–40. Durham, NC: Duke University Press.

Graham, Laura R. 2011. "Quoting Mario Juruna: Linguistic Imagery and the Transformation of Indigenous Voice in the Brazilian Print Press." *American Ethnologist* 38(1): 164–83.

Graham, Sandra Lauderdale. 1988. *House and Street: The Domestic World of Servants and Masters in Nineteenth-Century Rio de Janeiro.* New York: Cambridge University Press.

Gualtieri, Sarah M.A. 2009. *Between Arab and White: Race and Ethnicity in the Early Syrian American Diaspora.* Berkeley: University of California Press.

Guimarães, Antonio Sérgio Alfredo. 1995. "Racism and Anti-racism in Brazil: A Post Modern Perspective." In *Racism and Anti-racism in World Perspective.* Benjamin P. Bowser, ed. Pp. 208–26. Newbury Park, CA: Sage.

———. 2003. "Racial Insult in Brazil." *Discourse and Society* 14(2): 133–51.

Guterl, Matthew Pratt. 2013. *Seeing Race in Modern America.* Chapel Hill: University of North Carolina Press.

Hale, Charles R. 2006. *Más Que un Indio: Racial Ambivalence and Neoliberal Multiculturalism in Guatemala.* Santa Fe, NM: School of American Research Press.

Hall, Stuart. 1997. "The Spectacle of the 'Other.'" In *Representation: Cultural Representations and Signifying Practices.* Stuart Hall, ed. Pp. 223–90. New York: Sage.

Hanchard, Michael George. 1994. "Black Cinderella? Race and the Public Sphere in Brazil." *Public Culture* 7(1): 165–85.

———. 1998. *Orpheus and Power: The Movimento Negro of Rio de Janeiro and São Paulo, Brazil, 1945–1988.* Princeton, NJ: Princeton University Press.

Haney-López, Ian. 1998. "Chance, Context, and Choice in the Social Construction of Race." In *The Latino/a Condition: A Critical Reader.* Richard Delgado and Jean Stefancic, eds. Pp. 9–16. New York: New York University Press.

————. 2006. *White by Law: The Legal Construction of Race.* New York: New York University Press.

Harris, Cheryl I. 1993. "Whiteness as Property." *Harvard Law Review* 106(8): 1707–91.

Harris, Marvin. 1952. "Race Relations in Minas Velhas: A Community in the Mountain Region of Central Brazil." In *Race and Class in Rural Brazil.* Charles Wagley, ed. Pp. 47–81. Paris: UNESCO.

————. 1970. "Referential Ambiguity in the Calculus of Brazilian Racial Identity." *Southwestern Journal of Anthropology* 26(1): 1–14.

Harris, Marvin, Josildeth Gomes Consorte, Joseph Lang, and Bryan Byrne. 1993. "Who Are the Whites? Imposed Census Categories and the Racial Demography of Brazil." *Social Forces* 72(2): 451–62.

Hartigan, John, Jr. 2005. *Odd Tribes: Toward a Cultural Analysis of White People.* Durham, NC: Duke University Press.

Hasenbalg, Carlos, and Nelson do Valle Silva. 1988. *Estrutura Social, Mobilidade e Raça.* São Paulo: Vértice.

Hebdige, Dick. 1979. *Subculture: The Meaning of Style.* New York: Routledge.

Hellwig, David. 1992. *African-American Reflections on Brazil's Racial Paradise.* Philadelphia: Temple University Press.

Heneghan, Bridget T. 2003. *Whitewashing America: Material Culture and Race in the Antebellum Imagination.* Jackson: University Press of Mississippi.

Hewitt, Roger. 1986. *White Talk Black Talk: Inter-racial Friendship and Communication amongst Adolescents.* New York: Cambridge University Press.

Hill, Jane H. 2008. *The Everyday Language of White Racism.* Malden, MA: Wiley-Blackwell.

Holston, James. 2008. *Insurgent Citizenship: Disjunctions of Democracy and Modernity in Brazil.* Princeton, NJ: Princeton University Press.

————. 2011. "Contesting Privilege with Right: The Transformation of Differentiated Citizenship in Brazil." *Citizenship Studies* 15(3–4): 335–52.

Holston, James, and Teresa P. R. Caldeira. 1998. "Democracy, Law, and Violence: Disjunctions of Brazilian Citizenship." In *Fault Lines of Democracy in Post-Transition Latin America.* Felipe Agüero and Jeffrey Stark, eds. Pp. 263–96. Miami: University of Miami North-South Center Press.

Hordge-Freeman, Elizabeth. 2015. *The Color of Love: Racial Features, Stigma, and Socialization in Black Brazilian Families.* Austin: University of Texas Press.

Htun, Mala. 2004. "From 'Racial Democracy' to Affirmative Action: Changing State Policy on Race in Brazil." *Latin American Research Review* 39(1): 60–89.

Huggins, Martha K. 2000. "Urban Violence and Police Privatization in Brazil: Blended Invisibility." *Social Justice* 27(2): 113–34.

Ignatiev, Noel, and John Garvey. 1996. *Race Traitor.* New York: Routledge.

Inda, Jonathan Xavier. 2000. "Performativity, Materiality, and the Racial Body." *Latino Studies Journal* 11(3): 74–99.

Inoue, Miyako. 2003. "Speech without a Speaking Body: 'Japanese Women's Language' in Translation." *Language and Communication* 23: 315–30.

Irvine, Judith T., and Susan Gal. 2000. "Language Ideology and Linguistic Differentiation." In *Regimes of Language: Ideologies, Polities, and Identities.* Paul V. Kroskrity, ed. Pp. 35–83. Santa Fe, NM: School of American Research Press.

Irving, Katrina. 2000. *Immigrant Mothers: Narratives of Race and Modernity, 1890–1925.* Chicago: University of Illinois Press.

Jabor, Arnaldo. 1998. "Racionais MC's são os 'Manos' contra os 'Playboys': Finalmente um Fato Político Novo Aparece na Paisagem Pop." *O Globo.* August 18, 1998. Segundo Caderno, p. 12.

Jacobs, Margaret D. 2009. *White Mother to a Dark Race: Settler Colonialism, Maternalism, and the Removal of Indigenous Children in the American West and Australia, 1880–1940.* Lincoln: University of Nebraska Press.

Jacobs-Huey, Lanita. 2006. *From the Kitchen to the Parlor: Language and Becoming in African American Women's Hair Care.* New York: Oxford University Press.

Jacobson, Matthew Frye. 2001. *Whiteness of a Different Color: European Immigrants and the Alchemy of Race.* Cambridge, MA: Harvard University Press.

Jaguaribe, Beatriz. 2014. *Rio de Janeiro: Urban Life through the Eyes of the City.* New York: Routledge.

Jones–de Oliveira, Kimberly F. 2003. "The Politics of Culture or the Culture of Politics: Afro-Brazilian Mobilization, 1920–1968." *Journal of Third World Studies* 22(1): 103–20.

Joseph, Tiffany. 2015. *Race on the Move: Brazilian Migrants and the Global Reconstruction of Race.* Stanford, CA: Stanford University Press.

Kamel, Ali. 2006. *Não Somos Racistas: Uma Reação aos que Querem nos Transformar numa Nação Bicolor.* Rio de Janeiro: Editora Nova Fronteira.

Khan, Shamus Rahman. 2011. *Privilege: The Making of an Adolescent Elite at St. Paul's School.* Princeton, NJ: Princeton University Press.

Kosek, Jake. 2006. *Understories: The Political Life of Forests in Northern New Mexico.* Durham, NC: Duke University Press.

Kroskrity, Paul V. 2000. *Regimes of Language: Ideologies, Politics and Identities.* Santa Fe, NM: School of American Research Press.

Landes, Ruth. 1986 [1970]. "A Woman Anthropologist in Brazil." In *Women in the Field: Anthropological Experiences.* Peggy Golde, ed. Pp. 119–42. Berkeley: University of California Press.

———. 1994. *The City of Women.* Albuquerque: University of New Mexico Press.

Larkins, Erika Robb. 2015. *The Spectacular Favela: Violence in Modern Brazil.* Oakland: University of California Press.

Leão, Danuza. 1992. *Na Sala com Danuza.* São Paulo: Editora Siciliano.

Leeds, Anthony, and Elizabeth Leeds. 1970. "Brazil and the Myth of Urban Rurality: Urban Experience, Work, and Values in 'Squatments' of Rio de Janeiro and Lima." In *City and Country in the Third World: Issues in the Modernization of Latin America.* Arthur J. Field, ed. Pp. 229–72. Cambridge: Schenkman.

Lesser, Jeffrey. 2013. *Immigration, Ethnicity, and National Identity in Brazil, 1808 to the Present.* New York: Cambridge University Press.

Levinson, Stephen C. 1988. "Putting Linguistics on a Proper Footing: Explorations in Goffman's Participation Framework." In *Goffman: Exploring the Interaction Order.* Paul Drew and Anthony Wootton, eds. Pp. 161–227. Oxford: Polity Press.

Lippi-Green, Rosina. 2011. *English with an Accent: Language, Ideology, and Discrimination in the United States.* New York: Routledge.

Lipsitz, George. 1998. *The Possessive Investment in Whiteness: How White People Profit from Identity Politics.* Philadelphia: Temple University Press.

MV Bill. 1999. *Traficando Informação.* São Paulo: BMG International.

Maio, Marcos Chor. 2001. "UNESCO and the Study of Race Relations in Brazil: Regional or National Issue?" *Latin American Research Review* 36(2): 118–36.

Mauss, Marcel. 1973. "Techniques of the Body." *Economy and Society* 2(1): 70–88.

McCallum, Cecilia. 2005. "Racialized Bodies, Naturalized Classes: Moving through the City of Salvador da Bahia." *American Ethnologist* 32(1): 100–117.

McCann, Bryan. 2002. "Black Pau: Uncovering the History of Brazilian Soul." *Journal of Popular Music Studies* 14: 33–62.

———. 2014. *Hard Times in the Marvelous City: From Dictatorship to Democracy in the Favelas of Rio de Janeiro.* Durham, NC: Duke University Press.

McClintock, Anne. 1995. *Imperial Leather: Race, Gender, and Sexuality in the Colonial Contest.* New York: Routledge.

McElhinny, Bonnie. 2005. "'Kissing a Baby Is Not at All Good for Him': Infant Mortality, Medicine, and Colonial Modernity in the U.S.-Occupied Philippines." *American Anthropologist* 107(2): 183–94.

McIntosh, Janet. 2009. "Stance and Distance: Social Boundaries, Self-Lamination, and Metalinguistic Anxiety in White Kenyan Narratives about the African Occult." In *Stance: Sociolinguistic Perspectives.* Alexandra Jaffe, ed. Pp. 72–91. New York: Oxford University Press.

Mendoza-Denton, Norma. 2011. "The Semiotic Hitchhiker's Guide to Creaky Voice: Circulation and Gendered Hardcore in a Chicana/o Gang Persona." *Journal of Linguistic Anthropology* 21(2): 260–78.

Milroy, James, and Lesley Milroy. 2012. *Authority in Language: Investigating Standard English.* New York: Routledge.

Mitchell, Michael J., and Charles H. Wood. 1999. "Ironies of Citizenship: Skin Color, Police Brutality, and the Challenge to Democracy in Brazil." *Social Forces* 77(3): 1001–20.

Mitchell, Sean T. 2016. "Whitening and Racial Ambiguity: Racialization and Ethnoracial Citizenship in Contemporary Brazil." *African and Black Diaspora* (July). http://www.tandfonline.com/doi/abs/10.1080/17528631.2016.1189693. Accessed August 19, 2016.

Moreton-Robinson, Aileen. 2011. "Bodies That Matter: Performing White Possession on the Beach." *American Indian Culture and Research Journal* 35(4): 57–72.

Morgan, Marcyliena. 2002. *Language, Discourse and Power in African American Culture.* New York: Cambridge University Press.

Nascimento, Abdias do. 1978. *O Genocídio do Negro Brasileiro: Processo de um Racismo Mascarado. Coleção Estudos Brasileiros.* Rio de Janeiro: Paz e Terra.

Nascimento, Elisa Larkin. 2001. "It's in the Blood: Notes on Race Attitudes in Brazil." In *Beyond Racism: Race and Inequality in Brazil, South Africa, and the United States.* Charles V. Hamilton, Lynn Huntley, Neville Alexander, Antonio Sérgio Alfredo Guimarães, and Wilmot James, eds. Pp. 509–24. Boulder, CO: Lynne Rienner.

———. 2007. *The Sorcery of Color: Identity, Race, and Gender in Brazil.* Philadelphia: Temple University Press.

Nobles, Melissa. 2000. *Shades of Citizenship: Race and the Census in Modern Politics.* Stanford, CA: Stanford University Press.

Nogueira, Oracy. 1942. "Atitude Desfavorável de Alguns Acunciantes de São Paulo em Relação aos Empregados de Côr." *Sociologia* 4(4): 328–58.

———. 1959. "Skin Color and Social Class." In *Plantation Systems of the New World.* Pan American Union Social Science Monographs No. 7. Vera Rubin, ed. Washington, DC: Pan American Union.

———. 1985. *Tanto Preto Quanto Branco: Estudos de Relações Raciais.* São Paulo: T.A. Queiroz Editora.

Norvell, John M. 2002. "A Brancura Desconfortável das Camadas Médias Brasileiras." In *Raça como Retórica: A Construção da Diferença.* Yvonne Maggie and Claudia Barcellos Rezende, eds. Pp. 245–67. Rio de Janeiro: Civilização Brasileira.

O'Dougherty, Maureen. 2002. *Consumption Intensified: The Politics of Middle-Class Daily Life in Brazil.* Durham, NC: Duke University Press.

Ochs, Elinor. 1992. "Indexing Gender." In *Rethinking Context: Language as an Interactive Phenomenon.* Alessandro Duranti and Charles Goodwin, eds. Pp. 335–58. New York: Cambridge University Press.

Otovo, Okezi T. 2016. *Progressive Mothers, Better Babies: Race, Public Health, and the State in Brazil, 1850–1945.* Austin: University of Texas Press.

Owensby, Brian P. 1999. *Intimate Ironies: Modernity and the Making of Middle-Class Lives in Brazil.* Stanford, CA: Stanford University Press.

———. 2005. "Toward a History of Brazil's 'Cordial Racism': Race beyond Liberalism." *Comparative Studies in Society and History* 47(2): 318–47.

Paixão, Roberta, and Virginie Leite. 1996. "Guerra na Areia: O Subúrbio Invade as Praias da Zona Sul do Rio e Expõe o Muro Invisível do Preconceito." *Veja* (November 20): 72–75.

Pardue, Derek. 2008. *Ideologies of Marginality in Brazilian Hip Hop.* New York: Palgrave Macmillan.

Patai, Daphne. 1988. *Brazilian Women Speak: Contemporary Life Stories.* New Brunswick, NJ: Rutgers University Press.

Penglase, R. Ben. 2007. "Barbarians on the Beach: Media Narratives of Violence in Rio de Janeiro, Brazil." *Crime Media Culture* 3(3): 305–25.

———. 2014. *Living with Insecurity in a Brazilian Favela: Urban Violence and Daily Life.* New Brunswick, NJ: Rutgers University Press.

Perlman, Janice E. 2010. *Favela: Four Decades of Living on the Edge in Rio de Janeiro.* New York: Oxford University Press.

Perry, Keisha-Khan Y. 2013. *Black Women against the Land Grab: The Fight for Racial Justice in Brazil.* Minneapolis: University of Minnesota Press.

Philips, Susan U. 2004. "The Organization of Ideological Diversity in Discourse: Modern and Neotraditional Visions of the Tongan State." *American Ethnologist* 31(2): 231–50.

Pierson, Donald. 1942. *Negroes in Brazil: A Study of Race Contact at Bahia.* Chicago: University of Chicago Press.

Pinheiro-Machado, Rosana, and Lucia Mury Scalco. 2014. "Rolezinhos: Marcas, Consumo e Segregação no Brasil." *Revista de Estudos Culturais* 1. Universidade de São Paulo. http://www.revistas.usp.br/revistaec/article/view/98372. Accessed August 19, 2016.

Pinho, Patricia de Santana. 2009. "White but Not Quite: Tones and Overtones of Whiteness in Brazil." *Small Axe: A Caribbean Journal of Criticism* 13(2:29): 39–56.

———. 2010. *Mama Africa: Reinventing Blackness in Bahia.* Durham, NC: Duke University Press.

Pino, Julio César. 1997. *Family and Favela: The Reproduction of Poverty in Rio de Janeiro.* Westport, CT: Greenwood Press.

Postero, Nancy. 2006. *Now We Are Citizens: Indigenous Politics in Postmulticultural Bolivia.* Stanford, CA: Stanford University Press.

Racionais MC's. 1990. *Holocausto Urbano.* São Paulo: Zimbabwe.

———. 1998. *Sobrevivendo no Inferno.* São Paulo: Zambia.

Racusen, Seth. 2004. "The Ideology of the Brazilian Nation and the Brazilian Legal Theory of Racial Discrimination." *Social Identities* 10(6): 775–809.

Rafter, Nicole. 2006. "Apes, Men, and Teeth: Earnest A. Hooton and Eugenic Decay." In *Popular Eugenics: National Efficiency and American Mass Culture in the 1930s.* Susan Currell and Christina Cogdell, eds. Pp. 249–68. Athens: Ohio University Press.

Ramos, Alcida Rita. 1998. *Indigenism: Ethnic Politics in Brazil.* Madison: University of Wisconsin Press.

Ramos, Guerreiro. 1995. *Introdução Crítica à Sociologia Brasileira.* Rio de Janeiro: Editora UFRJ.

Ramos, Silvia, and Leonarda Musumeci. 2005. *Elemento Suspeito: Abordagem Policial e Discriminação na Cidade do Rio de Janeiro.* Rio de Janeiro: Civilização Brasileira.

Ramos-Zayas, Ana Y. 2007. "Becoming American, Becoming Black? Urban Competency, Racialized Spaces, and the Politics of Citizenship among Brazilian and Puerto Rican Youth in Newark." *Identities: Global Studies in Culture and Power* 14(1–2): 85–109.

Rampton, Ben. 1995. *Crossing: Language and Ethnicity among Adolescents.* New York: Longman Group.

Rezende, Cláudia Barcellos, and Márcia Lima. 2004. "Linking Gender, Class and Race in Brazil." *Social Identities* 10(6): 757–73.

Rickford, John Russell, and Russell John Rickford. 2000. *Spoken Soul: The Story of Black English.* New York: John Wiley and Sons.

Roediger, David R. 1991. *The Wages of Whiteness: Race and the Making of the American Working Class.* New York: Verso.

———. 1998. "What to Make of Wiggers: A Work in Progress." In *Generations of Youth: Youth Cultures and History in Twentieth-Century America.* Joe Austin and Michael Nevin Willard, eds. Pp. 358–66. New York: New York University Press.

———. 2003. *Colored White: Transcending the Racial Past.* Berkeley: University of California Press.

Roland, L. Kaifa. 2013. "T/racing Belonging through Cuban Tourism." *Cultural Anthropology* 28(3): 396–419.

Rosa-Ribeiro, Fernando. 2000. "Racism, Mimesis and Anthropology in Brazil." *Critique of Anthropology* 20(3): 221–41.

Rose, Tricia. 1994. *Black Noise: Rap Music and Black Culture in Contemporary America.* Hanover, NH: Wesleyan University.

———. 2008. *The Hip Hop Wars: What We Talk about When We Talk about Hip Hop—And Why It Matters.* New York: Basic Civitas Books.

Roth-Gordon, Jennifer. 2007a. "Racing and Erasing the *Playboy:* Slang, Transnational Youth Subculture, and Racial Discourse in Brazil." *Journal of Linguistic Anthropology* 17(2): 246–65.

———. 2007b. "Youth, Slang, and Pragmatic Expressions: Examples from Brazilian Portuguese." *Journal of Sociolinguistics* 11(3): 322–45.

———. 2009a. "Conversational Sampling, Race Trafficking, and the Invocation of the *Gueto* in Brazilian Hip Hop." In *Global Linguistic Flows: Hip Hop Cultures, Youth Identities, and the Politics of Language.* H. Samy Alim, Awad Ibrahim, and Alastair Pennycook, eds. Pp. 63–77. New York: Routledge.

———. 2009b. "The Language That Came Down the Hill: Slang, Crime, and Citizenship in Rio de Janeiro." *American Anthropologist* 111(1): 57–68.

———. 2011. "Discipline and Disorder in the Whiteness of Mock Spanish." *Journal of Linguistic Anthropology* 21(2): 210–28.

———. 2012. "Linguistic Techniques of the Self: The Intertextual Language of Racial Empowerment in Politically Conscious Brazilian Hip Hop." *Language & Communication* 32(1): 36–47.

———. 2013. "Racial Malleability and the Sensory Regime of Politically Conscious Brazilian Hip Hop." *Journal of Latin American and Caribbean Anthropology* 18(2): 294–313.

Roth-Gordon, Jennifer, and Antonio José B. da Silva. 2013. "Double-Voicing in the Everyday Language of Brazilian Black Activism." In *The Persistence of Language: Constructing and Confronting the Past and Present in the Voices of Jane H. Hill*. Shannon T. Bischoff, Deborah Cole, Amy V. Fountain, and Mizuki Miyashita, eds. Pp. 365–88. Philadelphia: John Benjamins.

Rottenberg, Catherine. 2003. "Passing: Race, Identification, and Desire." *Criticism* 45(4): 435–52.

Sansone, Livio. 2003. *Blackness without Ethnicity: Constructing Race in Brazil.* New York: Palgrave Macmillan.

Santos, Sales Augusto dos. 2006. "Who Is Black in Brazil? A Timely or a False Question in Brazilian Race Relations in the Era of Affirmative Action?" *Latin American Perspectives* 33(4): 30–48.

Scheper-Hughes, Nancy. 2006. "Death Squads and Democracy in Northeast Brazil." In *Law and Disorder in the Postcolony*. Jean Comaroff and John L. Comaroff, eds. Pp. 150–87. Chicago: University of Chicago Press.

Schieffelin, Bambi B., Kathryn A. Woolard, and Paul V. Kroskrity. 1998. *Language Ideologies: Practice and Theory.* New York: Oxford University Press.

Schucman, Lia Vainer. 2014. *Entre o Encardido, o Branco e o Branquíssimo: Branquitude, Hierarquia, e Poder na Cidade de São Paulo.* São Paulo: Annablume.

Schwarcz, Lilia Moritz. 1998. "Nem Preto nem Branco, Muito pelo Contrário: Cor e Raça na Intimidade." In *História da Vida Privada no Brasil: Contrastes da Intimidade Contemporanea*, vol. 4. Lilia Moritz Schwarcz and Fernando A. Novais, eds. Pp. 173–244. São Paulo: Companhia das Letras.

Schwartzman, Luisa Farah. 2009. "Seeing like Citizens: Unofficial Understandings of Official Racial Categories in a Brazilian University." *Journal of Latin American Studies* 41(2): 221–50.

Segato, R.L. 1998. "The Color-Blind Subject of Myth; Or, Where to Find Africa in the Nation." *Annual Review of Anthropology* 27: 129–51.

Seigel, Micol. 2003. "Comparable or Connected? Afro-Diasporic Subjectivity and State Response in 1920s São Paulo and Chicago." In *Race and Democracy in the Americas*. Georgia A. Persons, ed. Pp. 64–75. New Brunswick, NJ: Transaction.

———. 2009. *Uneven Encounters: Making Race and Nation in Brazil and the United States.* Durham, NC: Duke University Press.

Sheriff, Robin E. 2001. *Dreaming Equality: Color, Race, and Racism in Urban Brazil.* New Brunswick, NJ: Rutgers University Press.

———. 2003. "Embracing Race: Deconstructing Mestiçagem in Rio de Janeiro." *Journal of Latin American Anthropology* 8(1): 86–115.

Silva, Ana Paula. 2014. *Pelé e o Complexo de Vira-Latas: Discursos sobre Raça e Modernidade no Brasil.* Niterói: Editora da UFF.

Silva, Denise Ferreira da. 1998. "Facts of Blackness: Brazil Is Not (Quite) the United States ... and Racial Politics in Brazil?" *Social Identities* 4(2): 201–34.

———. 2001. "Towards a Critique of the Socio-logos of Justice: The Analytics of Raciality and the Production of Universality." *Social Identities* 7(3): 421–54.

Silva, Hédio, Jr. 1998. "Crônica da Culpa Anunciada." In *A Cor do Medo: Homicídios e Relações Raciais no Brasil.* Dijaci David de Oliveira, Elen Cristina Geraldes, Ricardo Barbosa de Lima, and Sales Augusto dos Santos, eds. Pp. 71–90. Brasília: Editora UnB.

Silva, Luiz Antonio Machado da. 2015. "A Experiência das UPPs: Uma Tomada de Posição." *Dilemas: Revista de Estudos de Conflito e Controle Social* 8(1): 7–24.

Skidmore, Thomas E. 1974. *Black into White: Race and Nationality in Brazilian Thought.* New York: Oxford University Press.

———. 1999. *Brazil: Five Centuries of Change.* New York: Oxford University Press.

Smith, Christen A. 2015. "Blackness, Citizenship, and the Transnational Vertigo of Violence in the Americas." *American Anthropologist* 117(2): 384–87.

———. 2016. *Afro-Paradise: Blackness, Violence, and Performance in Brazil.* Urbana: University of Illinois Press.

Smith, Mark M. 2006. *How Race Is Made: Slavery, Segregation, and the Senses.* Chapel Hill: University of North Carolina Press.

Smitherman, Geneva. 1998. "Word from the Hood: The Lexicon of African-American Vernacular English." In *African-American English: Structure, History, and Use.* Guy Bailey, John Baugh, Salikoko S. Mufwene, and John R. Rickford, eds. Pp. 203–25. New York: Routledge.

Sollors, Werner. 2000. *Interracialism: Black-White Intermarriage in American History, Literature, and Law.* New York: Oxford University Press.

Sovik, Liv. 2009. *Aqui Ninguém é Branco.* Rio de Janeiro: Aeroplano.

Stepan, Nancy Leys. 1991. *"The Hour of Eugenics": Race, Gender, and Nation in Latin America.* Ithaca, NY: Cornell University Press.

Stoler, Ann Laura. 1995. *Race and the Education of Desire: Foucault's History of Sexuality and the Colonial Order of Things.* Durham, NC: Duke University Press.

———. 1997. "Racial Histories and their Regimes of Truth." *Political Power and Social Theory* 11: 183–206.

———. 2002. *Carnal Knowledge and Imperial Power: Race and the Intimate in Colonial Rule.* Berkeley: University of California Press.

Sweetland, Julie. 2002. "Unexpected but Authentic Use of an Ethnically-Marked Dialogue." *Journal of Sociolinguistics* 6(4): 514–36.

Tannen, Deborah. 1983. "'I Take out the Rock—DOK!': How Greek Women Tell about Being Molested (and Create Involvement)." *Anthropological Linguistics* 25(3): 359–74.

———. 1989. *Talking Voices: Repetition, Dialogue, and Imagery in Conversational Discourse.* New York: Cambridge University Press.

Tavolaro, Lília. 2008. "Affirmative Action in Contemporary Brazil: Two Institutional Discourses on Race." *International Journal of Politics, Culture, and Society* 19(3–4): 145–60.

Telles, Edward Eric. 2004. *Race in Another America: The Significance of Skin Color in Brazil.* Princeton, NJ: Princeton University Press.

Tuan, Mia. 1998. *Forever Foreigners or Honorary Whites? The Asian Ethnic Experience Today.* New Brunswick, NJ: Rutgers University Press.

Turra, Cleusa, and Gustavo Venturi. 1995. *Racismo Cordial: A Mais Completa Análise sobre o Preconceito de Cor no Brasil.* São Paulo: Editora Ática.

Twine, France Winddance. 1998. *Racism in a Racial Democracy: The Maintenance of White Supremacy in Brazil.* New Brunswick, NJ: Rutgers University Press.

Ultraje a Rigor. 1985. *Nós Vamos Invadir Sua Praia.* Warner.

Urciuoli, Bonnie. 1996. *Exposing Prejudice: Puerto Rican Experiences of Language, Race, and Class.* Boulder, CO: Westview Press.

Van Leeuwen, Lizzy. 2011. *Lost in Mall: An Ethnography of Middle-Class Jakarta in the 1990s.* Leiden: KITLV Press.

Vargas, João Costa. 2004. "Hyperconsciousness of Race and Its Negation: The Dialectic of White Supremacy in Brazil." *Identities: Global Studies in Culture and Power* 11: 443–70.

———. 2011. "The Black Diaspora as Genocide: Brazil and the United States—A Supranational Geography of Death and Its Alternatives." In *State of White Supremacy: Racism, Governance, and the United States.* Moon-Kie Jung, João H. Costa Vargas, and Eduardo Bonilla-Silva, eds. Pp. 243–70. Stanford, CA: Stanford University Press.

———. 2014. "Black Disidentification: The 2013 Protests, *Rolezinhos,* and Racial Antagonism in Post-Lula Brazil." *Critical Sociology* 42(4–5): 1–15.

Vargas, João Costa, and Jaime Amparo Alves. 2010. "Geographies of Death: An Intersectional Analysis of Police Lethality and the Racialized Regimes of Citizenship in São Paulo." *Ethnic and Racial Studies* 33(4): 611–36.

Veloso, Leticia. 2008. "Universal Citizens, Unequal Childhoods: Children's Perspectives on Rights and Citizenship in Brazil." *Latin American Perspectives* 35(4): 45–59.

———. 2010. "Governing Heterogeneity in the Context of Compulsory Closeness: The 'Pacification' of Favelas in Rio de Janeiro." In *Suburbanization in Global Society.* Mark Clapson and Ray Hutchison, eds. Pp. 253–72. Bingley, UK: JAI Press.

———. 2011. "Class as Everyday Imagination and Practice in Brazil." Paper presented at the seminar New Middle Classes and Low Carbon Mobilities, Lancaster University, Lancaster, UK.

Ventura, Zuenir. 1994. *A Cidade Partida.* São Paulo: Companhia das Letras.

Wagley, Charles. 1952. *Race and Class in Rural Brazil.* Paris: UNESCO.

Wald, Gayle. 2000. *Crossing the Line: Racial Passing in Twentieth-Century U.S. Literature and Culture.* Durham, NC: Duke University Press.

Warren, Jonathan W. 2001. *Racial Revolutions: Antiracism and the Indian Resurgence.* Durham, NC: Duke University Press.

Weinstein, Barbara. 2015. *The Color of Modernity: São Paulo and the Making of Race and Nation in Brazil.* Durham, NC: Duke University Press.

Weismantel, Mary. 2001. *Cholas and Pishtacos: Stories of Race and Sex in the Andes*. Chicago: University of Chicago Press.

Weismantel, Mary, and Stephen F. Eisenman. 1998. "Race in the Andes: Global Movements and Popular Ontologies." *Bulletin of Latin American Research* 17(2): 121–42.

Willems, Emílio. 1949. "Racial Attitudes in Brazil." *American Journal of Sociology* 54(5): 402–8.

Windsor, Liliane Cambraia. 2007. "Deconstructing Racial Democracy: A Personal Quest to Understand Social Conditioning about Race Relations in Brazil." *Social Identities* 13(4): 495–520.

Wirtz, Kristina. 2014. *Performing Afro-Cuba: Image, Voice, Spectacle in the Making of Race and History*. Chicago: University of Chicago Press.

Woolard, Kathryn A. 1998. "Introduction: Language Ideology as a Field of Inquiry." In *Language Ideologies: Practice and Theory*. Bambi B. Schieffelin, Kathryn A. Woolard, and Paul V. Kroskrity, eds. Pp. 3–47. New York: Oxford University Press.

Woronov, T. E. 2015. *Class Work: Vocational Schools and China's Urban Youth*. Stanford, CA: Stanford University Press.

Wray, Matt. 2006. *Not Quite White: White Trash and the Boundaries of Whiteness*. Durham, NC: Duke University Press.

Young, Christie T. 1916. *The Black Princess and Other Fairy Tales from Brazil*. London: The Sheldon Press.

Zakabi, Rosana, and Leoli Camargo. 2007. "Eles São Gêmeos Idênticos, Mas . . ." *Revista Veja* (June 6). http://planetasustentavel.abril.com.br/noticia /atitude/conteudo_235546.shtml?func=2. Accessed August 14, 2016.

Zaluar, Alba. 1993. "Urban Violence, Citizenship and Public Policies." *International Journal of Urban and Regional Research* 17(1): 56–66.

———. 1994. *Condomínio do Diabo*. Rio de Janeiro: Editora Revan.

Index

abolition, 4, 16–17

activism, 162, 163–64, 179–81, 183–84, 201n4 (chap. 6), 202n7; Marcha Nacional Contra o Genocídio do Povo Negro (National March Against the Genocide of Black People), 183; NGOs, 162, 167; *rolezinhos* ("little strolls" peaceful protest), 128–29, 139; *#somostodosmacacos*, 3; *Teatro Experimental do Negro* (Black Experimental Theater) (TEN), 22, 90, 202n6

affirmative action, 17, 25–26, 162, 180, 181–84, 189, 201n1; Universidade de Brasília and, 181

Afonso Arinos Law (1951), 2

Africa: descendants in Brazil, 4, 16, 19, 146–48, 162, 163, 167, 180, 199–200n1, 202n1; apartheid in, 182

African Americans, 16, 171; in Brazil, 2, 130, 168, 197n1, 201n3 (chap. 5), 202n4

Afro hairstyle, 164–66

Afro-Brazilian history, teaching of, 8–9, 162, 188

Alagoas, 9

Alberto, Paulina, 22–23, 90, 145, 163–64; "When Rio was Black," 164–65

Alves, Daniel, 3

Alves, Jaime Amparo, 24, 48, 49, 52, 62, 107, 194

Amorim, Paulo Henrique, 1, 3–4, 25–26, 188, 195n1, 195n3

Angeli: "Feriado: Dia da Consciência Negro" cartoon, 8–11, 10*fig.*

antiracism, 1, 3–4, 196n7

appearance: *"boa aparência"* (good appearance), 38, 44, 46–48, 50–52, 63–66, 124–25, 129–30, 170–72; dress, 6, 47, 125–26, 170–71*ex.*, 173; hairstyle, 164–66, 169–72, 170–71*ex.*, 175, 201n2. *See also* comportment; phenotypical features

Aqui Ninguém é Branco (There are no whites here) (Sovik), 18, 74, 92, 190

Arpoador (Ipanema Beach area), 111*fig.*

arrastões (group theft on the beach), 114–15, 123–24, 126, 127

asfalto, 24, 32, 82

"assuming one's blackness" (*assumir a negritude*), 65, 170–72

Banck, Geert, 115, 120, 122–23

Bagno, Marcos, 79, 157

Bahia, 19, 46, 55, 67, 74, 132, 165

"barbarism," 15–16

Barickman, Bert, 75, 108, 125

Barra de Tijuca (neighborhood), 122–23

baseball, 171

basketball, 148, 176

Bastide, Roger, 131

beaches, 8, 108, 109*fig.*, 201n7; access to, 116, 117*map*, 119, 125–27; and *"boa aparência"* (good appearance), 124–25; manners at the, 113–14, 115, 119–22, 124–26; racial contact at the, 108–16, 110*fig.*, 119–20, 122, 123–24, 132, 142; structural racism at the, 8–11, 10*fig.*, 39–40, 201n6; violence at the, 116, 118–19, 121, 126–27

beauty, 120, 123–24; blackness and, 165, 186, 188, 191

black consciousness, 8–9, 90, 165, 167, 180; *negro assumido* (black person who has "assumed" their blackness), 65, 170–72; *Teatro Experimental do Negro* (Black Experimental Theater) (TEN), 22, 90, 202n6

Black Consciousness Day, 8–9, 162

Black Experimental Theater (Teatro Experimental do Negro, TEN), 22, 90, 202n6

Black into White (Skidmore), 4, 15–17, 42, 129, 172

"black is beautiful" movement, 41, 164

Black Lives Matter campaign, 184, 198n5

blackness, 27–31, 40–41, 55, 61–62, 170, 198n2, 196n16; as "barbarism," 15–16; black "inferiority," ideas of, 6–7, 8, 15, 17–18, 44, 46, 63–64, 85, 91, 131, 165; black visibility, 41, 163–67, 171, 173–79, 181, 184, 186–87, 189; brownness and, 13; *"cheiro de negro"* ("black smell"), 47, 76; criminality and, 53, 100, 148; *negro* (black), 145, 162, 179–80*ex.*, 186–88, 202n6; *negro assumido* (black person who has "assumed" their blackness), 65, 170–72; *negro comportado* (well-behaved black person), 167, 169; *negro de alma branca* (black with a white soul), 1–4, 45, 195n3, 201n5 (chap. 5); slang associated with, 28, 30–31, 39–40, 64–66, 65*ex.*, 77, 80–82,

80–81*ex.*, 148, 192, 193; violence and, 176. *See also* racial difference, noticing

blackness, avoidance of, 23, 38, 40, 44–45, 74, 158–60, 194; and fear of racial contact, 94, 95–97, 121–22, 126–27, 129–33, 139, 140–41*ex.*, 144–48

blackness, preference for, 145–49, 149–53*ex.*, 153–54, 155*ex.*, 156, 158*ex.*, 159–60, 163, 176, 179, 179–80*ex.*, 201n7

"Black Rio: O orgulho (importado) de ser negro no Brasil" (Black Rio: The [imported] pride of being black in Brazil) (Frias), 164

"boa aparência" (good appearance), 38, 44, 46–48, 50–52, 63–66, 129–30, 170–72; at the beach, 124–25

bodies, reading of, 6, 18–19, 27–31, 40, 181, 188; at the beach, 113; grammar and, 65–66, 86; and "personal whiteness," 73–75; phenotypical features and, 6, 30, 38, 44, 66–67, 189–91; rappers', 134, 164–65, 167, 168–73; racial crossing and, 159–60, 176–78; racial discourse and, 27–29, 121; for safety, 94, 96, 107–08, 121; and "seeing" race, 162, 184, 191–94. *See also* comportment

Bourdieu, Pierre, 6, 67–68, 72, 78–79, 113, 142, 165, 170

brancura and *branquitude*, 18, 69, 92–93, 190

brasilidade (harmonious mixing of African, European, and Native heritage), 21, 163

Brazil: colonial, 7–11, 15–17; "comfortable racial contradiction" in, 3–7, 20, 25, 162, 184, 187, 191, 194; constitution (1934), 16; constitution (1988), 2; as a "disjunctive democracy," 53, 62; nationalism, 21; "redemocratization," 23, 52, 97–98, 107, 126, 167; race relations, current state of, 2, 20, 23, 146, 160, 162, 182–

83, 185–88; as a racial democracy, 3–5, 20–22, 24, 43, 100, 129, 162–63, 182; racial eugenics, 16, 45; racial tolerance, challenges to, 40–41, 163, 180–84, 202n7; racism, denial of, 1, 4–6, 16, 20, 25, 41, 44, 196n14; regional identity, development of, 19

Brazil: Five Centuries of Change (Skidmore), 4

Brazilian MTV Music Video Awards (1998), 161, 167

Brazilian Worker's Party (Partido dos Trabalhadores, PT), 72

Brizola, Leonel, 108

Brown, Mano, 161–62, 167, 170–71*ex.*, 171–72*ex.*, 172, 175–76, 183. *See also* Racionais MC's (The Rationals)

buses, 108, 117*map*, 125–26. *See also* transportation, public

Caldeira, Teresa, 23, 52–53, 101, 129; *City of Walls*, 52, 96–98, 122, 138, 156

Camargo, Leoli (*Veja* journalist), 181–82

Cameron, Deborah, 76, 78, 199n4

Cano, Ignácio, 32, 52, 96

"Capítulo 4, Versículo 3" (Chapter 4, Verse 3) (Racionais MC's), 55–56, 64–65, 173, 175*ex.*, 175–76, 199n12, 201n5 (chap. 6)

Carbado, Devon, 63

Cardoso, Fernando Henrique, 22, 153

Carr, E. Summerson, 79

Caribbean, the, 90, 146–47, 167

Cavanaugh, Jillian, 199n13

census, 69–70, 91–93, 162, 179; 1970, 22; 2000, 199n2; 2010, 12*map*, 199–200n1

"*cheiro de negro*" ("black smell"), 47, 76

Chevigny, Paul, 61

child-rearing, 76, 77*ex.*, 88, 131, 156–59, 158*ex.*, 185–88, 189–90

Cicalo, André, 13, 47, 57, 130

Cidade de Deus (City of God) (film), 133

Cidade de Deus (City of God) (suburb), 23, 48, 64

Cidade dos Homens (City of men), 133

citizenship rights, 24, 44, 53, 61–62, 67, 97–98, 126

City of Walls (Caldeira), 52, 96–98, 122, 138, 156

civilization, 15

"Civilization and Barbarism" (Sarmiento), 15

class, socioeconomic, 5–6, 8–9, 13–15, 30, 34, 42–44; "*classe C*" ("C class," working class), 138; in colonial Brazil, 7–8, 15–16; elite, 4, 34*fig.*, 35, 61, 74, 92–93, 131; language and, 6–7, 39, 57, 157–58; markers, 71–72; middle class, new lower, 143–45; middle class, upper, 144–45; privilege, and the ease of, 67, 90, 137; race and, 38–40, 42–44, 61–62, 71–72, 88–93, 133–35, 140–45, 154, 174*ex.*, 192, 193–94, 202n3. *See also* lower class; middle class

Coates, Ta-Nehisi: "Fear of a Black President," 94

cobertura (penthouse apartment), 34*fig.*

Collins, John F., 66–67, 73, 138, 193

colonialism, 66, 73–74, 87, 156, 159

Color of Modernity, The (Weinstein), 19

comportment, 90–91; at the beach, 113–14, 115, 119–22, 124–27; bodily control, 47, 62–63, 66, 67–68, 73–74, 76, 110; in hairstyle, 169–70; *negro comportado*, 167; at malls, 128–19, 143–45; "patterns of propriety," 122; and race, 114, 160, 194. *See also* "*boa aparência*" (good appearance); language

"compulsory closeness," 31–35, 34*fig.*, 39, 49–50, 51*fig.*, 95–96, 97, 124–25, 138–39

comunidade, 33, 132. *See also* Cruzada São Sebastião; *favela*

Constitution of Brazil: 1934, 16; 1988, 2

"conversational sampling," 174–76, 175ex., 179

Copacabana, 11, 35, 108, 115, 123, 125, 165

Corrêa, Sílvia Borges, 120

correlation, art of, 99–101

Costa Brava Clube, 124

"courtesy stigma," 146

Covin, David, 22, 24, 145, 164, 165

crime, 97–98, 107, 110; *arrastões* (group theft on the beach), 114–15, 123–24, 126, 127; crime talk, 97, 101; lower class and, 95–96, 100, 101–107, 118, 122; middle class and, 101–103, 121; robbery, 80–81, 95–96, 98, 101–102

criminality: blackness and, 53, 100, 148; hairstyles and, 169–70; language and, 57, 62–63, 66, 76, 84–85ex., 98–99, 102ex., 102–104, 104–105ex., 105–106ex.

"crossing," 153, 154, 159–60

Cruzada São Sebastião, 33–35, 36map, 50fig., 51fig., 76–77, 139fig., 142, 166; as *comunidade*, 11, 33, 132; as housing project, 11, 83; male youth of, 48–57, 58, 66–67, 78–79, 80–82, 85–86, 89, 98–99, 100ex., 102, 103–105, 122–23, 133–35, 139–40, 145–46, 148–49, 151–53, 154–58, 166, 174–80, 175ex., 177–78ex., 179–80ex.

cultural capital, 78, 113, 124, 137, 165

"cultural censorship," 3, 25, 187

cultural practices, 6, 38, 44–45, 69, 72–75, 125, 142, 164, 169–72, 184, 192, 194; racial display, 27–30, 172–73

cultural refinement, 24, 71–72, 89–90, 93, 114, 116, 120–22, 189–90, 192–94

Damasceno, Caetana, 46, 47, 191

DaMatta, Roberto, 21, 32, 61, 62

Daniel, G. Reginald, 21, 22, 42, 44

da Silva, Denise Ferreira, 9, 74–75

Dávila, Jerry, 22, 42, 73–74, 164, 172; *Diploma of Whiteness: Race and Social Policy in Brazil, 1917–1945,* 45

Davis, Darien, 7, 15–17, 20–21, 42, 44–45, 132, 172

Degler, Carl, 42–44, 121; *Neither Black nor White,* 147–48

democracy: "disjunctive," 53, 62; "redemocratization," 23, 52, 97–98, 107, 126, 167

dictatorships: military, 21–23, 26, 164, 167; Vargas, 21

"Dinheiro embranquece" ("Money whitens"), 43–44, 191, 202n3

Diploma of Whiteness: Race and Social Policy in Brazil, 1917–1945 (Dávila), 45

discipline, bodily. *See* comportment

discrimination, 18, 27, 128–29; *"boa aparência"* as, 46, 48; class, 14; correlation, and art of, 99–101; laws, 2–3, 16, 20–21, 164

DJTR (rapper), 63–67, 64ex., 65ex., 167–70, 169ex.

Dolozal, Rachel, 199n3

do morro (from the hill, or from a *favela*), 32, 83, 101, 114. *See also favela*

Dreaming Equality (Sheriff), 3, 5, 23, 25, 129, 146, 187, 196n16

Dreisinger, Baz: *Near Black,* 73, 154, 189

dress, 6, 47, 125–26, 170–71ex., 173

drug gangs, 32, 37, 49, 104, 118–19, 166

Du Bois, W. E. B., 71

Dunham, Katherine, 2

Eckert, Penelope, 79

education, 93, 153; higher education, 56–57, 72, 176, 198–99n9; private school, 13–15, 71–72, 76, 95–97, 143fig., 156, 176, 185–86; public school, 37, 45, 76. *See also* grammar

Ehrenreich, Barbara: *Fear of Falling: The Inner Life of the Middle Class,* 157

Eisenman, Stephen F., 29, 159

elite, 4, 34*fig.*, 35, 61, 74, 92–93, 131
embranquecimento (whitening),
    15–18, 42–48, 66, 69–70, 129, 131,
    145–46, 191, 196n15, 202n3
employment, 65–66, 139; "*boa
    aparência*" and, 38–39, 46, 50,
    198n3; *concursos* (contests), 14;
    domestic, 47, 89–90, 91–92*ex.*, 131,
    183, 188–89; manual labor, 10*fig.*,
    35–37, 76, 161–62, 190; *trabalhador-
    bandido* (worker-bandit) divide, 62,
    199n11
English language, 140-41*ex.*, 142–43,
    143*fig.*, 164–65, 190
enregisterment of slang, 83
eugenics, 16, 45, 73
Europe: influence of, 7, 15–16;
    immigrants, 19, 42, 159
exceptionalism, Brazilian, 5, 179, 187

facial features, 6, 18, 27, 46, 69–71
fairy tales, 17–18, 196–97nn17–18
Fanon, Frantz, 29
Farias, Patricia, 75, 108, 113, 115, 119,
    124, 127, 142
farofeiro, 124–25
favelas (shantytowns), 9, 12*map*, 19,
    36*map*, 197n26; and blackness, 23–25;
    "compulsory closeness," 31–35,
    34*fig.*, 49, 51*fig.*; crime and, 95–96, 98,
    102, 103–106, 118–19, 122; *do morro*
    (from the hill), 32, 83, 101, 114; and
    Flamengo soccer team, 99–100;
    middle-class youth in, 136–37, 147,
    154–56, 159–60; Rocinha (*favela*), 95,
    104–105; slang in, 66, 80–82, 83–85,
    192–93; South Zone *favelas*, 32–33.
    See also Cruzada São Sebastião
"Fear of a Black President" (Coates),
    94
*Fear of Falling: The Inner Life of the
    Middle Class* (Ehrenreich), 157
"Feriado: Dia da Consciência Negro"
    cartoon (Angeli), 8–11, 10*fig.*
Fernandes, Florestan, 5, 22, 131
financial means, 93, 96–97, 122, 144,
    149, 155*ex.*, 191

Fischer, Brodwyn, 23, 74, 96, 98, 100
Flamengo (neighborhood), 93, 101
Flamengo soccer team, 99–100, 100*fig.*
Folha de São Paulo (São Paulo), 8
Fordham, Signithia, 65–66, 67
Freeman, James, 124–25, 127
French, Jan Hoffman, 26, 52, 61, 63,
    101, 200n4
Freyre, Gilberto, 21
Frias, Lena: "*Black Rio: O orgulho
    (importado) de ser negro no Brasil*"
    (Black Rio: The [imported] pride of
    being black in Brazil), 164
Fry, Peter, 3, 129, 130, 163, 166, 179,
    183

Gama Filho University, 56
gender, 29, 50
genocide, cultural, 183–84, 202n7
Germany, 17, 45, 182
gíria (slang), 48, 115–16; blackness
    associated with, 28, 30–31, 39–40,
    64–66, 65*ex.*, 77, 80–82, 80–81*ex.*,
    148, 192, 193; criminality and, 66,
    76, 84–85*ex.*, 102*ex.*, 102–104, 104–
    105*ex.*, 105–106*ex.*; enregisterment
    of, 83; *playboy* use of, 155*ex.*,
    156–58, 158*ex.*, 178–79, 192;
    pragmatic markers, 80, 82–86,
    82–83*ex.*, 103, 153, 155*ex.*; "sound
    words," 175–76
Globo, O (Rio de Janeiro), 172–73,
    174*ex.*, 182
Goffman, Erving, 143, 146, 178
Goldstein, Donna, 52, 89–90, 183
Gomes, Laurentino, 7
grammar, 199n5; middle class,
    importance to, 71, 75–80, 77*ex.*,
    78*ex.*, 82, 84–89, 142–43, 153, 156–
    57, 178; lower class usage: 14, 62,
    63–67. *See also* Portuguese, standard
"Guerra na Areia . . ." (War in the
    sand . . .) (Paixão and Leite), 108,
    115–16, 118–22, 126
Guimarães, Antonio, 2, 76, 167, 188,
    194
Guterl, Matthew Pratt, 27

hairstyle, 169–72, 170–71*ex.*, 175, 201n2; Afro, 164–66; criminality and, 169–70

Hanchard, Michael, 5, 22–23, 27, 35, 45, 164, 165, 183, 187

Haney-López, Ian, 72–73, 197n25

harassment, police, 48–49, 52–57, 54–55*ex.*, 58

Harris, Marvin, 22, 43, 48, 70, 131, 191

Hartigan, John, 73

Heneghan, Bridget T., 27, 75

"HB" ("Hot Buttered") (Australian chain store), 144*fig.*

higher education, 56–57, 72, 176, 198–99n9; affirmative action and, 25, 162, 180–81, 189; Universidade do Estado do Rio de Janeiro (Rio de Janeiro State University, UERJ), 189; Universidade de Brasília, 181

highway improvement, 117*map*, 119, 126

hip-hop, 40–41, 63–65, 133, 161–67, 171–73, 174–79, 184, 201n4 (chap. 6); "conversational sampling," 174–76, 175*ex.*, 179; MV Bill (rapper), 52, 52*ex.*, 63, 133–34*ex.*, 166–67, 168–70, 169*ex.*, 172, 201n5 (chap. 5); rap, 38, 40–41, 63–64, 133–34, 166–72, 168*ex.*, 173–76, 184; U.S., imported from, 166–67, 171, 201n3 (chap. 5). *See also* Racionais MC's (The Rationals)

Holston, James, 23, 52–53, 55, 62, 98, 126–27

Hordge-Freeman, Elizabeth, 43, 44, 46, 164, 172

Hospital Municipal Miguel Couto (Rio de Janeiro), 95–96

housing project, 11, 83. *See also* Cruzada São Sebastião; *favela*

hygiene, 75–76, 79; verbal hygiene, 199n4

Ianni, Octávio, 22

identification (document), 165–66; request for, 53–55, 58–61*ex.*

ideology, language, 28–29, 39, 76–78

imitation, cultural, 121

immigration, 16, 19, 42

indigenous ancestry, 19, 21, 45, 146, 197n20, 199n5

Indonesia, 137–38

interracial relationships, 51; marriage, 42–43, 130, 131–32, 199n2. *See also* racial contact

interviews, metalinguistic, 35, 77, 86, 154

Ipanema, 11–12, 35, 95, 108, 110*fig.*, 111*fig.*, 115–16, 123, 185, 190

Isabel, Princess of Brazil, 8, 162

Jabor, Arnaldo, 173

jeitinho, 199n10

Jim Crow laws, 94, 130

Kamel, Ali: *Não Somos Racistas: Uma Reação aos que Querem nos Transformar numa Nação Bicolor* (We are not racist: A reaction to those who want to turn us into a black-white nation), 25–26, 182

Khan, Shamus, 6, 67, 90, 113, 137

KLJay (DJ), 64–65. *See also* Racionais MC's (The Rationals)

language: class and, 6–7, 39, 57, 157–58; language ideology, 28–29, 39, 76–78; optional variability, suppression of, 78; pragmatic markers, 80, 82–84, 82–83*ex.*, 86, 103, 153, 155*ex.*; profanity, 175, 176, 178–79; race and, 84–85*ex.*, 142–43, 193–94, 202n4; racially tinged, 24, 98, 100–101, 114, 122, 124; verbal hygiene, 199n4. *See also gíria* (slang); grammar

languages: English language, 140–41*ex.*, 142–43, 143*fig.*, 164–65, 190; among poor, 30. *See also* Portuguese

Larkins, Erika Robb, 32, 49, 57, 96, 197n26

Latin America, 15–16, 90, 146–47

law: Afro-Brazilian history, on teaching of, 8, 162; citizenship rights, 24, 44, 53, 61–62, 67, 97–98,

126; death penalty, 98; about *favelas*, 23; immigration (1945), 16; legal rights, 55; *prisão especial* (special prison), establishing, 57; runaway-slave colonies, returning land to former, 162

laws, discrimination, 2–3, 16, 20, 164; affirmative action, 17, 25–26, 162, 180–84, 189, 202n1; Afonso Arinos Law (1951), 2; antimiscegenation, 130, 201n4 (chap. 5); blackness, acknowledgment of, 162–63; racial insult, 1–3, 25–26, 194, 195n4

Leão, Danuza, 120

Leblon, 11, 13, 35, 36*map*, 49, 108, 123, 133, 136, 140*fig.*, 149. *See also* Cruzada São Sebastião

Leeds, Anthony and Elizabeth, 84, 103

legal system, 53, 107; Commission of Military Inquiry, 22; Superior Tribunal de Justiça (Superior Court of Justice), 1, 195n1; Supreme Federal Court, 57

Leite, Virginia: "Guerra na Areia . . . " (War in the sand . . .), 108, 115–16, 118–22, 126

Lima, Márcia, 47

linguistic anthropology, 27–28, 54, 78–79, 83

linguistic practices, 29–31, 38, 41, 75–76, 154–56, 164, 172, 184, 188, 192–94, 199n4; "conversational sampling," 174–76, 175*ex.*, 179; metalinguistic labor, 79

linguistic strategy, 57, 58, 62, 64–67

Lost in Mall (Van Leeuwen), 137–38

lower class, 14–15, 61–62; at the beach, 108, 111–13, 118–20, 125; crime and, 95, 100–101, 103–106; language and, 30, 193; middle class, in contrast to, 33–37, 76, 89–94, 106–107, 114, 118–20, 125, 132, 137–38, 191; white, 73, 154. *See also favelas* (shantytowns); poverty

lyrics, 166; "A Noite" (The night) (MV Bill), 52*ex.*, 63; "Nós Vamos Invadir Sua Praia" (We are going to invade your beach) (Ultraje a Rigor), 110–14; "*Pare de Babar*" (Stop Sucking Up) (MV Bill), 133–34; "conversational sampling," 174–76, 175*ex.*, 179

Malheiro, Perdigão, 4

malls, shopping, 39, 88, 128–30, 132, 137–39, 142, 144–45; Rio Sul mall, 138–39; Shopping Leblon, 139*fig.*, 140*fig.*; VillageMall, 138

manners. *See* comportment

mano (black brother), 164, 170–71*ex.*, 170–73, 174*ex.*, 176, 178

Marcha Nacional Contra o Genocídio do Povo Negro (National March Against the Genocide of Black People), 183

marriage: interracial, 42–43, 130, 131–32, 199n2

"matched guise" tests, 30

McCallum, Cecilia, 13, 34, 38, 66, 89

McElhinny, Bonnie, 121

media, 16, 161; *Folha de São Paulo* (São Paulo), 8; *O Globo* (Rio de Janeiro), 172–73, 174*ex.*, 182; radio, 64–65, 64*ex.*, 65 *ex.*, 158–59; Rede Globo, 1; social media, 3, 8, 128–29; *Veja*, 116–22, 181–83

melhorar a raça (improving the race), 16, 129

Mello, André: "Racionais MC's are the 'brothers' against the '*playboys*'" (*Racionais MC's são os 'manos' contra os 'playboys'*) (cartoon), 172–73, 174*ex.*

mestiçagem (race mixture), 21–24, 42, 53, 129–30, 145, 146–48, 178

middle class: at the beach, 113, 115–16, 118; blackness, avoiding, 94, 95–97, 99; children, 13–15, 71–72, 76, 95–97, 143*fig.*,159, 185–86; crime and, 101–103, 121; grammar and, 39, 67, 69–72, 76–79; lower class, in contrast to, 33–37, 76, 89–94, 106–107, 114, 118–20, 125, 132, 137–38, 191; new lower, 143–45; "personal whiteness" and, 69–72, 76–79; race,

middle class *(continued)*
  readiness to discuss, 187, 189, 192;
  reactions to *favela* crime, 103–106,
  118; slang and, 82–89, 148, 156–57;
  soul and, 164; upper, 144–45; youth,
  132, 136–39, 147–48, 154–56, 159–
  60. *See also playboys*
military police force (*Polícia Militar,*
  PM), 52, 58–61, 112, 200n4;
miscegenation, 8, 15–16, 45, 129
moreno (light brown or tan), 8, 69,
  177–78
Morgan, Marcyliena, 58
"mulatto," 17, 42–44, 147–48
music, 172, 175–76; funk, 118, 120–21;
  rock íní roll, Ultraje a Rigor, 108,
  110–16, 111–12*ex.*; soul, 145, 163–
  65, 169–70. *See also* hip-hop
MV Bill (rapper), 166–67, 168–70,
  169*ex.*, 201n5 (chap. 5); "A Noite"
  (The Night), 52*ex.*, 63; "*Pare de
  Babar*" (Stop Sucking Up), 133–
  34*ex.*, 172; *Traficando Informação*
  (Trafficking information), 167, 168*ex.*

Nabuco, Joaquim, 4, 16
*Não Somos Racistas: Uma Reação aos
  que Querem nos Transformar numa
  Nação Bicolor* (We are not racist: A
  reaction to those who want to turn
  us into a black-white nation)
  (Kamel), 25–26, 182
Nascimento, Abdias do, 5, 22, 195n3,
  202n7
Nascimento, Elisa Larkin, 16, 53, 69,
  129, 147, 186
nationalism, 21
Near Black (Dreisinger), 73, 154, 189
negão (big, strong or intimidating
  black guy), 61
negro (black), 145, 162, 179–80*ex.*,
  186–88, 202n6
negro assumido (black person who
  has "assumed" their blackness), 65,
  171–72
negro comportado (well-behaved black
  person), 167, 169

negro de alma branca (black with a
  white soul), 1–4, 45, 195n3, 201n5
  (chap. 5)
"*Negro Drama*" (The drama of black
  people) (Racionais MC's), 158*ex.*
Neither Black nor White (Degler),
  147–48
Neymar, 3
NGOs, 162, 167
Nobles, Melissa, 22, 164, 199n2
Nogueira, Oracy, 43–44, 45–46, 76,
  131, 132, 160, 191
"*Noite*" (The Night) (MV Bill,
  rapper), 52*ex.*, 63
nordestinos (northeasterners), 19, 93,
  98, 101
North America, 26–27, 72–73, 130,
  142, 157, 179, 183, 187; import of
  hip-hop from, 148, 163–65, 166–67,
  171. *See also* United States
North Zone (Rio de Janeiro), 32, 56,
  108, 125–26
"*Nós Vamos Invadir Sua Praia*" (We
  are going to invade your beach)
  (Ultraje a Rigor), 108, 110–16, 111–
  12*ex.*

O'Dougherty, Maureen, 19, 72, 90, 124
one-drop rule, 26, 43, 73
optional variability, suppression of, 78

Paixão, Roberta: "Guerra na Areia . . .
  " (War in the sand . . .), 108, 115–
  16, 118–22, 126
pardo (brown), 44, 69–71, 93, 149
Pardue, Derek, 63, 133, 168
"*Pare de Babar*" (Stop Sucking Up),
  133–34*ex.*, 172
"passing," 153, 154
Patai, Daphne, 90
Penglase, Ben, 24, 32, 96, 101, 126
Pereira, Heraldo, 1–2
periferia, a (the periphery), 32,
  117*map*, 128, 179
Performing Afro-Cuba (Wirtz), 18, 27,
  146, 197n24
Perry, Keisha-Khan, 11, 52

"personal whiteness," 39, 67–68, 69–75, 77, 79, 88, 93–94, 153, 154, 159, 190

phenotypical features, 18–19, 26–27; alteration of, 46–47; bodies, and reading of, 6, 30, 38, 44, 66–67, 189–91; facial features, 6, 18, 27, 46, 69–71; flexibility of, 2, 27, 29, 43, 91–93, 154, 164, 169, 172, 193–94; propriety and, 63, 127; skin color, 93, 146–47, 149–53ex., 177, 181–82, 185–87

Philips, Susan, 28–29

Pinheiro-Machado, Rosana, 88

Pinho, Patricia de Santana, 27, 46–47, 53, 65, 70, 75–76, 129, 146–47, 167, 170, 172

playboys: avoiding blackness, 133–37, 133–34ex., 135–36ex.; "crossing," 139–40, 140–41ex., 145–46, 148–53, 149–53ex., 154–60; *manos* and, 164, 170–73, 171–72ex., 174ex., 174–76; slang term, use of, 155ex., 156–58, 158ex., 178–79, 192

"pobreza tem cor" (poverty has a color), 11

police: on the beach, 111fig., 115–16; on buses, 126; harassment, 48–49, 52–57, 54–55ex., 58; military police force (*Polícia Militar*, PM), 52, 58–61, 112, 200n4; secret, 165; Unidades de Polícia Pacificadora (Pacifying Police Units), 96

political consciousness: hip-hop movement and, 38, 40–41, 56, 63, 82, 133–34, 160, 163–67, 170–79, 174ex., 184, 192, 201n4 (chap. 6). *See also* race consciousness

population: Brazil, 15; North Zone, 125; Rio de Janeiro, 6, 7, 12map, 52, 98

Portugal, 7, 19

Portuguese, 18, 28, 47, 54, 65–67, 82, 85–86, 103, 145; standard, 62, 76, 79, 84, 87–88, 157, 192, 193

poverty, 11, 19, 32–35, 43, 100–101, 138–39, 173, 194. *See also favelas* (shantytowns); lower class

pragmatic markers, 80, 155ex., 153; *bum*, 82–84, 82–83ex., 86; *na moral* (seriously), 103

preto (black), 179–80ex., 186

"preto por fora, branco por dentro" (black on the outside, white on the inside), 134, 172, 201n5 (chap. 5)

"preto tipo A" (class A black person), 177–78ex., 179

"Princesa Negrina" (The Black Princess), 17–18

profanity, 175, 176, 178–79

propriety. *See* comportment

prisons, 57, 147

privilege, the ease of, 67, 90, 137. *See also* class, socioeconomic; race, and class

Quilombo dos Palmares, 9, 162

race: and class, 38–40, 42–44, 61–62, 71–72, 88–93, 133–35, 140–45, 154, 174ex., 192, 193–94, 202n3; and comportment, 114, 160, 194; and language, 193–94, 202n4; not mentioned, 113–14, 118, 122, 124, 127, 140, 173, 183, 188; "seeing" race, 162, 173, 184, 187, 189, 191–94; and skin color, 185–87; as fixed, 18, 70

race consciousness, 163, 170, 180; black consciousness, 8–9, 63–65, 165, 167, 170–72, 180; Black Consciousness Day, 8–9, 10fig., 162; hyperconsciousness, 25; "*preto tipo A*," 177–78ex., 179. *See also* political consciousness

Race and Social Policy in Brazil, 1917–1945 (Dávila), 45

"race trafficking," 167

racial anxiety, 39, 73–74, 146, 147, 154, 157–58, 159–60

racial censorship, 22–23, 26

racial classification, 132, 180–82

racial contact, fear of, 94, 95–97, 121–22, 126–27, 129–33, 139, 140–41ex., 144–48; at the beach, 108–16, 110fig., 119–20, 122, 123–24, 132, 142

"racial contradiction, comfortable,"
3–7, 20, 25, 162, 184, 187, 191, 194
racial democracy, 3–5, 20–21, 24, 43,
100, 129, 162–63; critiques of, 22,
182
racial difference: noticing, 24–28, 30,
41, 61, 91, 97–98, 162–63, 167, 173,
185–91, 193–94; affirmative action
and, 181–84; downplaying, 180–82
racial discourse, 2, 27–29, 121
racial displays, 28–30, 172–73. See also
blackness; whiteness
racial hierarchy, 4–6, 18, 26, 28–29, 70,
91, 147, 169, 188, 189–91
racial identification, 91–92ex., 93, 149–
53ex., 154, 177–78ex., 193, 199n2;
self-identification, 24, 70–71ex., 181,
189, 202n1
racial ideologies: Brazilian, 5, 39,
44–45, 66, 96, 122, 131, 142, 145,
193; U.S., 130, 164
racial inequality, 5–6, 8–9, 22–23, 26,
56, 87–88, 162, 166, 187, 199n10
racial injury, 1–3, 25–26, 194, 195n4,
201n5 (chap. 5)
racial meaning, 6, 27–30, 99, 127, 142,
169–170, 193
racial privilege, 8, 18, 39–40, 69–71, 75,
137, 170
racial purity, 74, 130, 146–47, 198n2;
one-drop rule, 26, 43, 73
racial reforms, 162
racial revolution, 170–71
racial tolerance, 16, 20–22, 25–26, 145,
160, 163, 166–68, 188, 189, 190–92;
challenges to, 40–41, 163, 180–84,
202n7; "cordial" racism, 3–4, 20–21,
41, 145, 162–63, 166–67, 184, 191,
194, 196n8, 202n8
Racionais MC's (The Rationals), 172–
73, 174ex., 175, 178–79; Brown,
Mano, 161–62, 167, 170–71ex., 171–
72ex., 172, 175–76, 183; "Capítulo 4,
Versículo 3" (Chapter 4, Verse 3),
55–56, 64–65, 173, 175ex., 175–76,
199n12, 201n5 (chap. 6); KLJay (DJ),
64–65; "Negro Drama" (The drama

of black people), 158ex., 159;
Sobreviviendo no Inferno
(Surviving in hell), 161–62, 166
"Racionais MC's são os 'manos'
contra os 'playboys'" (Racionais
MC's are the 'brothers' against the
'playboys') (Mello), 172–73, 174ex.
racism, 13–15, 99–100, 122, 128–29,
135, 139, 140–41ex., 145, 146, 159–
60, 186, 188–89, 196n14; antiracism,
1, 3–4, 196n7; denial of, 1, 4–6, 16,
20–26, 41, 43–44, 184, 196n14;
scientific racism, 15. See also
discrimination
racism, "cordial," 3–4, 20–21, 41, 145,
162–63, 166–67, 184, 191, 194,
196n8, 202n8
racism, structural, 6, 8, 13–15, 20,
23–26, 41, 53, 56ex., 184, 188; at the
beach, 8–11, 10fig., 39–40, 201n6;
critique of, 167, 181
Racusen, Seth, 1–2, 194, 195n4
radio, 64–65, 64ex., 65 ex., 158–59
Ramos, Guerreiro, 74, 129, 147
rap, 38, 40–41, 63–64, 133–34, 166–72,
168ex., 173–76, 184. See also hip-hop
Rede Globo, 1
Rezende, Cláudia, 47
Rio de Janeiro, 5–7, 29–30, 31–38,
36map, 48; soul movement in, 164;
beaches, 8, 108, 109fig., 114, 116,
123–25, 142; cariocas (residents), 96;
favelas in, 23–25; Hospital
Municipal Miguel Couto, 95–96;
North Zone, 32, 56, 108, 125–26;
population, 6, 7, 12map, 52, 98;
racial groups, 193–94; shopping
malls of, 138–39, 144–45;
Universidade do Estado do Rio de
Janeiro (Rio de Janeiro State
University, UERJ), 189; West Zone,
122–24. See also Cruzada São
Sebastião; South Zone
robbery, 80–81, 95–96, 98, 101–102
Rocinha (favela), 95, 104–105
rolezinhos ("little strolls" peaceful
protest), 128–29, 139

Rosa-Ribeiro, Fernando, 2, 53, 146, 182

Sansone, Livio, 3, 44, 46, 50–51, 63, 166–67
São Paulo, 2, 19, 31, 45–46, 90, 97–98, 114, 122, 196n12, 198n3
São Paulo School of Race Relations, 22
Sarmiento, Domingo: "Civilization and Barbarism," 15
Scalco, Lucia Mury, 88
Schucman, Lia Vainer, 18, 92, 190
Schwarcz, Lilia Moritz, 17, 69, 146
security, 52, 58, 95–97, 101; middle class concern for, 37–38, 84–85ex., 94, 97–98, 107–108, 115, 121–22, 123–24, 127
Segato, Rita, 74
segregation, 98; laws, 8, 16, 43, 183; residential, 110, 130, 159, 193; "symbolic," 40, 97, 126, 190
Seigel, Micol, 4, 16, 21, 71
Sheriff, Robin: *Dreaming Equality,* 3, 5, 23, 25, 129, 146, 187, 196n16
Silva, Denise Ferreira da, 26, 30, 74, 186, 189, 194
"situational whiteness," 38–39, 44, 47, 67
Skidmore, Thomas: *Black into White,* 4, 15–17, 42, 129, 172; *Brazil: Five Centuries of Change,* 4
skin color, 93, 146–47, 149–53ex., 177, 181–82, 185–87. *See also* race
slang. *See gíria* (slang)
slavery, 4, 7, 153; abolition, 4, 16–17; end of, 8–9, 15, 16–17, 24, 42, 130; legacy of, 24, 75–76, 180
Smith, Christen A., 24, 48, 52, 55, 62, 107, 183, 194
Smith, Mark, 26, 76
Sobrevivendo no Inferno (Surviving in Hell) (Racionais MC's) (album), 161–62, 166
soccer fandom, 99–100, 100fig., 110fig.
"social face, cool," 58ex., 61
social media, 3, 8, 128–29

social mobility, 5, 9, 15, 43–44, 147–48, 195n3
socioeconomic class. *See* class, socioeconomic
sociolinguistics, 30, 78–79, 154
#somostodosmacacos, 3
soul, 145, 163–65, 169–70
"sound words," 175–76
South Zone (Rio de Janeiro), 12map, 35, 36map, 37–38, 117map, 126; beaches, 8, 108, 109fig., 114, 116, 123–25, 142; Copacabana, 11, 108, 115, 123, 125, 165; *favelas,* 32–33; Flamengo, 93, 101; Ipanema, 11–12, 95, 108, 110fig., 111fig., 115–16, 123, 185, 190; Leblon, 11, 13, 49, 108, 123, 133, 136, 140fig., 149. *See also* beaches; Cruzada São Sebastião
Sovik, Liv: *Aqui Ninguém é Branco* (There are no whites here), 18, 74, 92, 190
spaces, private, 13–14, 28, 35, 96–97, 125, 132; clubs, 49, 93, 123–24, 148; domestic, 37, 73, 159; Costa Brava Clube, 124; white elite spaces, 56–57, 63, 66, 71–72, 96, 122–23, 130–31, 137, 190–91
spaces, urban, 32–35, 48, 83, 125, 130–32, 119n13; beaches, 108–14, 119–20, 126–27; black spaces, 23–24, 32, 40, 160, 179; semiprivatized, 128–30, 137–39; struggle for, 11, 39–40, 44, 51, 142–43, 188, 201n7. *See also favelas;* malls, shopping
sports: baseball, 171; basketball, 148, 176; soccer fandom, 99–100, 100fig., 110fig.; surfing, 134, 142–43, 144fig., 172
Stoler, Ann, 27, 66, 72–74, 87, 93, 120, 156, 190
surfing, 134, 142–43, 144fig., 172

Tannen, Deborah, 58, 82
Teatro Experimental do Negro (Black Experimental Theater) (TEN), 22, 90, 202n6

Telles, Edward, 17, 43–44, 110, 129, 130–31, 160, 193

Traficando Informação (Trafficking Information) (MV Bill) (album), 167, 168ex.

transcription conventions, 54, 198n8

transportation, public, 32, 35, 37; to beach, 116, 117map, 119, 125–27; buses, 108, 117map, 125–26; highway improvement, 117map, 119, 126; Túnel Rebouças, 108

travel, 70, 93

Túnel Rebouças, 108, 117map

Universidade do Estado do Rio de Janeiro (Rio de Janeiro State University, UERJ), 189

Ultraje a Rigor: "*Nós Vamos Invadir Sua Praia*" (We are going to invade your beach), 108, 110–16, 111–12ex.

UNESCO studies, 20, 22, 43

Unidades de Polícia Pacificadora (Pacifying Police Units), 96

United States, 45, 63, 94, 146; Civil Rights Movement, 145, 166, 182; influence of, 130, 148, 166–67, 171, 201n3 (chap. 5); South, antebellum and postbellum, 26, 73, 75, 154, 202n8; transnational comparisons with, 5–6, 15, 22, 65–67, 72, 182–84, 186–87, 193, 196n15, 197n19, 198n2, 201n4 (chap. 4), 202n4

Universidade de Brasília, 181

Van Leeuwen, Lizzy, 73; *Lost in Mall*, 137

Vargas, Getúlio, 21

Vargas, João Costa, 3, 23–25, 47–48, 52, 62, 129, 131, 138, 160, 187, 194

Veja, 116–22, 181–83

Veloso, Leticia, 33, 50, 55, 95–96, 124, 139, 143–45

violence, 39–40, 95–96, 97–98, 110, 122, 166, 194; at the beach, 116, 118–19, 121, 126–27; and blackness, 176; drug gangs and, 32, 37, 49, 104, 118–19; police harassment, 48–49, 52–57, 54–55ex., 58; racial, 182–83; symbolic, 170

Wagley, Charles, 20, 22

Wattstax, 164

Weinstein, Barbara: *The Color of Modernity*, 19, 92, 101

Weismantel, Mary, 27, 29, 159, 173

West Zone (Rio de Janeiro), 122–24

"When Rio was Black" (Alberto), 164–65

white flight, 122, 123ex.

whiteness, 27–31, 188, 194; avoidance of, 129, 170–72, 175–80, 177–78ex., 179–80ex., 199n1 (chap. 3); civility and, 99; *embranquecimento* (whitening), 15–18, 42–48, 66, 69–70, 129, 131, 145–46, 191, 196n15, 202n3; instability of, 72–73, 146–48, 154, 159, 192; investment in, 157–58; lightness and, 18–19, 69, 92–93, 190; "personal whiteness," 39, 67–68, 69–75, 77, 79, 88, 93–94, 153, 154, 159, 190; "situational whiteness," 38–39, 44, 47, 67

white privilege, 8, 18, 39, 44, 170

white "superiority," 4, 6–7, 8, 16, 45–48, 63–64, 76, 193

"white" traits, 2, 44, 74–75, 194

Willems, Emílio, 25, 45, 47, 130–31

Wirtz, Kristina: *Performing Afro-Cuba*, 18, 27, 146, 197n24

World Conference Against Racism (2001), 162

World Cup: 1958, 17; 2014, 21, 197n20

youth, 110fig., 115–116, 118, 122, 124–25, 128–29, 164–65, 170–71, 174; middle-class, 132, 136–39, 147–48, 154–56, 159–60. See also Cruzada São Sebastião, male youth of; *playboys*

Zakabi, Rosana (*Veja* journalist), 181–82

Zumbi dos Palmares, 9, 162

CPSIA information can be obtained
at www.ICGtesting.com
Printed in the USA
JSHW030207230221
11971JS00002B/40

9 780520 293809